Idealism and

Henry E. Allison is one of the foremost interpreters of the philosophy of Kant. This new volume collects all his recent essays on Kant's theoretical and practical philosophy. All the essays postdate Allison's two major books on Kant (*Kant's Transcendental Idealism*, 1983, and *Kant's Theory of Freedom*, 1990), and together they constitute an attempt to respond to critics and to clarify, develop and apply some of the central theses of those books. One is published here for the first time.

Special features of the collection are: a detailed defense of the author's interpretation of transcendental idealism; a consideration of the Transcendental Deduction and some other recent interpretations thereof; further elaborations of the tensions between various aspects of Kant's conception of freedom and of the complex role of this conception within Kant's moral philosophy.

This volume brings together a major body of recent Kant interpretation by one of its leading exponents. It will be of special interest to both scholars and graduate students.

Idealism and freedom
Essays on Kant's theoretical and practical philosophy

Henry E. Allison
University of California, San Diego

CAMBRIDGE
UNIVERSITY PRESS

Published by the Press Syndicate of the University of Cambridge
The Pitt Building, Trumpington Street, Cambridge CB2 1RP
40 West 20th Street, New York, NY 10011-4211, USA
10 Stamford Road, Oakleigh, Melbourne 3166, Australia

© Cambridge University Press 1996

First Published 1996

Printed in the United States of America

Library of Congress Cataloging-in Publication Data
Idealism and freedom : essays on Kant's theoretical and practical philosophy / Henry E. Allison.
p. cm.
Includes bibliographical references and index.
ISBN 0-521-48295-X – ISBN 0-521-48337-9 (pbk.)
1. Kant, Immanuel, 1724–1804.   2. Kant, Immanuel, 1724–1804 – Ethics.   3. Knowledge, Theory of.   4. Ethics.   I. Title.
B2798.A633   1995
193 – dc20   95-16774
                                                                 CIP

A catalog record for this book is available from the British Library.

ISBN 0-521-48295-X hardback
ISBN 0-521-48337-9 paperback

To Norma, who makes it all possible

Contents

Acknowledgments	*page* ix
Note on sources and key to abbreviations and translations	xi
Introduction	xiii

Part I: Kant's theoretical philosophy

1	Transcendental idealism: A Retrospective	3
2	Reflections on the B-Deduction	27
3	Apperception and analyticity in the B-Deduction	41
4	On naturalizing Kant's transcendental psychology	53
5	Gurwitsch's interpretation of Kant: Reflections of a former student	67
6	Causality and causal law in Kant: A critique of Michael Friedman	80
7	Kant's refutation of materialism	92

Part II: Kant's practical philosophy

8	Kant on freedom: A reply to my critics	109
9	Autonomy and spontaneity in Kant's conception of the self	129
10	On the presumed gap in the derivation of the categorical imperative	143
11	Kant's doctrine of obligatory ends	155
12	Reflections on the banality of (radical) evil: A Kantian analysis	169

Notes	183
Index	213

Acknowledgments

The following essays in this volume have been previously published and I would like to thank the editors and publishers for permision to reprint them here.

"Reflections on the B-Deduction" was originally published in *The Southern Journal of Philosophy*, 25, Supplement, The Spindel Conference, 1986.

"Apperception and Analyticity in the B-Deduction" was originally published in *Grazer Philosophische Studien*, 44 (1993).

"Gurwitsch's Interpretation of Kant: Reflections of a Former Student" was originally published in *Kant-Studien*, 83 (1992).

"Causality and Causal Law in Kant: A Critique of Michael Friedman" initially appeared in *Kant and Contemporary Epistemology*, edited by Paolo Parrini, Kluwer, 1994.

"Kant's Refutation of Materialism" is copyright 1989, *The Monist*, La Salle, Illinois, 61301. Reprinted by permission.

"Kant on Freedom: A Reply to My Critics" is reprinted from *Inquiry*, 36 (1993), by permission of the Scandinavian University Press, Oslo, Norway.

"Autonomy and Spontaneity in Kant's Conception of the Self" first appeared in *The Modern Subject*, edited by Karl Ameriks and Dieter Sturma, State University of New York Press, 1995.

"On the Presumed Gap in the Derivation of the Categorical Imperative" was originally published in *Philosophical Topics*, 19, no. 1 (spring 1991).

"Kant's Doctrine of Obligatory Ends" was initially published in *Jahrbuch für Recht und Ethik*, 1 (1993).

"Reflections on the Banality of (Radical) Evil: A Kantian Analysis" was initially published in *Graduate Faculty Philosophy Journal*, 18, no. 2 (1995).

ACKNOWLEDGMENTS

I would also like to express my gratitude to Terry Moore of Cambridge University Press for his enthusiastic support of this project and to my students, former and present, Michelle Grier, Camilla Serck-Hanssen and Ian Eagleson for their helpful comments and suggestions concerning many of the essays in this volume. Finally, my thanks to Jeannette Filippone for her assistance in the preparation of the index.

Note on sources and key to abbreviations and translations

Apart from the *Critique of Pure Reason,* all references to Kant are to the volume and page of *Kants gesammelte Schriften* (KGS), herausgegeben von der Deutschen (formerly Königlichen Preuissischen) Akademie der Wissenschaften, 29 volumes [Berlin: Walter de Gruyter (and predecessors), 1902]. References to the *Critique of Pure Reason* are to the standard A and B pagination of the first and second editions. Specific works cited are referred to by means of the abbreviations listed below. The translations used are also listed below and, except in the case of the *Critique of Pure Reason,* are referred to immediately following the reference to the volume and page of the German text. It should be noted, however, that I have frequently modified these translations. Where there is no reference to an English translation, the translation is my own.

A/B	*Kritik der reinen Vernunft* (KGS 3 and 4). *Critique of Pure Reason,* trans. N. Kemp Smith, New York: St. Martin's Press, 1965.
Anthro	*Anthropologie in pragmatischer Hinsicht* (KGS 7). *Anthropology from a Practical Point of View,* trans. Mary J. Gregor, The Hague: Nijhoff, 1974.
Br	*Kants Briefwechsel* (KGS 10-13). *Kant Philosophical Correspondence, 1759–99,* trans. Arnulf Zweig, Chicago: University of Chicago Press, 1970.
Diss	*De Mundi sensibilis atquae intelligibilis forma et princippiis* (KGS 2). *Concerning the Form and Principles of the Sensible and Intelligible World* (The Inaugural Dissertation), trans. David Walford, in *The Cambridge Edition of the Works of Immanuel Kant, Theoretical Philosophy, 1755–1770,* Cambridge, New York: Cambridge University Press, 1992.
Fort	*Welches sind die wirklichen Fortschritte, die die Metaphysik seit Leibnizens und Wolfs Zeiten in Deutschland gemacht hat?* (KGS 20). *On the Progress of Metaphysics.*
Gr	*Grundlegung zur Metaphysik der Sitten* (KGS 4). *Groundwork of the Metaphysics of Morals,* trans. H. J. Paton, New York: Harper & Row, 1964.

xi

SOURCES, ABBREVIATIONS AND TRANSLATIONS

KprV   *Kritik der praktischen Vernunft* (KGS 5). *Critique of Practical Reason*, trans. Lewis White Beck, Indianapolis and New York: Bobbs-Merrill, 1956.

KU   *Kritik der Urteilskraft* (KGS 5). *Critique of Judgment*, trans. Werner Pluhar, Indianapolis: Hackett, 1987.

MAN   *Metaphysische Anfangsgründe der Naturwissenschaften* (KGS 4). *Metaphysical Foundations of Natural Science*, trans. James Ellington, Indianapolis and New York: Bobbs-Merrill, 1970.

MK_3 *Metaphysik K_3* (KGS 28).

ML_1 *Metaphysik L_1* (KGS 28).

MM   *Metaphysik Mrongovius* (KGS 29).

MS   *Die Metaphysik der Sitten* (KGS 6). *The Metaphysics of Morals*, trans. Mary Gregor, Cambridge: Cambridge University Press, 1991.

MSV   *Metaphysik der Sitten Vigilantius* (KGS 27).

Prol   *Prolegomena zu einer jeden künftigen Metaphysik die als Wissenschaft wird auftreten können* (KGS 4). *Prolegomena to any Future Metaphysics*, trans. Lewis White Beck, Indianapolis: Bobbs-Merrill, 1950.

R   *Reflexionen* (KGS 17–19).

Rel   *Die Religion innerhalb der Grenzen der blossen Vernunft* (KGS 6). *Religion within the Limits of Reason Alone*, trans. T. M. Greene and H. H. Hudson, New York: Harper & Row, 1960.

RSV   *Recension von Schulz's Versuch einer Anleitung zur Sittenlehre für alle Menschen, ohne Unterscheid der Religion, nebst einem Anhange von den Todesstrafen* (KGS 8). "Review of Schulz's 'Sittenlehre'."

UE   *Über eine Entdeckung nach der alle neue Kritik der reinen Vernunft duch eine ältere entbehrlich gemacht werden soll* (KGS 8). *The Kant-Eberhard Controversy*, trans. Henry E. Allison, Baltimore and London: The Johns Hopkins University Press, 1973.

Introduction

As the title indicates, the present volume contains a collection of my recent work on Kant's theoretical and practical philosophy. All of the essays dealing with the theoretical philosophy were written subsequently to the publication of *Kant's Transcendental Idealism* (1983); those dealing with the practical philosophy have been written since the appearance of *Kant's Theory of Freedom* (1990). Together, these essays constitute my efforts to reply to my critics and to clarify, develop and apply some of the ideas expressed in these two books. In some cases, this has led me to retract or significantly modify earlier views. Since most of these essays were written either for presentation at symposia or international conferences, or in response to an invitation to contribute to a volume of one sort or another, much of my recent work is scattered and not readily accessible. Of itself, however, this fact hardly justifies a collection of essays such as is contained in this volume. To my mind, at least, if such a collection is to be warranted it must be because its contents possess a certain thematic unity and advance the discussion in some significant way. I am confident that the first criterion is met by the contents of this volume, but I must leave it to the reader to judge with respect to the second.

I

Although the essays in this collection treat a fairly wide variety of topics in Kant's theoretical and practical philosophy, their main focus is on the central concerns of my ongoing work on Kant: the nature and significance of transcendental idealism, the spontaneity of the thinking and acting subject and the indispensability of Kant's radical conception of freedom to his moral theory. Not coincidentally, these are among the features of Kant's thought which are most widely rejected by contemporary Kantians. With few exceptions, philosophers within the analytic tradition working on Kant or Kantian themes tend to excise from their working picture of Kant virtually everything that cannot be readily naturalized, that is, fit into a broadly empirical framework. This perhaps leaves room for a certain notion of autonomy (albeit certainly not Kant's notion), but not for idealism or, more generally, anything having to do with the noumenal. I have challenged this dismissive treatment of much of Kant's thought in my two books, and I continue to do so in many of these essays. In so doing, I have consistently tried to show both that the standard criticisms often rest on crude misunderstandings of the Kantian texts and that, sympathetically construed, these same texts contain philosophical lessons that are still of value.

A case in point is the conception of spontaneity, which is inevitably downplayed or explained away on a naturalistic reading, but which is nonetheless central to Kant's theoretical and practical philosophy. With regard to the former, one need only note that the Transcendental Analytic of the *Critique of Pure Reason* is concerned with the operations of the understanding, which Kant defines in the very beginning as the *"spontaneity* of knowledge" (A51/B75). Thus, in spite of the near silence on the topic in many recent discussions, it is impossible to deal adequately with the major topics and sections of the Analytic, including the Transcendental Deduction, without taking this conception seriously.[1]

From a systematic point of view, however, perhaps the most interesting facet of Kant's conception of spontaneity concerns the question of the connection between its theoretical and practical dimensions (what I term epistemic and practical spontaneity). Although Kant anticipates Fichte in insisting that absolute spontaneity (or self-determination) is the defining feature of the self and in maintaining that this applies to the self both *qua* cognizer (subject of experience) and *qua* agent, he refrains from drawing the metaphysical conclusions from this that Fichte does. That is to say, he refrains from making spontaneity into the basis of a metaphysic of the subject. Instead, Kant's final position, as I read him, is more modest but (from a contemporary point of view) still highly controversial. Reduced to essentials, it amounts to the view that the idea of spontaneity is inseparable from (indeed constitutive of) our conception of ourselves as genuine cognizers and agents; but this does not license any ontological conclusions, since it leaves in place the epistemic possibility that we are nothing more than automata. Such a compromise position, which presupposes transcendental idealism, is not likely to satisfy either the Fichtean idealist or the committed naturalist. Nevertheless, this (or something very much like it) is what is required in order to reconcile the scientific "objective" conception of human beings as causally conditioned parts of nature with the "subjective," transcendental and normative conception of the self as the self-determining initiator of thought and action. At least that is what I attempt to argue in several of the essays in this collection.

A key to my basic argumentative strategy in these essays is to suggest that the function of the conception of spontaneity (in both theoretical and practical contexts) is a non-explanatory one. In other words, rather than being seen as part of an explanatory story about how the mind operates at either the phenomenal or noumenal level, this conception is regarded as the centerpiece of an essentially normative account of how the subject must conceive itself (or be conceived), if it is to take itself (or be taken) as a genuine subject of

INTRODUCTION

thought and action. If correct, this would explain why Kant refrains from drawing the expected ontological conclusions from his analyses, even though he takes them as sufficient to rule out in principle materialistic or mechanistic accounts of thought and action.[2] Moreover, although it hardly ends the debate, I do think that it also suffices to disarm the critic whose objection to the conception of spontaneity is predicated on the assumption that it is intended as part of some putative non-empirical explanation. In any event, an underlying assumption of my whole account is that there is an essential yet non-explanatory function for this conception.

II

So much, then, for the general orientation of the collection; it remains to say something about the two parts and the essays included therein. The first part is composed of seven essays dealing with Kant's theoretical philosophy. Many of these have a decidedly polemical tone, since they are addressed to specific criticisms of my views in *Kant's Transcendental Idealism*. This is particularly true of Chapter 1, "Transcendental idealism: A retrospective," which is written especially for this volume. It attempts to respond to the main lines of criticism that have been directed against my interpretation of transcendental idealism as an essentially epistemological or methodological rather than a metaphysical doctrine. Central to this interpretation is my analysis of Kant's transcendental distinction as concerned not with two worlds or sets of objects (appearances and things in themselves), but rather with two aspects or ways of considering the spatio-temporal objects of human experience: as they "appear" in connection with the sensible conditons of human cognition and as they may be "in themselves" independently of these conditions and as thought by a "pure understanding" not constrained by the conditions of sensibility.

Since my interpretation has been attacked by critics with widely different agendas of their own, I have found that a multi-faceted response is required. Thus, after an initial clarification and reformulation of my views on transcendental idealism, I take a fresh look at the problem of the so-called "neglected alternative" (that space and time might be both forms of sensibility and conditions, properties or relations of things as they are in themselves). I then attempt to defend my "double-aspect" reading on both textual and systematic grounds against the recent attack launched by Hoke Robinson. Finally, in the last two sections, I respond to the criticisms of Karl Ameriks and Paul Guyer, each of whom, albeit in quite different ways, claim that I have neglected the essentially ontological thrust of Kantian idealism. If this account does not convince my critics, I hope that it at least clarifies the issues.

Chapters 2 through 5 constitute a unit, since they all deal, in one way or another, with the Transcendental Deduction. Chapter 2, "Reflections on the B-Deduction," was originally presented at a Spindel Conference on the B-

INTRODUCTION

Deduction in the fall of 1986 and later published (Spring 1987) in the supplemental issue of *The Southern Journal of Philosophy* containing the proceedings of that conference. It attempts to provide what might be termed a "metatheory" of the deduction. Starting with the reflection that many philosophers before Kant had recognized the need for a prior justification of the possibility of knowledge claims but none had seen the necessity for anything resembling a Kantian transcendental deduction, I suggest that the project of a deduction in the Kantian sense rests on three presuppositions: the existence of pure concepts, the sensibility–understanding split and the principle that a concept must somehow be related to empirical intuition if it is to possess objective reality (sometimes termed Kant's "concept empiricism"). I also argue that together these presuppositions not only explain why Kant thought that a transcendental deduction is necessary, they also account for the form that it takes in the second edition of the *Critique*. And, in light of this, I criticize the interpretations of Dieter Henrich and Paul Guyer.[3]

Chapter 3, "Apperception and analyticity in the B-Deduction," was originally written for a *Festschrift* in honor of Henri Lauener, which was published in a volume of *Grazer Philosophische Studien* (1993). It is concerned with the analysis of Kant's surprising claim in the B-Deduction that the "principle of the necessary unity of apperception is . . . an identical, and therefore analytic proposition" (B 135; see also B 138). Whereas most commentators have either ignored this claim or dismissed it as a slip on Kant's part, in *Kant's Transcendental Idealism* I endeavored to take it seriously and to present it as the key to the much discussed division of the argument of the B-Deduction into two parts. The present essay is an attempt to develop further this line of thought and to defend the analyticity of the principle against the criticisms of Guyer and my colleague, Patricia Kitcher, who directed her critique specifically against my initial account. This defense involves explaining both how Kant can describe what seems to be the same principle (the synthetic unit of apperception) as synthetic in the first edition and as analytic in the second; and how the Transcendental Deduction can yield a synthetic *a priori* conclusion (the objective reality of the categories) when its initial premise is analytic.

Chapter 4, "On naturalizing Kant's transcendental psychology," was presented at a conference in Bern, again honoring Henri Lauener in the fall of 1993. It is devoted largely to a critique of Patricia Kitcher and her attempt to provide a naturalized picture of Kant as a protofunctionalist and cognitive scientist. Although I commend Kitcher for her efforts to rehabilitate Kant's transcendental psychology in the face of P. F. Strawson's wholesale and influential dismissal of this allegedly "imaginary subject," I argue that her uncompromising naturalism leads her (like Strawson) to dismiss essential features of Kant's account. I also suggest that this results in a blurring of the very contrast with Hume on mental activity that she endeavors to illuminate. In particular, I question her rejection of any proper role for self-awareness in cognition, her account of synthesis as an essentially causal process and her consequent refusal to grant anything more than a relative spontaneity (which Kant identifies with that of a turnspit) to the mind.

Chapter 5, "Gurwitsch's interpretation of Kant: Reflections of a former student," was first presented at a conference on the thought of Aron Gurwitsch at the New School in the fall of 1991 and later published in *Kant-Studien* (1992). It contains an analysis of Gurwitsch's posthumously published monograph, *Kants Theorie des Verstandes* (1990). Although known primarily as a phenomenologist, Gurwitsch was also deeply interested in the history of modern philosophy and made important contributions to this field.[4] Since it was in his seminars at the New School in 1960 and 1961 that I began my serious study of Kant, this piece may be viewed as an attempt to come to terms with my intellectual heritage. In addition to laying out Gurwitsch's views on Kant (and on Kant's relation to Leibniz), which certainly deserve to be more widely known, I attempt to suggest something of my debt to him and to indicate areas of disagreement. The debt is extensive and includes a general approach to philosophical texts as well as points of interpretation too numerous to mention. The disagreement concerns mainly the psychological dimension of his account of apperception (his phenomenologically inspired attempt to characterize how the synthetic activity of the mind must be "experienced" [*erlebt*]) and his essentially phenomenalistic reading of Kant's views on objective representation. The latter leads Gurwitsch to a critique of Kant along Husserlian lines, which in my judgment is not warranted.

Chapter 6, "Causality and causal law in Kant: A critique of Michael Friedman," was initially presented at a conference on Kant and contemporary epistemology in Florence in the spring of 1992 and later published in the proceedings of that conference (1994). It contains a defense of my reading of the Second Analogy against the critique of Michael Friedman and a corresponding critique of his alternative interpretation. In *Kant's Transcendental Idealism* I had argued (in agreement with Lewis White Beck, Gerd Buchdahl and others) that the Second Analogy adresses Hume's challenge to the general principle of causality ("every event has a cause"), but that it leaves open the question of the empirical lawfulness of nature, that is, whether nature contains a causal order discoverable by the human mind. Against this, Friedman argues that the Second Analogy guarantees both the existence and the necessity of (empirical) causal laws. His main concern, however, is to show that the transcendental principles of the first *Critique* receive their significance from the corresponding metaphysical principles of mechanics of the *Metaphysical Foundations of Natural Science*, that is, the Newtonian laws of motion as reconstructed by Kant. The result is a picture in which the metaphysical principles assume the grounding function usually assigned to their transcendental counterparts (the Analogies), since empirical regularities attain nomological status, which Friedman equates with genuine objectivity, only by being

INTRODUCTION

"nested" or framed in these principles. In spite of its elegance and initial attractiveness, I find this position deeply problematic in several respects. Chief among these is its inability to account for the objectivity of ordinary, pre-scientific experience.

The seventh and final chapter in Part I, "Kant's refutation of materialism," was written for an issue of *The Monist* on "Kant's critical philosophy" (April 1988), which I edited. It is perhaps my most ambitious and speculative essay in this collection and, therefore, probably the one most open to criticism. Although the focus is on the explication of Kant's perplexing claim to have shown the impossibility of a materialistic account of the mind, even while denying the possibility of any knowledge of the real natue of the "thing which thinks," I also attempt to show that Kant has provided the materials for a significant challenge to contemporary reductive and non-reductive versions of materialism, including the eliminative variety of my colleagues, Patricia and Paul Churchland. Thus, at crucial points this essay goes beyond Kant interpretation in an attempt to show the relevance of Kant's views to central issues in the philosophy of mind. At the same time, however, it also stands in essential continuity with the others, since the features of Kant's thought to which I appeal in my argument are the spontaneity of the understanding and the apperceptive nature of thought.

III

The second part of this collection contains five essays dealing with Kant's practical philosophy. They are all concerned in one way or another with the connection between morality and freedom, which was the main focus of *Kant's Theory of Freedom*. Of these, the first two attempt to defend and clarify some of the more controversial positions maintained in that work, while the last three explore further the complex and essential role played by Kant's conception of transcendental freedom within his moral theory. Much of the discussion concerns the nature, significance and interconnection of two theses regarding freedom, which played large roles in my book and which I have termed the "Incorporation Thesis" and the "Reciprocity Thesis." The former expresses what I take to be Kant's central insight regarding rational agency: inclinations or desires do not of themselves constitute a sufficient reason to act but do so only insofar as they are "taken up" or "incorporated" into a maxim by the agent. This means that an act of spontaneity or self-determination is involved even in inclination or desire based (heteronomous) action. I view this thesis as the key to both Kant's moral psychology and his conception of agency. The latter refers to Kant's claim in both the *Groundwork* and the *Critique of Practical Reason* that (transcendental) freedom and the moral law reciprocally imply one another. Its significance is that it makes freedom into a sufficient, not merely a necessary, condition of morality, since an agent that is transcendentally free is for that very reason already subject to the moral law (which does not mean, of course, that such an agent necessarily obeys that law).

Chapter 8, "Kant on freedom: A reply to my critics," is a somewhat revised version of a discussion that initially appeared in *Inquiry* (December 1993). Since it endeavors to respond to a set of diverse criticisms, it constitutes a counterpart to the initial essay in the first part. The first three sections respond to the criticisms that were raised against *Kant's Theory of Freedom* by Stephen Engstrom, Andrews Reath, and Marcia Baron at two symposia devoted to a discussion of the book. These criticisms were published together with my response in the issue of *Inquiry*. In a final section, I address the criticisms expressed by Karl Ameriks (who also participated in the second symposium) in a review article and by Paul Guyer in his review of my book. The major issues in these debates include the Incorporation and Reciprocity Theses and the complex question of the metaphysics of freedom in Kant. Even though these topics are also discussed elsewhere in this collection, I have decided to include this reply because it gives the reader a sense of both the kinds of difficulties that knowledgeable critics have found in my views and how I attempt to deal with these difficulties. I also believe that my analysis of some of these points (particularly those relating to the metaphysic of freedom) is fuller and perhaps somewhat more adequate than I offer elsewhere.

Chapter 9, "Autonomy and spontaneity in Kant's conception of the self," was initially presented at a conference on the concept of the self in Kant and post-Kantian idealism at Notre Dame in the spring of 1994. It explores at length the tension in Kant's thought between a conception of freedom based on a reflection on the general nature of rational agency (spontaneity) and one which is based on the specifics of Kant's view of moral agency (autonomy). I argue that, although in his later writings (from the *Critique of Practical Reason* onward) Kant tends to give priority to autonomy and to claim that it is only through our awareness of standing under the moral law that we are conscious of our freedom; the non-morally specific conception of freedom as spontaneity is never absent and, in fact, is presupposed by autonomy. In other words, the autonomy of the moral agent presupposes the spontaneity of the rational agent even though it cannot be derived directly from it. In contrast to my position in *Kant's Theory of Freedom* and to Kant's own explicit claims, I argue that Kant can at most derive freedom in the sense of autonomy from the moral law as the "fact of reason," so that freedom as spontaneity remains presupposed but not demonstrated. Consequently, the "deduction" of freedom in the full transcendental sense in the second *Critique* fails (assuming that this was Kant's intent), since the epistemic possibility that our freedom might be illusory remains untouched by this argument.

Chapter 10, "On a presumed gap in the derivation of the categorical imperative," was written as an invited article for *Philosophical Topics* (Spring 1991). It attempts to respond to the objection developed by Bruce Aune and

INTRODUCTION

Allen Wood (but already foreshadowed by Hegel) that Kant moves without apparent justification from the bare idea of conformity to universal law or from the mere concept of a universal practical law (neither of which is thought to be action guiding) to a contentful, action guiding categorical imperative. While granting Aune's contention that this fairly characterizes Kant's procedure in the *Groundwork,* where he proceeds analytically from a reflection on the ordinary, pre-philosophical views of morality, I deny that it applies to the *Critique of Practical Reason,* where Kant makes use of the synthetic method. The key difference is that in the latter work, but not the former, Kant introduces transcendental freedom before deriving the categorical imperative; and in light of this, I argue that this conception of freedom is necessary to fill in the gap to which Aune and Wood refer. In short, the problematic notion of transcendental freedom must be presupposed, if Kant is to arrive at a contentful, action guiding moral principle; but given such freedom, the derivation succeeds.

Chapter 11, "Kant's doctrine of obligatory ends," was presented at a symposium held at Jena in August 1992 on the timely topic of "Pre-positive law as a means of orientation in times of political upheaval." Together with the other papers from that symposium, it was first published in the *Jahrbuch für Recht und Ethik* (1993). Fortunately, this topic was construed liberally, since my essay certainly does not bear directly on it. It is rather concerned with an important but relatively neglected aspect of Kant's moral theory: the thesis expressed in the Introduction to the *Doctrine of Virtue* (the second part of the *Metaphysic of Morals* of 1797) that there are ends that are also duties to adopt, that is, obligatory ends. Expressed in imperatival form, it yields the synthetic principle: "Act according to a maxim of *ends* that it can be a universal law for everyone to have" (6: 395), which serves as the first principle of the doctrine of virtue. As such, it underlies Kant's arguments for positive duties, which are all duties to adopt certain ends or policies of action (such as beneficence) rather than to perform (or refrain from performing) specific actions. I contend that although Kant's actual arguments for this principle fail, a successful argument can be constructed, if we add transcendental freedom as an explicit premise.[5] I further contend that this inclusion is fully warranted by the fact that Kant himself connects end-setting with freedom. Thus, as in Chapter 10, we see that the conception of transcendental freedom not only serves as a foundation, but also plays a key and ineliminable role within Kant's moral theory. In a not sufficiently realized sense, Kant's moral theory stands or falls with this problematic conception.

Chapter 12, "Reflections on the banality of (radical) evil: A Kantian analysis," was written especially for a Hannah Arendt Conference at the New School in October 1993, devoted to the topic of freedom. In it I confront Arendt's conception of the banality of evil, made famous through her discussion of Eichmann, with my analysis of radical evil as developed in *Kant's*

INTRODUCTION

Theory of Freedom. In particular, I suggest that the thoughtlessness and self-deception, which for Arendt are both essential features of Eichmann's character and reasons for characterizing his evil as banal rather than diabolical, are in fact expressions of radical evil as understood by Kant. On the basis of this analysis, I argue that Arendt should not have denied the existence of radical evil and that this denial reflects a deep misunderstanding of what Kant intended by this conception. Whereas she apparently construes it as a great or deeply rooted, demonic form of evil (which would be at the opposite pole from banality), for Kant it refers to the root of *all* moral evil, whatever its extent. And since this root is located in freedom (a freely chosen propensity to evil), it follows that here, too, freedom plays a crucial role.

I

Kant's theoretical philosophy

1

Transcendental idealism: A retrospective

From the mid '70s to the early '80s, the period in which I was working on *Kant's Transcendental Idealism,* the dominant understanding of Kant's idealism, at least in the Anglo-American philosophical world, was what is generally termed the "two-object" or "two-world" view. According to this view, which can be traced back to Kant's immediate contemporaries, the transcendental distinction between appearances and things in themselves is construed as holding between two types of object: appearances or "mere representations," understood as the contents of particular minds, and things in themselves, understood as a set of transcendentally real but unknowable things, which somehow underlie or "ground" these appearances. Such a dualistic picture is easy to criticize, since it combines a phenomenalism regarding the objects of human cognition with the postulation of a set of extra-mental entities, which, in terms of that very theory, are unknowable. Thus, given the widespread acceptance of this reading of Kant's idealism, it is not difficult to understand the popularity of P. F. Strawson's *The Bounds of Sense* (1966), in which he taught a generation of analytical philosophers that, by focusing on the "analytic argument" of the *Critique,* it is possible to have one's Kant, or at least a scaled down version thereof, without the excess baggage of transcendental idealism.

Already in the late '60s, at the very beginning of my serious study of Kant, I was deeply suspicious of the Strawsonian approach, particularly the underlying assumption that one can so easily separate Kant's substantive philosophical claims concerning the conditions of experience from his idealism.[1] It was not until some years later, however, that the outlines of a radically different understanding of transcendental idealism began to emerge for me. According to this alternative understanding, which is usually termed the "double-aspect" or "two-aspect" view, Kant's transcendental distinction is primarily between two ways in which things (empirical objects) can be "considered" at the metalevel of philosophical reflection (transcendental reflection) rather than between the kinds of thing that are considered. Things can be considered either as they appear, that is, as they are in relation to the subjective conditions of human cognition, or as they are in themselves, independently of these conditions. Since it maintains that we know real, mind independent objects (although not considered as they are in themselves), the position is not phenomenalistic; and since things considered as they are in themselves are not ontologically distinct from the objects of human experience, there is no postulation of a separate realm of unknowable entities. At least no such postulation is entailed by the transcendental distinction.

In spite of its obvious philosophical advantages and significant textual support,[2] this view has itself been subjected to considerable criticism. Moreover, this criticism is addressed to both its inherent coherence (or lack thereof) and its adequacy as an interpretation of Kant. Although my prime concern here is with the clarification and defense of my own views, I shall attempt to address both lines of criticism. Since this requires me to deal with a number of distinct issues, the discussion is of necessity somewhat diffuse and is divided into five parts. The first presents a concise restatement of my understanding of transcendental idealism, including an account of the respects in which I have modified aspects of my earlier formulations. The second addresses a classical objection to Kant's central argument for idealism in the Transcendental Aesthetic: the so-called problem of the neglected alternative. The third part considers objections directed explicitly against the double-aspect view of transcendental idealism. It includes a brief summary of my previous treatment of such criticisms and a full response to the recent critique of my position by Hoke Robinson. The fourth attempts to answer the objection raised by Karl Ameriks, among others, that an essentially epistemological interpretation of Kant's idealism does not do justice to the difference in ontological status that Kant supposedly affirms between the phenomenal and the noumenal. Finally, the fifth part contains a reply to the critique of my views by Paul Guyer and to his unabashedly "dogmatic" and dismissive reading of transcendental idealism.

I

In order to emphasize what I take to be the essentially epistemological and methodological thrust of transcendental idealism, in *Kant's Transcendental Idealism* I introduced the conception of an epistemic condition as a heuristic device.[3] By this I meant a necessary condition for the representation of objects, that is, a condition without which our representations would not relate to objects or, equivalently, possess "objective reality." As such, it could also be termed an "objectivating condition," since it fulfills an objectivating function. As conditions of the possibility of representing objects, epistemic conditions were distinguished from both psychological and ontological conditions. By the former I understood primarily a propensity or mechanism of the mind which governs belief and belief acquisition. Hume's custom or habit is a prime example of such a condition. By the latter I understood a condition of the possibility of the existence of things, which conditions these things quite independently of their relation to the human (or any other) mind. Newton's absolute space and time are conditions in this sense. Epistemic conditions share with the former the property of being "subjective"; that is, they reflect the structure and operations of the human mind. They differ from them with respect to their objectivating function. Correlatively, they share with the latter the property of being "objective" or "objectivating." They differ in that they condition the objectivity of our *representations* of things rather than the very existence of the things themselves.

I also argued that the conception of an epistemic condition involves a certain idealistic commitment, one which is inseparable from Kant's transcendental method, and for that very reason quite distinct from the phenomenalistic and metaphysical versions of idealism usually attributed to Kant. The basic point is that the transcendental method requires one to consider objects in terms of the conditions of their representation, and this means that an object is understood idealistically as the correlate of a certain mode of representation. Moreover, I took this to be the sense of Kant's "Copernican hypothesis" that objects must "conform to our knowledge" (BXVI). On this reading, to say that objects must "conform to our knowledge" is just to say that they must conform to the conditions (whatever they may be) for the representation of objects; it is not to say that they exist in the mind in the manner of Berkeleian ideas or the sense data of phenomenalists.[4]

This, in turn, has led to two lines of criticism of my view. On the one hand, there are those critics who reject anything like what Karl Ameriks has termed a "short argument" to transcendental idealism from the mere conception of an epistemic condition.[5] For them, transcendental idealism is essentially a metaphysical position concerning the mode of existence of the sensible world of human experience. Typical of this approach (which, as we shall see, is also taken by Paul Guyer) is the critique of Malte Hossenfelder, who denies that there is any link between idealism and "the belief in certain conditions of our knowledge." As an empirical example, he points out that we know that our eyes can perceive things only if they reflect light of a certain wavelength; but as a fact about our visual capacities, this hardly brings with it any idealistic implications. On the contrary, Hossenfelder argues, these and similar claims, which could be made with respect to other sensory modalities, are more reasonably seen as applying to things in themselves and the conditions which they must meet in order to be perceived.[6] On the other hand, there are those critics (also including Guyer) who purport to be perplexed about where I stand on the idealism issue, since I seem to appeal both to a kind of short argument from epistemic conditions and to Kant's official arguments in the Aesthetic and Antinomies, which turn crucially on Kant's conception of sensibility.

With regard to the first point, it should suffice to note that not everything that might be labeled a "condition of knowledge" counts as an epistemic condition in the intended sense. Indeed, the kind of restriction on our sensory capacities appealed to by Hossenfelder is a case in point. A condition of this sort is not epistemic in the relevant sense, since it is not a means through which the mind can represent to itself objects. Like the Humean psychological conditions alluded to earlier, it has no objective validity or objectivating function. On the contrary, as empirical, it presupposes the existence of an objective, spatio-temporal world the representation of which is supposedly to be explained. Accordingly, it hardly follows from the fact that conditions of this sort do not entail any sort of idealism that properly epistemic conditions do not do so either.

Unfortunately, the second line of objection is more difficult to deal with, since it points to a genuine ambiguity in my previous analyses. The basic problem is illuminated nicely by Ameriks' distinction between "non-specific" and "specific" characterizations of transcendental idealism.[7] Proponents of the former, such as Hilary Putnam, Graham Bird, Gordon Nagel and Ralph Walker, tend to define idealism in very general epistemological terms as affirming the dependence of objects on our conceptual schemes, cognitive capacities, theories or the like. By contrast, proponents of the latter define idealism in more orthodox Kantian terms as a doctrine affirming the structuring of what is known by the mind's *a priori* forms, particularly the forms of sensibility. And since I make both sorts of claims, there has naturally arisen some perplexity regarding my own position.[8]

In an effort to clarify the situation, I should like to say that, although I stand by my claim that the generic notion of an epistemic condition brings with it a certain idealistic commitment of a non-phenomenalistic sort and is therefore useful as an introduction to the transcendental perspective, I no longer wish to suggest that it is sufficient to explicate what is distinctive in Kant's idealism. In particular, it is not adequate to ground the transcendental distinction between the two ways of considering things. The latter can be understood only in terms of Kant's account of human (indeed, all finite) cognition as discursive and ultimately the conception of sensibility and its *a priori* conditions that is inseparably linked to this account.

To claim that human knowledge is discursive is to claim that it requires both concepts and sensible intuition. Without the former there would be no thought and, therefore, no cognition; without the latter there would be no content to be thought. As Kant puts it in his oft cited phrase, "Thoughts without content are empty, intuitions without concepts are blind" (A51/B76).[9] Notoriously, Kant assumes rather than argues for the discursivity thesis, even while insisting that it is not the only conceivable kind of cognition.[10] Like so much else in his philosophy, he seems to regard it as an ultimate "fact," for which no explanation is either possible or necessary. Nevertheless, it has immense consequences for virtually every aspect of his thought. With respect to our current concern, it entails that there must be two distinct and heterogeneous sets of epistemic conditions to which any object cognized by the human mind must conform: sensible conditions, or "forms of sensibility," through which objects (or, better, the data for thinking objects) are given, and intellectual conditions, or categorial concepts, through which the data are referred to objects in judgment.

It may, perhaps, not be immediately obvious why the discursivity thesis commits one to the assumption that human sensibility has its own *a priori* forms and all that this entails. Why could one not simply hold that objects are given to the mind as they are in themselves, so that the mind's "contribution" is limited to the conceptual side? On this view it might seem that we would have discursivity (even pure concepts) without the need to add any distinct forms of sensibility. Although the issues raised by this question are far too complex to be dealt with adequately here, the main point is relatively clear: if one assumes that objects are given to the mind as they are in themselves, that is, if one denies the existence of any *a priori* forms of sensibility, then one also limits the role of conceptualization to the clarification and organization of this pre-given content. In short, one effectively denies the discursivity thesis, and instead views cognition as essentially a matter of "copying" a pre-given reality.

Moreover, precisely because it entails that sensibility has its own *a priori* forms, the discursivity thesis likewise leads to the transcendental distinction. To begin with, it is clear from the Transcendental Aesthetic, particularly from its critique of the Leibnizian theory of sensibility, that Kant's transcendental conception of appearance is the mirror image of his conception of sensibility. We can know objects only as they appear because we can know them only insofar as they are given in sensible intuition and because this intuition is structured according to our subjective forms of sensibility (space and time). Leibniz thus "falsified" the concept of sensibility (and appearance) because he viewed sensible representation as nothing more than a confused representation of things as they are in themselves (A43/B60).[11] And this falsification can be avoided only by regarding sensible intuition as providing access merely to things as they appear.

It also follows from this that to consider things as they are in themselves is to reflect on them in a way which ignores or abstracts from the subjective conditions of human sensibility; and, given the discursivity thesis, this amounts to considering them through the mere understanding or as some pure understanding might represent them. Here again, I am forced to modify my earlier view, which was that to consider things as they are in themselves is just to consider them independently of *all* epistemic conditions (conceptual as well as sensible). To be sure, there is an important sense in which this remains true, since a central claim of the Transcendental Analytic is that the categories are limited by their schemata as the sensible conditions of their realization. Thus, we cannot use the categories, any more than the forms of sensibility, to gain knowledge of things as they are in themselves.[12] Nevertheless, Kant clearly allows for a logical (as opposed to a real) use of the categories for the thought of things in general and/or as they are in themselves; and there are numerous passages in which Kant explicitly states that to think or consider things as they are in themselves is just to think them as some pure intellect might, that is, one not restricted by sensible conditions.[13]

This line of thought reflects Kant's doctrine of the Inaugural Dissertation, where he contrasts the sensible world of phenomena, which depends for its "form" on our modes of sensibility, with an intellectual world to which these sensible conditions do not apply. As he there succinctly puts it, sensible representations are of things "*as they appear* [*uti apparent*]," whereas "intellectual concepts are representations of things *as they are* [*sicuti sunt*]" (Diss 2: 392; 384). Although in the *Critique* Kant denied the possibility (at least for finite subjects) of a purely intellectual cognition, he maintained the view that to think things apart or in abstraction from the sensible conditions under which they are given in sensible intuition is to consider (think) them as they are in themselves.

Correlatively, if we (mistakenly) deny that space and time function as sensible conditions under which objects are given, then we are thereby regarding "mere appearances" as if they were things in themselves. In both cases, *an sich* status is viewed as the correlate of a purely conceptual representing, which ignores or rejects the distinctive contribution of sensibility and its *a priori* conditions. Thus, by viewing the transcendental distinction in light of the discursivity thesis, we not only confirm the view that this distinction is one between two ways of considering objects, we also see that these two ways of considering are defined in terms of the two sets of epistemic conditions required by the discursivity of human cognition. And this leads us back to the initial claim that Kant's idealism is fundamentally epistemological in nature.

II

If things considered as they are in themselves are unknowable, however, how can Kant claim that the things we intuit are not in themselves as we intuit them (A42/B59)? This is the root of the much discussed problem of the neglected alternative, made famous by Adolf Trendelenburg but traceable back to Kant's contemporaries. According to this objection, in moving from the thesis that space and time are forms of human sensibility to the conclusion that they cannot be conditions, properties or relations of things as they are in themselves, Kant simply overlooked the possibility that they might be both at once. I have dealt with this thorny question both in an early paper and in *Kant's Transcendental Idealism*, but since my analyses have been subject to a fair amount of criticism and since my views on the topic have evolved over the years, I shall take this opportunity to state my position and to indicate something of the route by which I have arrived at it.[14]

Initially, I attempted to derive the non-spatiality thesis directly from an analysis of the concept of a thing considered as it is in itself. If space and time are forms of human sensibility (which is granted by the neglected alternative objection) and if to consider things as they are in themselves is to consider them independently of these forms (which is stipulated as a matter of definition), then it follows that things so considered are not in space and time. Left at this point, however, the argument seems open to an obvious objection, which has been formulated by Paul Guyer. As Guyer bluntly puts it, "such an argument simply confuses claims about a *concept* with claims about things." From the fact that the *predicate* "spatiality" is abstracted from or ignored in a certain *concept* of things, it does not follow that the *property* of spatiality is absent from the things themselves.[15]

Although Guyer's point can hardly be denied, its relevance to my analysis is another matter. In fact, far from being oblivious to the problem, as Guyer's critique suggests, I explicitly posed and attempted to deal with it in my earliest treatment of the neglected alternative issue.[16] Following Gerold Prauss, I there pointed out that, when construed transcendentally (rather than empirically), the phrase *"an sich selbst"* in *"Ding an sich selbst betrachtet"* functions adverbially to modify *"betrachtet"* rather than adjectivally to modify *"Ding."*[17] In short, it characterizes *how* one considers things in transcendental reflection rather than the *kind* of things (those that exist in themselves) being considered. If the latter were the case, Guyer would be correct, since we would then have to distinguish between the thing being considered (or conceived) and our conception of it. On the adverbial reading, however, there is no room for this distinction and no such confusion, since all that is at issue is the how of considering. Accordingly, the entire force of Guyer's objection on this point rests on his own understanding of Kant's transcendental distinction, and this, as we shall see later, is itself highly questionable.

Of itself, this is not sufficient to establish the non-spatiality thesis, however, since it leaves open the question of why forms of sensibility or, more properly, the content of such forms, must be assigned solely to the cognitive apparatus of the human mind and, therefore, could not also be attributed to things considered as they are in themselves. This is a substantive claim and it cannot be derived from the analysis of a way of considering without begging the question. Accordingly, in *Kant's Transcendental Idealism* I took up the matter afresh, focusing this time on the conception of a "form of sensibility." Very briefly, the essential point is that a form of sensibility, understood as a form of sensibly intuiting, involves an essential reference to mind. This rules out the possibility of either a numerical or a qualitative identity between empirical space as the content of a form of sensibility and some putative transcendentally real space. Since, *ex hypothesi*, they would be two different spaces, they obviously could not be numerically identical; and since mind-dependence is a defining feature of the former and mind-independence of the latter, they could not be qualitatively identical either.

Admittedly, this still appears to leave open the possibility of a similarity or analogy between the two spaces; and this is a more difficult matter to deal with, since it now becomes a question of what degree of similarity is required in order for the neglected alternative to count as a viable option. Clearly, to deny categorically the possibility of *any* similarity or analogy between the content of a form of human sensibility and putative properties or relations of things considered as they are in themselves would be to maintain more than is warranted and, indeed, more than Kant might wish to claim.[18] Nevertheless, in *Kant's Transcendental Idealism,* I attempted to rule out the possibility of any relevant similarity or analogy by noting that it would have to be between something that involves an essential reference to mind and something that, *ex hypothesi,* is completely independent of mind. And I further suggested that the claim for such a similarity could avoid contradiction only at the cost of its utter vacuity.

It has been pointed out by Lorne Falkenstein, however, that such a response is inadequate.[19] The problem is that mind-dependence is only one property of empirical space (and a relational property at that). Consequently, excluding it as a property of any putative transcendentally real space does not of itself rule out the possibility of a significantly strong analogy between them to justify the neglected alternative hypothesis. Why couldn't there be a transcendentally real surrogate of space that is just like our space except for the fact that is has no relation to mind?

In order to exclude such a possibility, it is necessary to appeal to certain features of "our space," that is, of the representation of space (and time) as analyzed in the Metaphysical and Transcendental Expositions of the Transcendental Aesthetic. This is the main focus of Falkenstein's paper, and his response turns on a distinction between two types of order: "presentational orders," that is, orders in which the mind receives its data in intuition, and "comparative orders," which are orders of properties such as colors. Given this distinction, he argues that space and time are orders of the former sort and that an order of things as they are in themselves would have to be a comparative order of internal properties (much as in the Leibnizian monadology). The question thus becomes whether it is meaningful to affirm an isomorphism between two such radically distinct types of order. Falkenstein denies this on the grounds that the presentational (spatio-temporal) order of phenomena is indifferent to the internal properties of the objects ordered therein (presumably, Kant shows this in the Expositions and in his appeal to incongruent counterparts).

I believe that Falkenstein's analysis is essentially correct and that his conception of a presentational order nicely captures a major feature of Kant's conception of a form of sensibility. It is, indeed, a form or order in which the mind receives its data. For that same reason, however, I also believe that his analysis corroborates and fills out rather than conflicts with the main thrust of my own account. The claim, after all, was that the non-spatiality of things as they are in themselves follows from an analysis of the concept of a thing so considered *and* the conception of a form of sensibility. What Falkenstein does, and I view it as an important contribution, is to show just why there can be no isomorphism between a form of sensibility and an order of things as they are in themselves.

III

The neglected alternative objection, like most familiar criticisms, is directed against transcendental idealism in general rather than any particular interpretation thereof. The double-aspect interpretation has itself come under attack in the recent literature, however, and in an earlier paper I considered two such attacks.[20] One was by Richard Aquila, who takes Kant's distinction to be between two ways of *existing* rather than two ways of *considering*.[21] According to Aquila, to exist as an appearance is to exist in what he calls a "phenomenalistic sense," that is, "merely intentionally," while to exist in itself is to exist in a non-phenomenalistic sense."[22] Given this, he then rejects the double-aspect reading on the grounds that, on the only interpretation in which it is intelligible (which he takes to be the "noumenalistic" view that grants ontological priority to things as they are in themselves), it is not possible to assume that the same thing could exist in two such incompatible ways.

In my response to Aquila, I questioned both the above mentioned critique of the double-aspect view and his alternative interpretation of the transcendental distinction. But since this critique turns on the claim that the distinction is between two ways of existing, we need only consider that point here. Aquila's main support for this claim stems from his reading of the idealism argument of the Antinomy, where Kant asserts that a contradiction would emerge if one regards the world (the sum-total of all appearances) as a "whole existing in itself." He maintains that this argument must be taken as making a claim about how to regard the *existence* of appearances, since if we take Kant to be referring to the sum-total of things considered as they appear we succeed only in trivializing it. In rebuttal, I claimed that this rests upon a misreading of Kant's argument, and that properly construed it not only is compatible with but requires my reading.[23] I also pointed out that the textual evidence for the linguistic claim is slim, since there are relatively few passages in which *'an sich selbst'* is explicitly linked with forms of *'existieren'* compared with those in which there is either an explicit or implicit reference to a mode of consideration.

The second line of objection, which was noted by Ameriks in a review article on the recent Kant literature, is similar in spirit to Aquila's, although it focuses on the contrast between phenomenal and noumenal properties rather than between ways of existing.[24] The basic assumption underlying the critique is that on the double-aspect reading Kant is committed to the thesis that every object in the phenomenal world is identical to one in the noumenal world. In other words, there must be a one to one mapping or strict isomorphism between the sets of objects constituting the membership of the two worlds. In addition to the obvious problem that this seems to claim more than the "critical" limits on knowledge would allow (a claim also made by Aquila), this isomorphism is said to raise deep puzzles about identity and individuation. Since phenomenal objects are supposed to be individuated on the basis of their spatio-temporal location, the great problem is to explain how one can claim that such objects are numerically identical to objects which, *ex hypothesi*, lack spatio-temporal properties altogether. More generally, is it not simply incoherent to suggest that two objects with no common properties are identical?

In my response to this line of objection, I first tried to show that certain recent attempts to deal with these problems by appealing to the resources of possible world semantics were largely beside the point. Although initially promising, since it allows for the assignment of inconsistent pairs of predicates to the same object as well as transworld identity between objects lacking in any common properties, this strategy operates with a metaphysical conception of the transcendental distinction which I regard as alien to Kant.[25] The major thrust of my analysis, however, was to deny that the double-aspect reading commits Kant to a full or even a partial isomorphism between the phenomenal and the noumenal. It is, after all, one thing to distinguish between things as they are for us in virtue of the sensible conditions of human knowledge and things as they are thought independently of these conditions, and quite another to affirm an isomorphism between the members of two domains. Moreover, I called attention to two passages in which Kant himself seems to deny explicitly any such isomorphism.[26]

Recently, however, my interpretation of transcendental idealism, including this response to the earlier critics of the double-aspect reading, has been challenged afresh on both textual and systematic grounds by Hoke Robinson.[27] The textual challenge mainly concerns my alleged inability to deal adequately with the passages in which Kant identifies appearances with representations or "mere representations." Robinson lists thirty-three passages from the *Critique* and the *Prolegomena* in which this identification is supposedly "clear and unequivocal" and states that there are several others in which it is implicit.[28] He claims both that these passages constitute a major challenge to my interpretation, since they seem to commit Kant to a two-object view, and that I fail to deal with them in a convincing way. According to Robinson, the problem with my analysis is two-fold: first, I consider only a single passage and extend the results to the other texts without further argument; second, my interpretation of this passage is itself questionable.

In the passage in question Kant writes: "All objects of any experience possible to us are nothing but appearances, that is, mere representations, which, in the manner in which they are represented, as extended beings, or as series of alterations, have no independent existence outside our thoughts" (A490–91/B518–19). Robinson suggests that my reading turns on taking the phrase "in the manner in which they are represented" as modifying "appearances, that is, mere representations." In fact, I take the phrase in question to refer back to the objects of possible experience that are characterized as appearances. Questions of syntax aside, however, my main point (both in *Kant's Transcendental Idealism* and now) is that Kant is here identifying appearances with objects *qua* sensibly represented rather than, as might initially seem to be the case, with "mere representations." And it this which Robinson thinks constitutes a questionable reading of the text.

On Robinson's alternative reading, the phrase "as they are represented" [*so wie sie vorgestellt werden*] belongs to the following relative clause, since it falls within the scope of that clause. According to Robinson, this makes the sentence claim that the objects of possible experience are "nothing but appearances (i.e. mere representations); these have no independent existence outside our thoughts insofar as they are represented as extended or in alteration."[29] On this reading, however, Kant would seemingly be speaking nonsense, since the claim is that appearances (now identified with "mere representations") have no independent existence outside our thoughts insofar as they are *represented* (italics mine) as extended or in alteration. Would appearances so construed then have independent existence insofar as they are *not* represented in the manner specified, and do we wish to attribute to Kant the view that appearances are represented representations? I gladly leave it to the reader to decide which interpretation of this passage is more plausible.

This does not end matters, however, for, as Robinson notes, even if my reading is correct, this still leaves us with only a single passage which identifies appearances with things considered insofar as they are sensibly represented. And this is to be compared with the many in which they are seemingly equated directly with representations. Nevertheless, I believe that there is more to be said in support of the reading I favor, even though it may not suffice to resolve the textual dispute once and for all. To begin with, the passage in question is far from peripheral. On the contrary, it is one of the two places in the *Critique* in which Kant defines transcendental idealism and the only one retained in the second edition.[30] Accordingly, it seems reasonable to grant it some weight in an interpretation of the transcendental distinction.

Moreover, this is hardly the only place in which Kant construes appearances in roughly the way I have suggested, that is, as things *qua* sensibly represented or as objects of sensible representation (which leaves conceptual space for a non-sensible representation of the same thing). Thus, confining ourselves to the Transcendental Aesthetic, we note that Kant tells us that, "[A]ppearance . . . always has two sides [*zwei Seiten*], the one by which the object is viewed in and by itself (without regard to its mode of intuiting it – its nature therefore remaining always problematic), the other by which the form of intuition of this object is taken into account" (A38/B55). And, in the very next paragraph, after reminding the reader that space and time as "*a priori* sources of knowledge" (epistemic conditions in my terminology) are "merely conditions of our sensibility," he states that this very fact entails that "[T]hey apply to objects only insofar as objects are viewed [*betrachtet*] as appearances, and do not present [*darstellen*] things as they are in themselves" (A39/B56). And, finally, at the beginning of the "General observation on Transcendental Aesthetic," by way of explicating his idealistic conclusions, Kant writes: "What we have meant to say is that all our representation is nothing but the representation of appearance; that the things which we intuit are not in themselves what we intuit them as being" (A42/B59).[31]

Robinson's major challenge to my interpretation, however, is systematic rather than textual. Like earlier critics of the double-aspect view, he maintains that there is at least a *prima facie* implausibility in the claim that phenomenal and noumenal properties or features could be aspects of the *same* underlying thing. But unlike the earlier critics, he specifically takes issue with my previous attempt to deal with the problem. As he correctly notes, this attempt turned largely on an appeal to Prauss's understanding of the transcendental distinction as one between two ways of considering one and the same thing. In spite of his overall sympathy with Prauss's approach, Robinson thinks that this is inadequate because in order to have distinct non-vacuous ways of considering the same thing, the thing must somehow itself embody both aspects being considered. To cite his own example, Michaelangelo's *Pietà* can be considered as, among other things, both a great work of art and a lump of marble; but this is only because it really is both. Thus, the problem remains, since we supposedly cannot non-vacuously attribute both phenomenal and noumenal or *an sich* aspects to the same thing.[32]

In addition to this basic critique, Robinson offers a diagnosis of how I have gone wrong. The major problem seems to be that my view of the relation between subject and object is unclear. More specifically, I am charged with sliding from a conception of an object which is completely mind-dependent, since it holds of whatever is represented in accord with an epistemic condition, and one which is mind-independent in the sense that it is a self-subsisting thing that appears to us in accordance with our forms of sensibility.[33] Then, in an effort to determine how I might explain the relation between a cognitive subject equipped with epistemic conditions and a dual-aspected object, he attributes to me what he terms a "filtration model." According to this model, at least some objects possess both *an sich* (noumenal) and "representation-enabling features" (those which conform to epistemic conditions). The mind then acts like a filter, excluding all those objects lacking the appropriate features and selecting as members of the phenomenal world those that do. Finally, he remarks that although a dual-aspect theory employing the filtration model can deal successfully with the problem of phenomenality (the existence of unperceived objects), it fails to resolve the isomorphism problem and is particularly vulnerable on the non-spatiality issue.[34]

The great irony of Robinson's critique is that the filtration model which he attributes to me (at least by implication) is similar in many respects to the view defended by Paul Guyer, who is perhaps my staunchest critic on the idealism issue (and many others). Nevertheless, given his presuppositions, it is easy to see why Robinson thinks that I must be committed to something like this bizarre model, which has nothing to do with Kant's idealism. At the heart of the matter is Robinson's assumption about what a coherent double-aspect theory must involve. As is clear from his example of the *Pietà*, Robinson's underlying assumption is that any non-vacuous consideration of a thing must reflect some pre-given, real aspect of the thing being considered. And this leads directly to the conclusion that the object must possess in its own right the so-called "representation-enabling features," as well as to the previously noted puzzles about identity and isomorphism.

It therefore seems that for Robinson a double or dual-aspect theory is one which assigns distinct properties to distinct aspects of some underlying thing. Now, admittedly, this is how such theories are usually construed. Most notably, with regard to the mind–body problem, "dual-aspectism" is often regarded as a competitor to both dualism and materialism; and Spinoza's account of the mind as constituting one and the same thing with the body is perhaps the classical example of a dual-aspect theory in this metaphysical sense.[35]

If anything is clear in this murky subject, however, it is that Kant's transcendental distinction is not to be understood as involving a theory of this type. That is to say, transcendental idealism, on a double-aspect reading, does not require that phenomenal and noumenal properties be assigned to the same things, as is suggested by the metaphysical version of dual-aspectism and Robinson's *Pietà* example. Nor does it even entail the weaker view, suggested by Robinson's talk of "representation-enabling features," that things are such as to be representable by beings like us as spatio-temporal and by beings with a different cognitive apparatus (perhaps a pure understanding operating independently of sensible imput) in some non–spatio-temporal manner. Since (on Kant's view) being representable in these disparate ways is a function of different modes of representing rather than of the nature of the things represented, it is not (except in a trivial sense) a property of the things themselves.

What transcendental idealism is committed to on the reading advocated here is first of all the possibility and indispensability of distinguishing between two epistemic relationships in which things can be considered in a philosophical reflection on the conditions of their cognition. Once again, it is between a consideration of things in relation to the sensible conditions of human knowledge (as they appear) and a consideration of the same things as putative objects of some "pure understanding" (as they are in themselves). And, given this distinction, such idealism is further committed to the thesis that the spatio-temporal aspects, features or properties of objects (at this point the precise terminology is unimportant) pertain to these objects only *qua* considered in the first of these two ways. Granted, one may very well find Kant's arguments for this thesis unpersuasive; I nonetheless maintain that the underlying distinction between these two ways of considering things is itself perfectly coherent and fully grounded in Kant's discursivity thesis. I further maintain that if one does reject this distinction, one will also have to reject the entire framework of the *Critique of Pure Reason*.

At this point it might be objected that I have still not addressed the problem of sameness, which is perhaps the main thrust of Robinson's critique (as well as that of other critics of the double-aspect interpretation). Even if, as I have argued previously, transcendental idealism does not assert an isomorphism between the phenomenal and noumenal, the fact remains that it does commit one to the claim that it is in some sense the *same thing* that is to be considered from two points of view. And this raises the question of how this sameness is to be understood.

The problem is not that there is a manifest contradiction, as if the same thing that is considered an appearance is also considered a non-appearance.[36] It is rather that these two conflicting ways of considering do not seem to leave room for the conception of some single underlying thing that is being considered. The obvious response, the one certainly suggested by the metaphysical version of dual-aspectism, is that it is the thing as it is in itself or, more simply, the thing in itself (the "real" thing) that is being considered from two points of view. The difficulty here, however, is that "as it is in itself" is itself one of the ways of considering the thing. Thus the problem remains: how are we to characterize that which can be considered in two such disparate manners – as it appears and as it is in itself? This apparently requires a conception of the thing from no point of view, and that seems incoherent.

Although to my knowledge Kant never addressed this problem explicitly, the resources of the *Critique* can provide only one conceivable answer: the thing must be characterized as a "transcendental object = x." In this respect, the *concept* of the transcendental object is not equivalent to the *concept* of the thing considered as it is in itself. And insofar as I tended to identify the two in *Kant's Transcendental Idealism*, Robinson is correct in challenging me on this point.[37] What this suggests, however, is not the rejection of any connection between the thing in itself and transcendental object, but rather the necessity for a further distinction between the thing in itself *simpliciter*, which for us (as finite discursive intellects) can be thought merely as a transcendental object = x, and the thing *considered* as it is in itself, which is thought through pure categories. The basic difference is that the former must be characterized as "= x" because it remains inaccessible to all of the resources of a discursive intellect, while the latter, as involving independence merely from sensible conditions, can at least be thought problematically. I am not sure that Kant ever had quite this distinction in mind, but it is very close to the distinctions between transcendental object and noumenon and between negative and positive conceptions of a noumenon, which he drew in the first and second editions of the *Critique* respectively.[38] More importantly, it is precisely what Kant needs in order to deal with the sameness problem.

IV

Perhaps the most basic fault that critics have found in my essentially epistemological rendering of the transcendental distinction is its failure to do justice to what they take to be the ontological thrust of Kantian idealism. In fact, this line of objection has been advanced by both those who are somewhat sympathetic to transcendental idealism and those who dismiss it out of hand. Foremost in the former group is Karl Ameriks, who, in his most recent discussion of the topic, remarks that on my reading there is "no reason to think that the non-ideal has a greater ontological status than the ideal."[39] And this, Ameriks thinks, flies in the face of the fact that Kant believed in and spoke of (which he is careful to distinguish from making particular theoretical assertions about) "the absolute reality of things in themselves with substantive non–spatio-temporal characteristics."[40]

At first glance, at least, there is much to favor an ontological reading of the sort Ameriks recommends. Indeed, the very language of Kant's transcendental distinction would seem to require it. "Appearance talk" is, after all, meaningful only if it is contrasted with talk about things as they "really are." Thus, even granting that the distinction is between two ways of considering things rather than between two kinds of thing, it would still seem that whatever can be said of things on the basis of the first way of considering them would have lesser ontological import than claims (if there were any) based on the second. In short, it would seem that under any interpretation, the transcendental distinction must be seen as in some way incorporating the classical ontological contrast between appearance and reality.

Such a reading also seems to draw support from the previously noted fact that in the Inaugural Dissertation, Kant explicitly contrasted sensible to intellectual cognition as a knowledge of things as they appear to a knowledge of "things as they are." Even though the "critical" Kant denied that we can have knowledge of the latter type, his continued adherence to the Dissertation's doctrine of sensibility and his equation of a consideration of things as they are in themselves with a consideration of things as some pure understanding might think them certainly suggest that the ontological contrast of the earlier work is still operative.

Further support for the ontological reading appears to come from Kant's moral philosophy, particularly his practical metaphysics of the supersensible.[41] By affirming the primacy of practical reason or, what amounts to the same thing, denying knowledge in order to make room for faith (Bxxx), Kant is offering an *entrée* through practical reason to the very same ultimate reality which he had foreclosed to speculation. Or so it would seem.

Nevertheless, I still maintain that a straightforwardly ontological reading of the sort that Ameriks (together with many others) favors is to be rejected. In dealing with this issue, I shall first address the general points noted above which supposedly speak in favor of such an ontological reading, and then consider some of the specifics of Ameriks' analysis.

Since I have discussed the issue of "appearance talk" at some length in *Kant's Transcendental Idealism*, I shall here be quite brief. The basic point is simply that if we take the contrast between things as they appear and as they are in themselves as a distinction between how things *seem* to beings with our cognitive apparatus and how they *really are*, it becomes difficult, if not impossible, to preserve the robust empirical realism on which Kant so clearly insists. Preserving this realism requires not abandoning transcendental idealism (as Guyer, for one, would have it), but rather deontologizing the transcendental distinction. Properly deontologized, the denial that spatio-temporal properties are predicable of things considered as they are in themselves amounts neither to the thesis that things only appear to us to be in space and time (whereas "really" they are not) nor to the claim that things so considered possess a distinct set of noumenal properties, which are more real than the phenomenal properties revealed in experience. It rather consists essentially in a scope limitation on spatial and temporal concepts, a limitation which reflects the epistemic functions of the representations of space and time. To this extent, at least, transcendental idealism is, in Guyer's terms, a doctrine of epistemological modesty, but this is surely no more than Kant himself asserts when he insists that the concept of a noumenon is "a merely *limiting concept*, the function of which is to curb the pretensions of sensibility" (A255/B311).[42]

Similarly, I deny that the connection between the Dissertation's doctrine of intellectual cognition as yielding knowledge of things as they really are and the *Critique*'s conception of the nature of a consideration of things as they are in themselves points to an ontological reading of transcendental idealism. On the contrary, I take it that Kant's project in the *Critique* involves the radical deontologization of the doctrine of the Dissertation. In other words, in the *Critique* Kant does not merely deny the possibility of knowledge of the sorts of things he had previously viewed as knowable in a non-sensory manner (although he certainly does that), he also regards as problematic the very conception of the object (a noumenon) on which the earlier conception rests. Moreover, this can be seen as a direct consequence of the discursivity thesis. Once it is recognized that thought apart from its relation to sensible intuition is "empty," and that the "real use" of the intellect is possible only in connection with experience,[43] then the consideration of things as they are in themselves loses any claim to being a thought (much less a cognition) of them as they "really are." It becomes instead a reflection on how we are constrained to think things, once we abstract from the sensible conditions through which they are given in experience.

I also maintain that this lack of ontological priority extends to claims made from the "practical point of view," where Kant most clearly seems to be making substantive ontological claims about the noumenal, particularly with respect to freedom. In fact, I think that it is precisely here that we find the strongest considerations against the type of ontological reading favored by Ameriks. Although Kant certainly holds that from the practical point of view we are entitled to predicate transcendental freedom or absolute spontaneity of the will and that this is possible only because transcendental idealism allows us to consider the will (or self) from two points of view, he never takes this to mean that we *really are* free and only *appear* to be causally determined. That would amount to as great a perversion of Kant's view as the contrary claim that we really are causally determined and only believe that (or act as if) we are free. On the contrary, Kant is committed to the thesis that we are both causally conditioned and free (in an indeterminist sense), albeit *qua* considered from different points of view. Granted, this is a difficult doctrine and it has been subjected to considerable criticism from Kant's time to the present. But regardless of what one thinks of Kant's doctrine, it should at least be clear that the problem is one of reconciling competing claims and that this is not to be accomplished by assigning them to different levels on an ontological hierarchy.

Admittedly, Kant does speak on occasion, particularly in *Groundwork III* and the *Critique of Practical Reason,* of the idea of freedom or the consciousness of the moral law as giving us *entrée* to an intelligible world or higher order of things, quite distinct from the sensible world of experience. Nevertheless, it is clear from the context that the superiority of the former to the latter is to be construed in axiological rather than ontological terms. In other words, what we become aware of is a higher set of values and a vocation (*Bestimmung*) to pursue them, not of our membership in some higher order of being. Similarly, in connection with his discussion of the postulates in the second *Critique,* Kant speaks of the primacy of practical reason in relation to the speculative (KprV5: 119–21; 125–27). But this means only that our practical interest (in morality and the conditions of its possibility) is entitled to override our speculative interest in avoiding ungrounded claims and that the latter must therefore submit to the former. Once again, then, there is no thought of any access (cognitive or otherwise) to an ontologically superior order of being.

This brings us to Ameriks' specific claim that Kant believed in and spoke about "the absolute reality of things in themselves with substantive non–spatiotemporal characteristics." Since what Kant may or may not have believed (as a matter of private opinion) is not really germane, the operative question is how one is to construe those places in which Kant apparently makes substantive claims about things as they are in themselves, even while denying that, properly speaking, we can possess any knowledge of things so considered. Although in his discussion of my views Ameriks refers only to Kant's transcendental theology as an example of such a claim, it is clear from his other writings that he also has in mind the claims about the self (its immateriality, identity, etc.), which Kant makes in connection with his critique of rational psychology in the Paralogisms. According to Ameriks, Kant continued to maintain an essentially rationalist (Leibnizian) view of the self even after his "critical turn." Consequently, what he rejects in the Dialectic of the first *Critique* is not the rationalist position *in toto*, but merely some of its more extravagant claims and the flawed arguments in support of them.[44]

Since I analyze Kant's case for one of these "substantive" claims (immateriality) in Chapter 7 ("Kant's refutation of materialism"), it would be redundant to pursue that topic here. Instead, I shall attempt to address Ameriks' objection by appealing to some general considerations regarding the Dialectic. From this point of view, what is distinctive about the kind of claim that Ameriks has in mind is that it involves transcendental ideas. By such an idea, Kant understands "a necessary concept of reason to which no corresponding object can be given in sense experience" (A327/B383). Such ideas are deemed "necessary" because they are concepts of the unconditioned (or totality of conditions), which must be thought in connection with the conditioned appearances. For present purposes, however, the crucial point is that even though by their very nature these ideas involve the thought of something intelligible or supersensible, they are not to be identified (at least not straightforwardly) with concepts of things as they are in themselves. On the contrary, apart from the idea of the world (which is just the idea of the sum-total of appearances), they are concepts of objects that are ontologically distinct from appearances. Thus, even assuming for the sake of argument that Kant ontologically privileges the purely intelligible objects of these ideas, it does not follow that he likewise privileges things considered as they are in themselves. Moreover, it should not be assumed that this distinction conflicts with the double-aspect interpretation advocated here. This interpretation does not deny that Kant refers to noumena that are ontologically distinct from the phenomenal objects of human experience (e.g. God and the soul); it rather merely affirms that the transcendental distinction, on which Kant's idealism turns, is not to be equated with the distinction between these two types of object.[45]

But what of these intelligible objects corresponding to the transcendental ideas with respect to which Kant appears to be making substantive claims? In order to understand Kant on this point, we must consider, however briefly, the Dialectic's doctrine of transcendental illusion. Simply put, this doctrine maintains that reason inevitably falls prey to illusion when pursuing its endemic quest to find the unconditioned for every conditioned, thereby securing the completeness and systematicity required for the ultimate coherence of our knowledge.[46] This illusion consists in taking subjective principles as objective; and it is manifested in the use of the transcendental ideas (God, freedom and the soul) through which reason attempts to think the unconditioned. Although a transcendental idea is defined as "a necessary concept of reason to which no possible object can be given in sense experience" (A327/B383), Kant claims that reason necessarily posits a noumenal object for these ideas, and herein lies the illusion.

As Michelle Grier has pointed out in her study of Kant's doctrine of transcendental illusion, what is really interesting about this doctrine is that Kant maintains both that the illusion itself is inevitable and that we can nonetheless avoid succumbing to it.[47] The means for avoiding this fate is, of course, a critique of pure reason, such as Kant provides in the book with that name. But since the tendency to hypostatize and the apparent ontological privileging of claims about noumenal grounds that goes with it remain in place even after a critique, it is not surprising to find passages in Kant fitting Ameriks' description. Far from conflicting with my understanding of Kant's "critical" modesty, however, they serve merely to explicate how reason is constrained to think the noumenal.

V

Like Ameriks, Paul Guyer affirms an ontological reading of Kant's idealism. Unlike Ameriks, however, he dismisses this idealism as incoherent and as irrelevant to Kant's genuine philosophical contribution: his transcendental theory of experience, which he regards as all that is worth preserving in the *Critique*.[48] Consequently, he is opposed not so much to the double-aspect view *per se* as to any attempt to interpret transcendental idealism in a sympathetic fashion. One aspect of Guyer's critique has already been discussed in connection with the neglected alternative objection, but since the issues at stake are central to the interpretation of Kant's theoretical philosophy, a fuller consideration is in order.

According to Guyer, my interpretation of Kant's idealism is completely wrongheaded. Far from being the "anodyne recommendation of epistemological modesty" that I (and others) supposedly take it to be, he construes it as the dogmatic doctrine that things in themselves are not spatial and temporal. Guyer grants that Kant makes this denial without postulating a second set of non-spatial and non-temporal objects in addition to the ordinary objects of human experience. However, he insists that Kant does something equally unsatisfactory, namely, "*degrade* ordinary objects to mere representations of themselves, or *identify* objects possessing spatial and temporal properties with mere mental entities."[49] In short, rather than attributing to Kant something like a double-aspect view, we are invited to regard him as beginning with the familiar Lockean dualistic ontology of ordinary objects such as tables and chairs and the representations of them and arriving at his idealism through the reassignment of spatial and temporal properties from the former (now denominated "things in themselves") to the latter (now termed "appearances"). Guyer recognizes that this is totally unacceptable, but, for the reason already noted, he claims not to be perturbed by it. Thus, in spite of his fundamentally different approach, Guyer ends up in virtually the same place as Strawson. Transcendental idealism is both untenable and superfluous, and any attempt (such as mine) to rehabilitate it is ill-conceived.

But where, in particular, does Guyer locate my error? Apart from the previously discussed charge that I am guilty of the crude mistake of confusing a claim about the *concept* of the thing in itself with a claim about its actual *properties* (or absence thereof), he maintains that I both misconstrue the actual course of Kant's reasoning from conditions of experience to ideality and attribute to him a fallacious argument. More specifically, he attacks two passages in *Kant's Transcendental Idealism* in which I argue that epistemic conditions must be construed as reflecting the constitution of the subject and cannot be viewed as based on the structure of things as they are in themselves. In the second of these, I argue in particular that the representation of space cannot *both* function as a condition of experience *and* be derived from the experience of spatially ordered things in themselves. As I there put it:

[T]here is a contradiction involved in the assumption that the representation of something that is supposed to function as a condition of the possibility of the experience of objects can have its source in the experience of these objects. This is contradictory because it entails that experience be possible apart from something that is stipulated to be a condition of its possibility.[50]

Guyer not only denies that there is any contradiction in the assumption that a condition necessary for the experience of objects is derived from the experience of these very objects, he contends that it provides the most plausible explanation of this necessity. The idea here is that cognition or experience occurs just in case what is required by the subject as a condition of experience is satisfied by the objects. And no idealistic assumptions, no conception of the mind imposing its forms on given data, are required to account for this possibility. Guyer does not, of course, deny that Kant moves from necessity to subjectivity, but he affirms that such a move is so counterintuitive that it must be seen as the conclusion, not as a premise, of Kant's argument for idealism. Thus, in sharp contrast to my view (and that of most commentators), Guyer contends that Kant argues not that space and time cannot be properties of things in themselves *because* they are subjective forms of representation, but rather the opposite thesis "that space and time can *only* be mere forms of representation because they *cannot* be properties of things as they are in themselves."⁵¹

As textual support for the claim that Kant actually argues in this way, Guyer cites the order of the two conclusions that Kant draws from the Metaphysical and Transcendental Expositions of space. Instead of taking them as complementary conclusions, mutually entailed by the arguments, which is surely the most natural reading, he maintains that the second conclusion ("space is nothing but the form of all appearances of outer sense . . .") is supposed to follow from the first ("space does not represent any property of things in themselves . . ."). This makes it appear as if Kant were, in fact, arguing from the dogmatic assertion of the non-spatiality of things in themselves to the subjective status of space as a form of sensibility.

But even if one were to accept this forced and implausible reading, it does little to support Guyer's claim. This would require not merely taking the conclusions in the way in which he does, but also completely ignoring the fact that both are explicitly presented by Kant as inferences from the premise that the representation of space is an *a priori* intuition.⁵² To be sure, he also refers to a number of other passages from the *Nachlass* in support of his reading. These prove to be of no help, however, since all that they do is to reiterate the familiar Kantian refrain that *a priori* knowledge of space is incompatible with the assumption that it is derived from things in themselves.⁵³ And, as Guyer is well aware, it is one thing to claim that our knowledge of space is not derived from things in themselves (which would make it empirical) and quite another to hold that things in themselves are non-spatial.

Moreover, direct evidence against Guyer's reading is found in *On a Discovery According to which Any New Critique of Pure Reason Has Been Made Superfluous by an Earlier One,* a text which he ignores completely. In response to his Leibnizian critic, J. A. Eberhard, who accused him of taking everything that is of value in the *Critique* from Leibniz (including his theory of sensibility), Kant there writes regarding space and time:

Given the nature of these original modes of representation, I can regard them only as merely subjective (but positive) forms of my sensibility (not merely as the deficiency of the clarity of the representations obtained through this sensibility), not as forms of *things in themselves,* therefore only as forms of objects of sensible intuition, and hence of mere appearances (UE 8: 240; 151).

Although the latter portion of this passage taken in isolation might seem to suggest Guyer's view that Kant first denies that space and time pertain to things in themselves and only then concludes that they are mere forms of appearances, the passage as a whole makes it quite apparent that both conclusions are derived from an analysis of these "original modes of representation," that is, from the analysis of the representations of space and time provided in the Metaphysical Expositions of the Transcendental Aesthetic. Moreover, on the next page, Kant reiterates the point, remarking that the ideality of space and time were deduced from the inner nature of the representations (UE 8: 241; 152).

Nevertheless, Guyer insists not merely that Kant in fact argued in the way he suggests, but that, given the implausibility of the straightforward move from apriority to subjectivity, he had to do so in order to establish his cherished but misguided ideality thesis. At the heart of the problem, according to Guyer, is Kant's deep confusion about necessity and *a priori* knowledge. Instead of recognizing that all that may be inferred from our putative *a priori* knowledge of space is the conditional and *de dicto* claim, "Necessarily, if we are to perceive an object then it is spatial and euclidean," Kant's confusion led him to affirm the absolute and *de re* thesis, "If we are to perceive an object, it is *necessarily* spatial and euclidean."[54] And since the latter, unlike the former, is supposedly incompatible with the assumption that things in themselves are spatial, it leads directly to idealism.

Guyer's reason for assuming that *a priori* knowledge requires only a conditional necessity and that this is compatible with such knowledge being of things in themselves is particularly instructive. It reduces to the bare assertion that, "[I]t seems at least possible to imagine that we could know because of certain constraints on our ability to perceive that any object we perceive must have a certain property."[55] Guyer is certainly correct in asserting that on this scenario there would be no need for idealism. The perceived properties might very well belong to things as they are in themselves, since whatever structure is attributed to the mind functions merely to restrict the kind of data it can receive or record (much as in Robinson's proposed filtration model), not to impose its own forms upon these data. He is incorrect, however, in assuming that the reason why Kant rejected such an account is that it entails that *a priori* knowledge applies only contingently to objects. On the contrary, the problem with Guyer's account is not that under it putative *a priori* knowledge would apply only contingently to objects but that it would not apply at all. At best, we might have *a posteriori* knowledge (in Lockean fashion) of the "natural constitution" of our cognitive faculties, not a knowledge of the world, either as it is in itself or as it appears. Moreover, Guyer himself virtually admits as much when, in a revealing passage, he states that a conditional necessity "would seem to be the only kind of necessity that we could ever arrive at by any investigation construed, in Lockean fashion, an *exploration of the limits of our own cognitive faculties* – which is to say by a Copernican revolution as Kant apparently intended that to be understood."[56]

So much, then, for Guyer's alternative, dogmatic interpretation of transcendental idealism and the line of reason leading to it; the next question is what survives of his critique of my view. Since this critique is based mainly on his denial of any contradiction in the supposition that a representation functioning as a condition of experience is also derived from a direct encounter with things as they are in themselves, a further consideration of his reasons for this denial seems called for.

To begin with, it must be emphasized that the issue currently before us is not whether epistemic conditions might somehow be *satisfied* by things as they are in themselves, but rather whether the representations that function as such conditions (in this case the forms of sensibility) might be *derived from* an experience of things so considered. Although I was admittedly not completely clear on this crucial point in *Kant's Transcendental Idealism*, it is only the latter that is claimed to be contradictory.[57] Indeed, it is precisely because there is no direct contradiction in the former claim that the problem of the neglected alternative arises. Thus, insofar as Guyer's denial of a contradiction turns on the claim that the conditions of knowledge might be satisfied by things as they are in themselves, he is guilty of an *ignoratio elenchi*.

But what are we to make of Guyer's claim that the conditions of knowledge might be satisfied by things as they are in themselves, which amounts to a kind of reaffirmation of the neglected alternative objection? Recall that by such conditions, Guyer means essentially constraints or limits on the mind's capacity to receive (and presumably process) its data. Now, admittedly, there is no difficulty in assuming that things as they are in themselves might satisfy *such* conditions; in fact, it is difficult to imagine what else could. The problem, however, is that Guyer seems to infer from this that they might likewise satisfy what I have termed epistemic conditions. Moreover, in so doing, he simply begs the question, not only against me, but also against transcendental idealism.

As should be clear from the preceding, the difference between Guyer and myself on the complex of issues concerning transcendental idealism turns largely on our quite distinct interpretations of Kant's transcendental conditions of experience. For Guyer, if I understand him correctly, these conditions function like guardians of the mind, denying access to whatever does not present the proper credentials (such as being ordered in three dimensional euclidean space). Consequently, it remains on this view an entirely contingent matter whether or not the data satisfy these conditions, but insofar as they do we are able to cognize things as they are in themselves. By contrast, for me (and I believe for Kant) they are more like *enabling* conditions. As forms or modes of representing things, they make it possible for the mind to represent to itself not only a public objective world, but even its own inner states. Moreover, on this view it is absurd to suggest that there is an element of contingency in the conformity of things to the conditions of our knowledge.[58] Things, *qua* known (phenomena), necessarily conform to these conditions, precisely because they constitute our forms of cognizing them. And, *pace* Guyer, I take this to be the whole point of Kant's "Copernican revolution."

Finally, on this interpretation, I think it obvious that there is, indeed, a contradiction in the supposition that these forms could themselves be derived from experience, for this would require that the mind be able to represent objects apart from the very conditions which are assumed to make such representation possible.[59] As Kant himself claims with respect to all our "pure *a priori* representations" (including space and time), "We can extract clear concepts of them from experience, only because we have put them into experience, and because experience is thus itself brought about only by their means" (A196/B241). To be sure, one might still maintain that Kant fails to establish that the representations of space and time (or anything else, for that matter) function in this way. As before, however, I am not here concerned to defend this result, but merely the thesis that the ideality of space and time follows from it.[60]

2

Reflections on the B-Deduction

The Transcendental Deduction in the *Critique of Pure Reason* is clearly among the most highly praised, often criticized and least understood items in the philosophical canon. The obscurity and complexity of the text have enabled philosophers of vastly different persuasions to find what they wish to find in it and to disregard the rest. Thus, for Kant's idealistic successors it was the main inspiration for a speculative metaphysic of the I that contained both the deepest truth of the "critical" philosophy and the key to the transcendence of its allegedly "dogmatic" elements, such as the conception of the *Ding an sich*. By contrast, in our day it has been thought to contain the germ of a powerful transcendental argument that, starting from some supposedly non-controversial premise about self-consciousness or the self-ascription of experience, arrives at substantive, anti-skeptical conclusions regarding the objectivity of experience, without any of the excess baggage of transcendental idealism or transcendental psychology.

Curiously enough, these radically different approaches to the text have more in common than one might at first assume. Specifically, they share the view that the crucial theme in the Deduction is the correlation between self-consciousness or the capacity to say 'I' (apperception) and the consciousness or experience of an objective, spatio-temporal world. Indeed, the root idea that these somehow mutually condition one another is the nerve center of the Transcendental Deduction in virtually every interpretation from the most metaphysical to the most analytic. Presumably, the widely shared intuition that there is some deep and important truth or near truth contained in this idea accounts for the continued fascination with the argument, while the difficulty of spelling out just what this truth is, or even what Kant himself thought it to be, is the source of the continued disagreement among his interpreters and critics.

The situation remains basically unchanged in the latest work. As Karl Ameriks points out in his review of the recent literature, the Strawson-inspired transcendental argument approach is still dominant, even though there is widespread disagreement about the nature of the premises, the strength of the conclusion and the cogency of the argument.[1] As Ameriks also points out, a curious feature of this approach is that it virtually ignores what Kant himself quite clearly states to be the main concern of the Deduction, namely, to establish the objective validity of the pure concepts of the understanding or categories.[2] Although not unrelated, this is certainly a different matter than refuting a skeptical challenge to the "objectivity" of experience or the reality of the "external world." Presumably, Ameriks' own work is intended as a corrective to this tendency, since he defends a "regressive" reading of the argument, that is, one that sees it as moving from a relatively strong (and, therefore, controversial) premise regarding the reality of empirical knowledge or experience to the affirmation of the pure concepts as necessary conditions of such knowledge or experience.[3]

The interpretive problem is, of course, compounded by the fact that the Deduction exists in two distinct versions in the first two editions of the *Critique*. For some, mainly analytically minded interpreters, the difference between the two versions is a matter of minor significance at best. As already indicated, their chief concern is to uncover and evaluate a core of transcendental argumentation that is presumably buried in the text. For others, however, it is a matter of prime importance. Although broad generalizations are always dangerous, it does seem to be reasonable to state that metaphysically or phenomenologically oriented students of the *Critique* tend to see in the first edition the authentic "critical" position, whereas epistemologically or methodologically oriented students usually favor the second edition because of the dominance of the "logical" over "psychological" factors.

Given this state of affairs, I think that it is encumbent on each of us to put our hermeneutical cards on the table. At least that is what I propose to do here. The paper is divided into three parts. The first presents a brief sketch of the problematic of the Deduction as I see it and of the kind of procedures dictated by this problematic. The operative assumption is that an account of the actual premises and goals of Kant's argument (as contrasted with some idealized and sanitized transcendental argument) must consider the presuppositions of Kant's belief that a transcendental deduction is both necessary and possible. The second part applies some of these considerations to the interpretation of the proof-structure of the B-Deduction. It consists largely of a discussion of my differences with Dieter Henrich on this score. The third part raises some further exegetical questions about the later work of Henrich and its development by Paul Guyer. The paper as a whole can be described as an attempt to clarify certain aspects of my own interpretation by spelling out the motivation for them and by juxtaposing them to some of the main alternatives in the recent literature. Where it fails to convince, I hope that it at least serves to make clear where I stand on the issues.

I

In spite of its frequent neglect in the recent literature, the explicit purpose of the Transcendental Deduction is easy enough to specify, namely, to establish and delimit the epistemic credentials for a set of pure concepts of the understanding or categories that have been previously identified and connected with the very capacity to judge in the Metaphysical Deduction. Appealing to the legal terminology that was so congenial to him, Kant maintains that this amounts to answering a *quid juris,* that is, establishing a right as opposed to determining a fact (A84–A85/B116–117). Kant suggests that until this is accomplished we can have no assurance that these concepts have any more legitimacy than "usurpatory" concepts such as fortune and fate. Moreover, since these concepts are supposedly intimately involved in all claims for *a priori* knowledge, he also insists that it is necessary to determine the sphere (if any) of their legitimacy "before taking a single step in the field of pure reason" (A88/B121).

It is also quite clear that Kant holds that the only way in which this goal can be achieved is to show that these categories function as necessary conditions of the possibility of experience and that this is supposed to occur by connecting both to self-consciousness or apperception. It is just at this point, however, that the exegetical questions alluded to previously arise. Thus, it remains to be determined (among other things): for what sense of 'experience' are the categories supposed to be necessary conditions of its possibility; does the argument proceed to experience, so conceived, as a conclusion, or does it begin with it as a premise; what conception of self-consciousness or self-knowledge is operative in the argument; how does it actually function; and how is it connected with the categories and with experience?

As already indicated, I think that some light can be shed on these questions by first considering the more basic question of the presuppositions underlying the very project of attempting a transcendental deduction. It is, after all, not immediately obvious that a transcendental deduction is necessary. In fact, no one prior to Kant had thought of attempting one; although there were certainly numerous related justificatory projects, e.g., the Cartesian one. Now there seem to be three presuppositions which conjointly make a transcendental deduction a matter of pressing concern, as well as others which dictate that the deduction must proceed by linking the concepts in question to the possibility of experience.

The first and most obvious presupposition is that there are such things as pure concepts of the understanding, that is, concepts that are derived from, and reflect the cognitive structure of the mind. Since any empiricist must deny this, this is hardly a trivial assumption; but it is not unique to Kant. In some form or another it can be found in virtually every rationalist. Kant's most important predecessor on this score, however, was clearly Leibniz. In his *New Essays,* a work which we know to have exerted a profound influence on Kant, Leibniz affirms that the mind possesses a set of concepts which reflect the structure of the understanding and which are accessible to it through apperception. Thus, already in Leibniz there are clear intimations of a connection between the possession of a set of concepts and the capacity to say 'I.'

Nevertheless, there is not in Leibniz any more than there is in the empiricists, the recognition of the need for anything like a transcendental deduction in the Kantian sense. From Kant's perspective this can be attributed largely to the Leibnizian theory of sensibility, according to which the distinction between intellectual and sensible representation is merely one of clarity and distinctness rather than (as it is for Kant) one of kind. Given this theory, it follows that there will necessarily be a conformity between what is sensibly apprehended and what is clearly and distinctly conceived. Consequently, the potential problem of a lack of cognitive fit between the two species of representations simply does not arise. For Kant, however, who insists that sensibility and understanding are radically, i.e. transcendentally, distinct and that each has its own irreducible set of *a priori* conditions, this is by no means the case. Thus, for Kant, unlike Leibniz, it remains entirely possible (at least prior to a transcendental deduction) that "appearances [sensible representations] might very well be so constituted that the understanding should not find them to be in accordance with the conditions of its unity" (A90/B123).

Together these two premises or presuppositions are certainly enough to generate a problem about the legitimacy of pure concepts, but not the specific problematic of the Transcendental Deduction. Also, they do not yet point toward the Kantian solution, which consists in connecting these concepts with the possibility of experience. One could still very well assume, as Kant in fact did in the Dissertation, that these concepts apply to a non-sensible reality. If this be assumed, then it could also be maintained that they are legitimated by the fact that they are necessary for the very conception of such a reality (an "intelligible world"). Clearly, then, in order to arrive at the full set of preconditions for the formulation of the problematic of the Deduction, it is necessary to add the premise that a concept or principle can be legitimated only if it can somehow be related to what is intuitively given. Since sensibility and understanding are now regarded as radically distinct, this may no longer be construed in the naive psychological way that it was by Hume, namely, as requiring one to supply the impression of which the putative idea is a "copy." *Ex hypothesi,* this could never be done for a Kantian pure concept (or even an empirical concept for that matter). But this serves only to sharpen the problem, not to obviate the necessity of showing the connection between pure concepts and sensible intuition.

These presuppositions not only generate the need for a transcendental deduction, they also dictate how it must be carried out. Kant must establish a necessary connection between the pure concepts and the manifold of sensible intuition. This would have the dual effect of both legitimizing these concepts and restricting their sphere of application to what can be sensibly intuited. Moreover, since these concepts are conditions under which objects are thought, not conditions under which they are given, their legitimation can consist only in showing that they function as necessary conditions for doing anything, cognitively speaking, with the sensible data given to the mind under the forms of space and time. Finally, since what the mind supposedly does with its data is to cognize objects, this suggests that the pure concepts must function as necessary conditions of the knowledge of objects by means of the data, that is, as necessary conditions of empirical knowledge, or, equivalently, as necessary conditions of experience.

If this project is to be feasible, however, two additional assumptions are required. Specifically, it must be presupposed both that the understanding is spontaneous in the sense that it has the capacity to impose its own ordering rules (pure concepts) on the sensible data and that the data do not, of themselves, provide all that is necessary for the knowledge of objects. Without spontaneity, which is its essential property for Kant, the understanding would not be able to do anything with the given data; correlatively, without the assumption that the mere reception of data does not of itself suffice for the representation of objects or experience there would be no first order (in Kant's terms "real" as opposed to "logical") task for the understanding to perform. Consequently, there would be no role for the pure concepts; they would be superfluous. But these two assumptions are themselves simply two sides of the more basic assumption that the human understanding is discursive. To claim that our understanding is discursive is to claim that it operates by means of the conceptualization of given data. As Kant makes clear at the very beginning of the Transcendental Analytic, this is a fundamental presupposition of the *Critique of Pure Reason* as a whole.

Finally, if one accepts this sketch of the assumptions underlying both the problematic of the Transcendental Deduction and the procedures for its execution, several exegetical implications emerge. First, the argument must be "regressive" in the sense that it presupposes the possibility of experience or, equivalently, empirical knowledge. As Ameriks quite correctly points out, however, this does not prevent it from also being "progressive" in the sense that it moves from a premise about the possibility of empirical knowledge to a conclusion affirming synthetic *a priori* principles as conditions of this possibility.[4] Moreover, as Ameriks also indicates, the sense of 'experience' at work is quite weak and cannot be equated with the experience of a public, spatio-temporal world, which is the *terminus ad quem* of the Deduction on a Strawsonian reading.[5] All that is presupposed is the capacity to think objects by means of the conceptualization of given data, and this capacity can be exercised even if the objects thought are not distinct from our subjective states.

Second, although it is not so obvious, it would seem that, in order to get started, the Deduction requires an analytic premise (or set of premises) about the understanding and its *modus operandi*. Any such premise must be analytic because it consists merely in the unpacking of what is already implicit in our conceptions of discursive or conceptual thinking. Since Kant explicitly identifies the understanding with apperception (B134n), this premise should also involve analytic claims about the nature and conditions of apperception. It would not, however, involve any claims about the conditions of empirical self-consciousness or the self-ascription of experience.

Third, it should be apparent from the above that the nerve of the Deduction must be a synthetic *a priori* premise linking apperception or the understanding and its conditions (the categories) with the sensible data given to the mind in intuition. As we have already seen, it does not follow from an analysis of the understanding (or apperception) and the conditions of its unity that the sensible data will conform to these conditions. Consequently, to show that and how such conformity is possible can be regarded as the essential task of the Deduction.

II

The main reason usually given in order to explain Kant's complete revamping of the Transcendental Deduction in the second edition is his desire to prune away the psychological and phenomenalistic features that figure so prominently in the initial version. This, in turn, is seen as part of an overall concern to recast his position in response to the charge of subjective idealism raised in the notorious Garve–Feder review of the first edition of the *Critique*.[6] There is undoubtedly a good deal of truth to this, but it is not the whole story. Indeed, I think that even greater significance must be attributed to the fact that the B-Deduction more readily fits the preceding account of the problematic, assumptions and procedures of a transcendental deduction. Admittedly, the fit is not complete and there remain plenty of ambiguities and tensions between conflicting lines of argument even in the revised version. Nevertheless, it is the case that in the B-Deduction, but not in its predecessor, one is able to discern the outlines of a single line of argument which, beginning with an analytic account of the understanding or apperception, and proceeding by means of synthetic *a priori* claims regarding the transcendental synthesis of the imagination, attempts to link the categories with the data of human sensibility, and through the data to experience.

Unfortunately, moving from its general outlines to the specific features of this argument is not an easy task. As Henrich has emphasized in a classic paper, a major interpretive problem is to account for the fact that Kant arrives at apparently identical conclusions concerning the role of the categories in two places, §20 and §26.[7] Of itself, this might suggest that he is offering two distinct proofs, as he did in the first edition. This is ruled out, however, by Kant's remark at the end of the first part that "a beginning is made of a *deduction* of the pure concepts of understanding" (B144). This indicates that the two parts are intended as two stages in a single proof. Thus, the challenge posed by Henrich to any interpretation of the B-Deduction is to explain how the two parts do in fact constitute – or, at least, how Kant might have thought that they constitute – two steps in a single proof. In *Kant's Transcendental Idealism* I accepted this challenge and offered my own reconstruction of the argument. I did not, however, except parenthetically, express my reasons for differing from Henrich on a number of crucial points. Accordingly, I would like to take this opportunity to state some of these reasons. In so doing, I also hope to be able to show in a bit more detail why I take the B-Deduction to embody the argument-schema sketched above.

Like many other interpreters, Henrich sees the central task of the Deduction to be the elimination of the dreaded possibility that "appearances might very well be so constituted that the understanding should not find them to be in accordance with the conditions of its unity." What is unique to his reading is the claim that the B-Deduction attempts to achieve this goal in a piecemeal fashion. The key here is his assumption that there is a restriction in the first part of the argument that is removed in the second. This restriction, according to Henrich, is expressed in the conclusion of the first part, where Kant states that "All the manifold, therefore, so far as it is given in a single empirical intuition [*in Einer empirischen Anschauung*] is determined in respect of one of the logical functions of judgment . . ." (B143). Taking the capitalization of *Einer* to indicate that Kant is referring to the unity of intuition (a point that is completely missed by Kemp Smith in his translation), he infers from this that the function of the first part is to establish the applicability of the categories to intuitions insofar as they already possess unity. Since this leaves undetermined "the range within which unitary intuitions can be found," a second step is necessary in order to overcome this restriction and to show that all our sensible intuitions are subject to the categories because they are all unitary. The latter is presumably established by arguing that, since space and time are themselves unities and since all our intuitions are in space and time (both points being shown in the Transcendental Aesthetic), it follows that all our intuitions contain unity.[8]

As I suggested in *Kant's Transcendental Idealism* and as Hoke Robinson has argued independently, there is something peculiar in Henrich's contention that the first part contains a restriction on the range of application of the categories that is removed in the second part.[9] The problem is that Kant clearly views the first part as concerned with the relation between the categories and the manifold of sensible intuition in general and the second as concerned with their relation to the manifold of human sensible intuition.[10] Since human intuition or sensibility is certainly a species of intuition or sensibility in general, it seems far more natural to assume that the first part contains the broader rather than the narrower claim. In fact, the heading for the very section in which Henrich claims to find the restriction states that "*All sensible Intuitions are subject to the Categories, as conditions under which alone their Manifold can come together in one consciousness"* (B143).

Beyond this general difficulty, there are also specific problems with each of the steps of the proof as Henrich conceives them. According to Robinson, the first step is fatally flawed by the fact that every intuition for Kant contains unity.[11] Consequently, the first step, of itself, already entails the applicability of the categories to all intuition, which means that it leaves no restriction to be removed by the second step. This difficulty can, perhaps, be avoided by noting, as Robinson himself does, that Kant's claim concerns the *manifold* of intuition, not intuition itself.[12] Unfortunately, since Kant holds that the manifold, as given, does not possess unity and that whatever unity it acquires must be imposed upon it by an act of synthesis, this leads to the opposite problem. The point here is simply that if the applicability of the categories is to be limited to the manifold of intuition insofar as that manifold *already,* i.e., independently of categoreal synthesis, possesses unity, then it follows that the categories would have no application at all. On neither reading, then, do we have a plausible case for the claim that the categories have a restricted range of application that is later removed. Moreover, the situation is even worse with respect to the proposed second step in the argument. Although Henrich's account of this step is extremely cryptic, what he does say suggests that it involves a gross *non sequitur.* Certainly, it does not follow simply from the fact that space and time are unities that whatever is intuited in them must likewise be a unity.

Not surprisingly, Henrich's interpretation of the proof-structure of the B-Deduction also requires him to engage in some rather fanciful exegesis in order to deal with the portions of the text that do not fit neatly into his scheme. In particular, he insists that the two step proof is combined with a distinction between a *that* and a *how* question that differs from the familiar version of this distinction in the A-Deduction. In the earlier version, it is correlated with the contrast between the objective and the subjective sides of the Deduction. As Kant describes the situation, the concern of the former is to prove that the categories have objective validity, whereas the function of the latter is "to investigate the pure understanding itself, its possibility and the cognitive faculties upon which it rests" (Axvi). In the B-Deduction, according to Henrich, the *that* question remains the same, but the *how* question is now concerned with "making intelligible the possibility of relating the understanding to sensibility."[13]

This is puzzling because one would have thought that an explanation of how the understanding, and with it the categories, can relate to human sensibility is precisely the task of the second part of the Deduction (rather than a side issue). Moreover, this is confirmed by the very passage cited by Henrich in support of his own interpretation. After describing what has been accomplished in the Metaphysical Deduction and the first part of the Transcendental Deduction, Kant states,

> We have now to explain the possibility of knowing *a priori*, by means of the categories, whatever objects may *present themselves to our senses*, not indeed in respect of the form of their intuition, but in respect of the laws of their combination, and so, as it were, of prescribing laws to nature, and even of making nature possible" (B159–60).

As the context makes clear, Kant is here describing the task of the second part of the Deduction, not posing a distinct *"how* question." In fact, the contrived nature of Henrich's reading is evident from his own admission that the crucial step in the resolution of the presumed *"how"* question is to show "that such categories can exercise synthetic functions in intuition itself."[14] There is no doubt that Kant is concerned to show this; the point is only that to do so is to establish the objective reality of the categories and, therefore, to complete the task of the second part of the Deduction.

The recognition of the problematic features of Henrich's reconstruction underscores the significance of another exegetical question: namely, assuming that the proof does consist of two parts, why isn't the conclusion of the second part simply a trivial inference from the first? Since, as already noted, human sensible intuition is a species of sensible intuition in general (albeit the only one with which we are acquainted), it would seem that if the categories are applicable to the former, then, *a fortiori*, they must also be applicable to the latter.[15] Indeed, Kant himself seems to have suggested as much in the *Metaphysical Foundations of Natural Science*, when he states that the problem of the Deduction "can be solved almost by a single conclusion from the precisely determined definition of a judgment in general (an act by which given representations first become cognitions of an object)."[16] What we find in the *Critique*, instead of the expected linear inference from genus to species, however, are the accounts of the transcendental synthesis of the imagination (§24) and the empirical synthesis of apprehension (§26). Certainly, a major problem for any interpreter of the B-Deduction is to explain why, in spite of his remark in the *Metaphysical Foundations of Natural Science*, Kant thought that accounts of these syntheses were necessary in order to complete the task of the Deduction.

In dealing with this problem in my own work, I endeavored to take more seriously than is usually done Kant's insistence on the analyticity of the apperception principle.[17] With this as my starting point, I attempted to show that the entire argument of the first part of the Deduction can be seen as the unpacking of an analytical principle. Whatever one may think of the specifics of this analysis, it is at least clear that if my main interpretive thesis is correct, then there is significant work to be done in the second part. In fact, it follows that it is only in the second part that Kant can hope to establish *any* synthetic *a priori* claims about the categories. Moreover, once this is acknowledged, it also becomes apparent that Kant's account of the transcendental synthesis of the imagination and its relationship to apperception and the categories constitutes the real nerve of the Deduction because it is there that the categories are connected with the forms of human sensibility. This, in turn, makes it possible to connect them with the actual data of human sensible intuition through the empirical synthesis of apprehension.

Obviously, I cannot rehearse here the details of my interpretation of the transcendental synthesis of the imagination, but the key points can be brought out without doing so. Let us consider once again the possibility that "Appearances might be so constituted that the understanding should not find them to be in accordance with the conditions of its unity." If the conclusion of the first part is analytic, as it must be if it is a logical consequence of an analytical principle, then far from removing this possibility for a certain range of appearances (or intuitions), it does not remove it at all. Instead, it shows merely that insofar as unity is introduced into the manifold of intuition by the understanding, that is, insofar as it is represented as *a* manifold, it must conform to the conditions of the unity of consciousness and, therefore, to the categories. This result leaves completely unsettled the question of whether data given in accordance with the forms of human sensibility are capable of being unified in a single consciousness according to the categories. This is no longer a question about the nature of the understanding, but rather about the nature of the sensibly given or, more precisely, about the manner or "form" in which data are given in human sensibility. It is not as Henrich suggests, however, a question about whether what is given is *unified*, but rather whether it is *unifiable*.

In the Transcendental Aesthetic, Kant does claim that appearances are unifiable in the sense that they are contained in a single time and a single space, and this result is certainly crucial for the argument of the second part of the Deduction. In order to complete the work of the Deduction, however, Kant must do more than simply "tack on" this result to the first and analytic part. He must also show that, since there can be no unity for the understanding except that which the understanding represents to itself as such, and, therefore, produces or "reproduces" through its own spontaneous activity, a categoreally governed synthesis is necessary if the understanding is to represent to itself the unity of space and/or time.[18] But since it is the unity of space and time that must be represented, not simply that of the understanding itself, a certain constraint or condition is imposed upon its synthetic activity by the given. For this reason Kant finds it necessary to distinguish this "figurative" or imaginative synthesis involved in the representation of space and time from "intellectual synthesis" or judgment, which was the focus of the first part of the Deduction. At the same time, he must also insist that, since this synthesis is required to bring the representations of the unity of time and space to the unity of consciousness, it must be governed by the categories. Finally, since all appearances in space and time are subject to the conditions of the representation of space and time, they are also subject to the categories.

In order to grasp the point of the complex line of argument sketched above, it may help to recall that in the Analogies Kant makes it clear that the applicability of the relational categories to appearances turns on the unifiability of appearances in a single time. But, as I argued in *Kant's Transcendental Idealism*, we cannot infer the unity of time (or space) from the unity of consciousness because there is no logical contradiction in the thought of appearances being given in different times (or spaces).[19] Consequently, we cannot argue directly from the unity of apperception to the applicability to appearances of the relational (or, indeed, any) categories. We can, however, reverse the process and argue from the unity of time to the necessary conditions of the consciousness of this unity.[20] I take this to be the crucial move in the second part of the B-Deduction. Moreover, since the argument begins with a synthetic *a priori* premise (the unity of time) rather than an analytic one (the unity of apperception), it can lead to a synthetic *a priori* result.

III

If my interpretation of the Transcendental Deduction can be described as an attempt to meet the challenge posed by Dieter Henrich in "The proof-structure of Kant's Transcendental Deduction," the work of Paul Guyer can be regarded as a response to the very different approach taken to the Deduction by Henrich in his subsequent monograph, *Identität und Objektivität*. Instead of concerning himself with a straightforward explication of the text of either edition, Henrich there adopts a method he terms "argumentative reconstruction" (*argumentierende Rekonstruktion*). Reduced to its simplest terms, this method consists in the systematic endeavor to uncover distinct premises and layers of argument and then, on their basis, to reconstruct various paths to the conclusions affirmed in the text. At one point Henrich describes such reconstruction as "a translation of a text into a schema of a truth-functionally determinate deduction."[21] This "translation" leads Henrich to locate two distinct types of argumentation in the deduction, each of which has many variants: (1) arguments from the nature of judgment; and (2) arguments from the nature of apperception. The latter, in turn, are divided into arguments from the unity and arguments from the numerical identity of apperception. Of these, the only one that Henrich finds to be at all adequate to the text is one that starts from the premise that a subject has "Cartesian certainty" of its "moderate numerical identity," that is, its identity throughout a temporal series of representative states, and that concludes from this that such certainty presupposes *a priori* rules for the synthesis of these states. These rules are, of course, the categories.[22]

IDEALISM AND FREEDOM

Guyer's approach is modeled on Henrich's in at least two major respects. First, although he is not very explicit about it, he seems to adopt something like Henrich's method of argumentative reconstruction. This is especially true in his most detailed treatment of the Deduction, "Kant's Tactics in the Transcendental Deduction," where he isolates various lines of argument or "tactics" by means of which Kant attempts to execute the "strategy" of proving that the categories are *a priori* conditions of the possibility of experience. Second, he seems to follow Henrich in assuming that the "Cartesian certainty" regarding numerical identity argument is, in fact, the chief tactic adopted by Kant. He differs from Henrich, however, in that he provides a criticism of the argument which is based on an alleged hidden ambiguity in its major premise. In addition, he offers a sketch of a somewhat different line of argument from the "empirical judgment that I have remained a single self through a period of diverse representations," which he claims to be the only ultimately successful tactic.[23] Although Guyer admits that only hints of this argument, which amounts to a weakened, "empiricized" version of Henrich's, are to be found in the actual text of the Deduction, he notes that Kant made considerable use of it in the *Reflexionen,* particularly those related to the Refutation of Idealism.

I do not propose to discuss here either the large methodological question of the viability of the Henrich–Guyer approach, which in many ways reminds me of the old fashioned "patchwork theory" (without its historical-philological underpinnings), or the adequacy of Guyer's own positive reconstruction. Instead, I would like simply to consider what I take to be the main assumptions of Guyer's interpretation, especially insofar as they contrast with my own. There are, I think, three such assumptions. The first, and most fundamental, is his agreement with Henrich that the main line of argument actually at work in the deduction (in both editions) turns on the premise that the mind has *a priori* knowledge (with "Cartesian certainty") of its own numerical identity over time and that this knowledge requires a synthesis according to the categories. The second assumption, the focal point of his difference from Henrich, is that this premise is ambiguous. He holds that it can be taken either as the hypothetical and analytic claim that if the mind is to be able to be conscious of its numerical identity throughout a successive series of representative states, then, necessarily, there must be some synthesis connecting them, or as the categorical and synthetic *a priori* claim that all my representations must be capable of being ascribed to an identical self.[24] The third assumption is that only the latter version is capable of getting the argument of the Deduction off the ground. Given this, he devotes most of his energies to showing that the key premise, so construed, is untenable, thereby paving the way for his own alternative.

Since the other assumptions obviously derive all of their plausibility from the first, I shall focus my remarks on it. To begin with, it should be noted that the textual support for this assumption is slim. Moreover, the main supporting passage is from the first edition, and, therefore, not without further argument applicable to the second. Finally, and most importantly, the passage itself is highly ambiguous. The passage in question states:

We are conscious *a priori* of the complete identity of the self in respect of all representations which can ever belong to our knowledge, as being a necessary condition of the possibility of all representations. For in me they can represent something only insofar as they belong with all others to one consciousness, and therefore must be at least capable of being so connected [A116].

As I noted in *Kant's Transcendental Idealism*, the ambiguity concerns just what we are supposed to be conscious of *a priori*.[25] The Henrich–Guyer interpretation, which focuses on the initial clause of the first sentence, takes it to be our numerical identity. On this reading, then, the main premise of the Deduction is that there is a "Cartesian certainty" of this identity "in respect of all representations which can ever belong to our knowledge." It would seem to be at least as plausible, however, to take the sentence to be claiming that what we are conscious of *a priori* is not our numerical identity, but rather the "fact" that this identity must be presupposed as "a necessary condition of the possibility of all representations." Certainly, this is suggested by the as-clause, as well as by the following sentence, which is merely a parenthetical clause in the German text. It is also in accord with the main thrust of the apperception principle in the B-Deduction, which, as I have argued, asserts merely the "necessity of a possibility," specifically, the necessity of the possibility of being conscious of an identical 'I think' with respect to each of my representations insofar as they collectively constitute a single complex thought.[26] Assuming that it is analytic that a single complex thought requires a single thinking subject (it takes one to have one), this principle is likewise analytic.

Guyer naturally rejects the analytic reading because, on his interpretation, it cannot do the job it is supposed to do. Accordingly, he likes to cite $A117_n$ where Kant seems to be claiming that the apperception principle is synthetic.[27] Although I am not as certain as Guyer that the proposition that Kant characterizes as synthetic in $A117_n$ is identical to the one that he regards as analytic in the B-Deduction, I do not wish to insist upon that here.[28] The important point is simply that Guyer's objection to the analytic reading becomes irrelevant, once one denies that the apperception principle states that we have a "Cartesian certainty" regarding our numerical identity with respect to any representations which we could ever possess. That principle is clearly synthetic; it is also clearly indefensible. Indeed, Guyer himself so convincingly demonstrates its indefensibility that one wonders why he follows Henrich so closely in insisting, on the basis of rather meager textual support, that it plays such a prominent role in Kant's actual argument.[29]

These brief remarks do not, of course, amount to a defense of my interpretation *vis-à-vis* Guyer's. In fact, to a considerable extent our interpretations work at cross purposes: his is concerned with uncovering lines of argument common to both editions (at least in his work which I have seen so far), while mine focuses narrowly and explicitly on the text of the B-Deduction. Most of us, I assume, would agree that these are equally legitimate approaches to the text. Nevertheless, I would like to close by saying in support of my own interpretation that it at least tries to take seriously and to establish a connection between two of the most puzzling features of the B-Deduction: namely, Kant's characterization of the apperception principle as analytic, and his claim, at a point at which it appears that the argument is complete, that only "a beginning is made of the deduction of the pure concepts of understanding." These, I suggest, are two features with which any serious interpretation of the B-Deduction must deal.

3

Apperception and analyticity in the B-Deduction

In the B-Deduction Kant states that, although it "reveals the necessity of a synthesis of the manifold given in intuition," the "principle of the necessary unity of apperception is . . . an identical, and therefore analytic proposition" (B135). Moreover, as if to emphasize that this was not a momentary slip, he remarks shortly thereafter that the proposition which "makes synthetic unity a condition of all thought . . . is, as already stated, itself analytic." This, he continues, is because:

[I]t says no more than that all *my* representations in any given intuition must be subject to that condition under which alone I can ascribe them to the identical self as *my* representations, and so can comprehend them as synthetically combined in one apperception through the general expression, '*I think*' (B138).

But, in spite of Kant's unambiguous pronouncements, this claim has proven to be a stumbling block for even the most sympathetic and thorough commentators.[1] To be sure, one could regard as analytic the trivial claim that all my representations must be subject to those conditions, whatever they may be, that allow them to be my representations. As the above citations indicate, however, Kant took the analyticity to extend also to the apparently substantive claim that the essential condition of the possibility of such self-ascription is that the representations be unifiable in a single self-consciousness. In short, Kant regards the principle of the necessary synthetic unity of apperception as itself analytic. And it is here that the problems begin, for it certainly seems strange that Kant, of all philosophers, would characterize what he terms "the highest principle in the whole sphere of human knowledge" (B135) as analytic. How could such a principle be analytic, and if it is, how could it ground the possibility of synthetic *a priori* knowledge?

In *Kant's Transcendental Idealism,* I attempted to take this claim seriously, making the analyticity of apperception into a key for interpreting the B-Deduction as a whole. In the present essay, I would like to return to this issue, considering the thesis in light both of Kant's overall teachings on apperception and of some of the literature that has appeared since the publication of my book. The essay is divided into three parts. The first sketches the main arguments against the thesis that the principle of apperception is analytic. The second attempts to show that the principle, in the form in which it appears in the first part of the B-Deduction, is in fact analytic and that this is consistent with the significance Kant attributes to it. The third considers the implications of the analyticity of the principle of apperception for the overall proof-structure of the B-Deduction. In particular, it argues that such an understanding of this principle is not only compatible with the two steps in a single proof schema noted by Dieter Henrich in his classical paper, but also serves to explain why the proof proceeds in two sharply distinguished steps.[2]

I

Perhaps the most serious discussion of Kant's claim for the analyticity of the principle of apperception in the recent literature is that of Paul Guyer, who considers this claim in light of his overall interpretation of the Transcendental Deduction. According to Guyer, the Deduction in both editions is a patchwork of radically different argumentative tactics. Some, resting on the presupposition of knowledge of objects, argue for the categories as necessary conditions of the possibility of such knowledge. Since this line of argument, which is prominent in the *Prolegomena* and many *Reflexionen,* involves strong assumptions about knowledge, it is obviously incapable of answering the skeptic. Others begin with apperception, understood as knowledge of the identity of the self, and attempt to argue that a synthesis governed by the categories is a necessary condition of the possibility of such knowledge. Breaking on this point with Dieter Henrich, who has advanced a similar interpretive scheme,[3] Guyer thinks that the second set of arguments fall into two classes: those which take the knowledge of the identity of the self to be *a priori,* and those which regard it as the empirical knowledge of the self's identity through time.[4]

For Guyer, only the latter tactic, which is found in the Refutation of Idealism and some related *Reflexionen* rather than the Deduction proper, holds out any hope for success. Nevertheless, he agrees with Henrich that it is the argument from the purportedly *a priori* knowledge of the identity of the self that predominates in the text of the Deduction. In other words, for Guyer (as for Henrich) the fundamental premise of the Deduction is that the self has *a priori* knowledge of its numerical identity, and this is supposed to entail knowledge of the categories.[5]

It is in connection with this premise and the line of argument stemming from it that Guyer considers the analyticity of the principle of apperception. In essence, Guyer's claim is that if the principle is taken as analytic, it can yield only a conditional necessity to the effect that I must be able to synthesize my representations, *if* I am to be conscious of them as belonging to my identical self. But for the argument of the Deduction to get off the ground, Kant needs to establish the quite distinct and unconditional necessity that all my representations are synthesizable and, therefore, ascribable to a single self, the numerical identity of which can be known *a priori.* This premise is needed, according to Guyer, if Kant is to be able to affirm the existence of a transcendental synthesis, governed by the categories, as a necessary condition of the knowledge of this identity. As Guyer points out, however, the claim that we have synthetic *a priori* knowledge of such identity is extremely implausible, which is why the basic tactic of the Deduction supposedly fails.[6]

On Guyer's reading, then, Kant's assertion of the analytic nature of the principle of apperception rests upon a confusion about his argumentative strategy, a strategy that is doomed to failure even when freed from this confusion. In support of this interpretation, Guyer points to an important footnote in the A-Deduction, where Kant explicitly affirms that the principle of the unity of apperception is synthetic.[7] As Kant there puts it: "The synthetic proposition, that all the variety of *empirical consciousness* must be combined in a single self-consciousness, is the *absolutely* first and synthetic principle of thought in general" (A117n). Taking this as equivalent to the principle that Kant characterizes as analytic in the second edition, Guyer in effect charges Kant with a further confusion regarding the status of his own first principle.

Although she devotes relatively little attention to the topic, Patricia Kitcher is equally emphatic in rejecting any analytic construal of the principle of apperception. In spite of what she acknowledges to be certain "remarks" to the contrary in the B-Deduction and Paralogisms, she holds that "Kant's own position on the synthetic nature of the doctrine of apperception is clear."[8] In support of this, she refers to the previously cited passage from the A-Deduction; the claim at B133 that "the *analytic* unity of apperception is possible only under the presupposition of a certain *synthetic* unity," together with the clarifying note attached to this claim (albeit without any explanation of what bearing this account of the relation between the analytic and synthetic *unities* of apperception is supposed to have on the analyticity of the *principle* of the synthetic unity of apperception[9]); and certain passages in the A-Paralogisms in which Kant allegedly endorses a manifestly synthetic claim. In this spirit, the places in which the analyticity of claims about the thinking subject are affirmed in the B-Paralogism are glossed by Kitcher as directed at rational psychologists of the Wolffian school, for whom (but not for Kant) such claims are in fact analytic.[10]

Clearly, however, the main reason for her refusal to take the analyticity of apperception seriously is its total incompatibility with her reading of the *Critique*. Kitcher's project is to rehabilitate Kant's transcendental psychology against both its wholesale dismissal by analytic interpreters such as Strawson (and Guyer) and the more apsychological, "logicized" reading of many of its central claims that I tend to favor.[11] Against both approaches, she maintains that Kant's doctrine of synthesis *cum* apperception is in reality a significant contribution to cognitive psychology, since it provides an account of mental unity far superior to Hume's. Indeed, the doctrine of apperception on her reading is neither a thesis about the necessary reflexivity of conscious thought nor an analytic claim regarding the *cogito*, but something like an inference to the best explanation of our capacity to perform the cognitive tasks that even a skeptic such as Hume must acknowledge we perform. In her own terms, "The doctrine of apperception is about the primary attribute of thinkers that is necessary for cognition."[12] As such, it constitutes the conclusion of Kant's argument rather than the initial premise of the Deduction.[13] So construed, the principle is obviously synthetic and the operative question is whether and to what sense it can also be *a priori*.

Moreover, in light of this understanding of apperception, Kitcher explicitly takes issue with my interpretation of the two-step proof of the B-Deduction on the grounds that it construes the analytic principle of apperception as the major premise of the first part of the proof. According to Kitcher, such a reading is hopelessly wrongheaded, for "If the first part of the Deduction is merely an analytic argument . . . then it could never make a contribution to the second, synthetic step, as Kant would be the first to point out."[14]

Whether Kant would in fact be the first to point this out remains to be seen, but for the present it seems clear that both Guyer and Kitcher have mounted a serious assault on the analyticity of the principle of apperception. If their analyses are correct, an analytic principle could neither serve the overt purpose of the Deduction, namely, to establish the validity of the categories, nor play a pivotal role in Kant's reply to Hume's skepticism regarding mental unity. The latter is undoubtedly true, but since I doubt very much that this was part of Kant's agenda in the Transcendental Deduction, I shall leave that issue untouched.[15] Instead, I shall focus on what I take to be the more serious and plausible objection that an analytic principle could not figure significantly in the argument of the Deduction.[16] Before turning to that, however, it is necessary to consider somewhat more closely the claim for analyticity itself.

II

As already noted, the principle of the synthetic unity of apperception is not simply the obvious tautology that all my representations are mine or even that they are necessarily subject to the conditions (whatever they may be) under which they can alone be mine. It is rather the claim that all my representations, in order to be representations for me, must possess synthetic unity, that is, they must be connected in such a way as to allow for the possibility of being grasped together in one consciousness by a single 'I think.' Moreover, since to grasp representations together is precisely to synthesize them, it follows that the doctrine of apperception entails the necessity of a synthesis.

As also noted, however, this characterization serves only to increase our perplexity, for this complex claim seems to be quite contentful and, as such, hardly a promising candidate for analyticity. In fact, since it refers to *all* my representations, it seems quite close to the principle designated by Guyer as obviously synthetic, not to mention its similarity to the one which Kant himself characterized as synthetic in the A-Deduction. Thus, applying Kant's own criterion of analyticity, it seems appropriate to ask: in what concept is this complex claim "contained" or, alternatively, from what concept does it follow by means of the law of non-contradiction alone?

Although Kant does not address this question directly in the Deduction, he does at least suggest his answer in the B-Paralogisms when he writes:

That the 'I' of apperception, and therefore the 'I' in every act of thought is *one* [*ein Singular*], and cannot be resolved into a plurality of subjects, and consequently signifies a logically simple subject, is something contained in the very concept of thought, and is therefore an analytic proposition (B407).

According to this passage, the claims about apperception and its necessary synthetic unity are supposed to be derived analytically from the concept of thought or, more precisely, from the concept of discursive thought.[17] Although I believe this to be the case, a good deal of preparatory work must be done before this answer can be made plausible. To begin with, it is essential to keep in mind that in the first part of the B-Deduction, where the account of apperception is developed, Kant explicitly abstracts from the nature of human sensibility, that is, from its spatio-temporal form. As Kant puts it, in a passage of inestimable significance for the understanding of his procedure in the B-Deduction:

[I]n this deduction [the first part, or §§15–20], since the categories have their source in the understanding alone, *independently of sensibility*, I must abstract from the mode in which the manifold for an empirical intuition is given, and must direct attention solely to the unity which, in terms of the category, and by means of the understanding, enters into the intuitions (B144).

By proceeding in this way, that is, by abstracting from the whole question of the relation of thought and its conditions to human sensibility and its *a priori* forms, Kant is also abstracting from the very conditions required to ground synthetic judgments. As Kant repeatedly insists, synthetic judgments require the relation of concepts to sensible intuitions and synthetic judgments *a priori* the relation of pure concepts to pure intuitions.[18] In the present instance, however, that requirement cannot be met. Instead of relating thought to human intuition, Kant is here relating it to the abstract notion of "sensible intuition in general." And far from being a specific mode of intuition, this is rather the *concept* of an unspecified mode of sensible intuition, which, as such, can neither ground a synthetic judgment nor establish a "real use" for the categories.[19] Thus, given Kant's own account of the conditions of synthetic judgment and assuming the exhaustiveness of the analytic–synthetic distinction, he had no choice but to regard the claims about apperception in the first part of the B-Deduction as analytic.

Moreover, this enables us to understand the difference in status assigned to the principle of apperception in the two versions of the Deduction. Rather than starting with the notion of a discursive intellect, which, as such, requires some unspecified mode of sensible intuition, the A-Deduction begins with an explicit reference to the temporal form of human consciousness. As Kant puts it at the very beginning of the "subjective deduction," "All our cognitions are ... subject to time.... In it they must all be ordered, connected, and brought into relation" (A98). And, by way of underscoring the significance of this claim, Kant remarks, "This is a general observation which, throughout what follows, must be borne in mind as being quite fundamental" (A99). Given this starting point, which links the accounts of apperception and synthesis directly to the temporal conditions of human cognition, we should not be surprised to find that the principle of the synthetic unity of apperception is characterized in the A-Deduction as synthetic. Indeed, an understanding of the principle as analytic became possible only with the methodological abstraction from the nature of human sensibility in the first part of the B-Deduction. But, given this abstraction, its analytic character is clear.

This is not, however, to suggest that the two versions of the Deduction operate with two radically distinct conceptions of apperception. At bottom, it is one and the same conception operative in both versions, but the A-Deduction appeals to it in what might be termed its "schematized" form and the B-Deduction its "pure" form. Moreover, just as the pure and the schematized categories are not two distinct sets of concepts, but rather one and the same set, considered in the first case in abstraction from the conditions of their realization or real use and in the second in relation to these conditions, so precisely the same might be said about the two versions of the conception of apperception.[20] Admittedly, there is no direct textual evidence for such a reading, since Kant never refers explicitly to a pure and a schematized version of the conception of apperception (nor to a distinction between pure and schematized categories for that matter). Nevertheless, it is certainly in accord with the basic thrust of Kant's thought and it does enable us to avoid an apparent contradiction between the characterizations of apperception in the two versions of the Deduction.

At most, however, the preceding analysis helps to explain why Kant could regard the same conception as yielding a synthetic principle in one version of the Deduction and an analytic one in the other. It does not show that this claim for analyticity is justified or even that there could be a "pure" (unschematized) conception of apperception analogous to the pure concepts of the understanding. In order to deal with this issue, we must take a closer look at Kant's account; and here it is helpful to begin with the best known and virtually canonical formulation of the principle:

It must be possible for the 'I think' to accompany all my representations; for otherwise something would be represented in me which could not be thought at all, and that is equivalent to saying that the representation would be impossible, or at least would be nothing to me. That representation which can be given prior to all thought is entitled intuition. All the manifold of intuition has, therefore, a necessary relation to the 'I think' in the same subject in which this manifold is found (B131–32).

Although Kant apparently regards this as a single principle, it is convenient to divide it into two parts. The first part, which is expressed in the first sentence, applies to all a subject's representations taken individually. It simply says in effect that any representation which I could not be aware of as mine, that is, which I could not think, would be nothing to me cognitively speaking. As I noted in *Kant's Transcendental Idealism*, this does not mean either that I must be explicitly aware of all my thoughts as mine or that I cannot have "representations" which are nothing to me cognitively speaking but which might nevertheless influence my behavior.[21] Kant is rather merely asserting the necessity of a possibility: the possibility of reflectively attaching the 'I think' to each of my representations that are involved in the thought of an object in the broadest sense.[22]

This necessity is based on the premise that having a thought involves the capacity to recognize it as one's own. Since a thought which I (in principle) could not recognize as my own would *ipso facto* not be a thought *for* me, and since a thought which is not a thought for me could not enter into my cognition, I take this claim to be obviously analytic. Moreover, I also take this portion of the doctrine of apperception to be applicable even to a problematic intuitive understanding, that is, to "an understanding which through its self-consciousness could supply to itself the manifold of intuition" (B138–39). For, as Kant's formulation indicates, even such an understanding is regarded as *self*-conscious, which means that it must be capable of becoming aware of the "manifold of [intellectual] intuition," which it somehow produces from itself, as its own. Otherwise, such an understanding would not count as an understanding in even the "widest sense of the term."[23]

The second and more problematic part of the principle of apperception concerns the requirement of synthetic unity and the necessity of a synthesis to bring it about. Since this refers directly to the manifold of *sensible* intuition (as the condition of its "relation to the 'I think' in the same subject in which this manifold is found"), it clearly does not apply to an intuitive intellect, a point which Kant himself makes at B145. Nevertheless, it follows from the first part of the principle, when combined with the assumption that the manifold of intuition is given from without or received rather than spontaneously generated by the understanding itself. Moreover, since the latter is definitional of a discursive intellect or discursive thought, this addition does not undermine the analyticity of the entire principle. Syntheticity would arise only if, for example, it were claimed that the human intellect is discursive. The latter is, of course, an underlying assumption of Kant's entire philosophy, but it is not at issue in the present stage of the argument. On the contrary, Kant is here doing pure conceptual analysis. His concern is with the "logical form" of discursive understanding, quite apart from any question of its instantiation.

Admittedly, however, the analysis is fairly complex, which is perhaps another reason why the analyticity thesis is usually not taken very seriously. First, it must be kept in mind that discursive thinking requires the unification of a manifold of given intuition through concepts (construed as rules for unification and recognition). It thus consists essentially in the production of single complex thoughts or, in Kant's terms, synthetic unities of representations. But a single complex thought or synthetic unity of representations logically requires a single thinker. Kant explicitly affirms both this principle and its analyticity in the previously cited passage in the Paralogisms, when he remarks that "the 'I' of apperception . . . is one and cannot be resolved into a plurality of subjects" (B407). This is also essentially the same as the point noted by William James, when he remarks that a set of distinct thoughts of the elements of a whole is not equivalent to the thought of the whole itself.[24] In other words, although each of the representations that collectively constitute the thought of the whole could conceivably be distributed among a variety of thinking subjects, the thought of the whole could not. On the contrary, the latter requires what Kant terms a "logically simple subject."

This is the feature of the principle of apperception emphasized in the Paralogisms, where, at least in the second edition, Kant's concern is to point out that such analytic claims about the unity, simplicity, identity and distinctness of the "logical subject of thought" (the 'I' of apperception, which constitutes the "sole text of rational psychology" [A343/B401]) are not to be confused with synthetic propositions about a real thinking subject or substance.[25] In the B-Deduction, however, the focus is on the converse of the above principle: that the identity of the 'I think' entails the synthetic unity of its representations. Although this further complicates the situation, we shall see that it does not really affect the analyticity of the principle.

To begin with, since the 'I' in question is not a substance, entity or even person, but merely the subject of thought considered as such, the identity conditions of the 'I' cannot be distinguished from the conditions of its consciousness of this identity. Moreover, the possibility of becoming aware of an identical 'I think' clearly requires that the representations with respect to which the 'I' is conscious of its identity constitute a synthetic unity in a single consciousness. Otherwise, the 'I' could not conceivably become aware of its identity with respect to these representations. Finally, if it is to be possible for the 'I' to become conscious of its identity, the synthetic unity must not only be *in* a single consciousness, it must also be *for* that same consciousness, that is, it must be a unity for the 'I.' But since for the 'I' to take its representations as unified is precisely for it to unify them, it likewise follows that it is only insofar as the 'I' is capable of unifying its representations in a single consciousness that it is capable of becoming conscious of its own identity.

In order to complete the argument of the first part of the B-Deduction, it is still necessary to connect this synthesis with judgment and therefore with the categories, understood as "concepts of an object in general, by means of which the intuition of an object is regarded as determined in respect of one of the logical functions of judgment" (B128). Admittedly, this is a fairly long and complex story, which cannot be dealt with adequately here. Nevertheless, as I argued in *Kant's Transcendental Idealism*, the key move is the introduction of the concept of an object as the correlate of this necessary synthetic unity (§17).[26] Very roughly, since by an "object" [*Objekt*] is here meant merely "that in the concept of which the manifold of a given intuition is *united*" (B137), it follows that this synthetic unity is not merely necessary but also sufficient for the representation of an object. And since this synthetic unity is, therefore, an "objective unity" (§18) and, as such, equivalent to a judgment (§19), it likewise follows that it is governed by the logical functions of judgment and, therefore, the categories (§20).

At least from §16 on, then, the first part of the B-Deduction might be regarded as a "synthetic" or "progressive" argument proceeding from the principle of the synthetic unity of apperception as its fundamental premise to the conclusion that the manifold of sensible intuition in general, insofar as it is brought to the unity of apperception and, therefore related to an object, is necessarily subject to the categories. But since this fundamental premise is itself an analytic truth, from which the subsequent steps are supposed to follow logically, in another sense the argument is entirely analytic. Or at least it must have been regarded as such by Kant.

III

This result brings us to the essential question: how can an analytical truth, even a uniquely complex one such as the principle of the synthetic unity of apperception, serve as a fundamental premise of the Transcendental Deduction? Clearly, it is this problem that has prevented most interpreters from taking Kant at his word on this point. It is usually dangerous not to take Kant at his word, however, particularly when, as in the present instance, he reiterates his claim. Accordingly, the task is to determine whether the argument of the B-Deduction as a whole, with its two step proof-structure, can be made intelligible on the assumption of the analyticity of the principle of apperception. In the remainder of this paper I shall attempt to show that it can. Although of itself this may not suffice to establish the analyticity of this principle, it does eliminate the most obvious and fundamental objection to it.

On most textually sensitive interpretations, the overall goal of the Deduction in both editions is to establish a necessary connection between the categories and the spatio-temporally informed data of human sensibility, that is, appearances. Why should what is given in sensible intuition conform to the conditions of thought is the basic question that Kant raises from about 1775 on.[27] Put negatively, the project involves eliminating the dreaded possibility that, "Appearances might . . . be so constituted that the understanding should not find them to be in accordance with the conditions of its unity" (A90/B123). In fact, a recent interpreter has claimed appropriately that this possibility constitutes the Kantian analogue of the Cartesian "evil genius," a specter that must be exorcized if the project of the Deduction is to succeed.[28]

Assuming, then, the two-step-in-one-proof reading of the B-Deduction, the operative question is the respective roles of the two steps in removing this specter. In his classical paper, Dieter Henrich argued that the threat was eliminated in the first part for a range of sensible intuition, for intuitions insofar as they already possess unity. He further argued that in the second part this restriction is removed and the result is affirmed for all human sensible intuition on the grounds that space and time are unities (as shown in the Transcendental Aesthetic) and all our intuitions are spatio-temporal.[29] Henrich's paper has been subject to considerable criticism, much of it focusing on his apparent attribution to Kant of the view that intuitions might already possess unity independently of the activity of the understanding.[30] In response to this criticism, Henrich has modified and refined his position somewhat, making clear that he never intended to attribute such a view to Kant. Thus, referring to B144n, where Kant discusses the ground of proof of the first part of the Deduction, Henrich suggests that what is shown in this part is merely that given intuitions contain a unity insofar as they are related to apperception, and that this relation to apperception cannot, without further argument, be affirmed of everything that is given in sensibility. This is an important clarification; but for our purposes, at least, what is noteworthy is that Henrich retains the basic idea that the first part of the B-Deduction affirms the validity of the categories under a restricting condition that is then removed in the second part.[31]

Clearly, however, any such interpretation of the relation between the two steps in the proof is incompatible with the assumption of the analyticity of the principle of apperception. For if, as argued, the first step affirms a merely analytic principle, then it cannot be thought to remove the specter or, equivalently, establish the reality of the categories for even a range of intuitions. On the contrary, one would seem to be forced to agree with Guyer that an analytic principle of apperception yields only a conditional necessity, roughly of the form: if (or insofar as) it is possible to become conscious of an identical 'I think' with respect to the thought of a manifold of intuition, then this manifold is necessarily subject to the categories as rules of synthesis. And since this leaves open the possibility that the condition is not fulfilled, it cannot of itself establish the objective reality of the categories for even a range of sensible intuition.

Nevertheless, this does not require us either to accuse Kant of confusion on this point or to abandon the attempt to take the principle of apperception as analytic. For an analytic first principle can contribute to a synthetic or progressive argument, yielding a synthetic *a priori* conclusion, in ways other than those considered so far. This is nicely illustrated by Kant's procedure in the Analytic of Pure Practical Reason of the second *Critique*, which was presumably written shortly after completion of the revisions for the second edition of the first *Critique*.[32] Kant there begins with what amounts to a stipulative definition of an unconditional practical law and proceeds to argue in the first eight sections of the Analytic that the moral law or categorical imperative is the only viable candidate for such a law and that the capacity to act on the basis of this law presupposes the autonomy of the will. The argument thus issues in the conditional result: if there is such an unconditional practical law, the categorical imperative is its formula and the will must be free in the absolute or transcendental sense required for autonomy. In the Deduction proper of the second *Critique*, Kant then proceeds to affirm the validity of the categorical imperative as a "fact of reason" and to derive the reality of freedom from it.

This example from Kant's moral philosophy suggests an alternative model for interpreting the relation between the two parts of the B-Deduction.[33] According to this model, just as the first eight sections of the Analytic of Pure Practical Reason spell out the implications of the concept of an unconditional practical law, so the first part of the B-Deduction spells out the implications of its first principle, the synthetic unity of apperception. And just as the former arrives at a conditional result regarding the reciprocity between the categorical imperative and freedom, so the latter affirms its own conditional conclusion, which includes a reciprocity between the synthetic unity of apperception and the representation of an object [*Object*] (the unity of consciousness and the consciousness of unity).[34] The pure concepts of the understanding enter into this picture as conditions of both the unity of apperception and the representation of objects. And since they make the latter possible, these concepts have an objectifying function, which justifies the attribution to them of objective validity.[35] Accordingly, in spite of its analytic major premise, the first part of the B-Deduction, like the first eight sections of the Analytic of Pure Practical Reason, can hardly be dismissed as trivial.

But, even if sound, this argument cannot be regarded as sufficient, for it does not establish that the objectivating functions expressed in the categories apply to the manifold of human sensibility. Thus, as Kant himself puts it, it remains to show "from the mode in which the empirical intuition is given in sensibility, that its unity is no other than that which the category ... prescribes to the manifold of a given intuition in general" (B144–45). Only such an argument would suffice to eliminate the specter of the nonconformity of appearances to the categoreal functions of the understanding, which is precisely what is required at this point.

Kant attempts to establish this result in two stages: first, in §24, he argues that the representations of space and time as unities require a transcendental synthesis of the imagination governed by the categories; then, in §26, he argues that the empirical synthesis of apprehension, which is constitutive of perception, is itself subject to the conditions of the transcendental synthesis. Together, they yield the conclusion that all of the manifold of human sensibility is subject to the categories, which completely eliminates the specter of nonconformity. As I argued in *Kant's Transcendental Idealism*, however, the key move, the very locus of syntheticity in the B-Deduction, occurs in §24 with the appeal to the transcendental synthesis of the imagination.[36]

This is not, of course, to say that this complex second part of Kant's argument, which involves, among other things, an explicit appeal to the results of the Transcendental Aesthetic, is entirely unproblematic. On the contrary, I have maintained that there are major gaps in the argument and that on even the most charitable interpretation (one which accepts as valid the results of the Aesthetic, the Metaphysical Deduction and the first part of the Transcendental Deduction), it falls far short of complete success.[37] Nevertheless, none of this need concern us here, for our present focus is on the proof-structure of the B-Deduction rather than on the validity or overall soundness of its argument. Moreover, to this end, it suffices to show that the analyticity of the principle of apperception is perfectly compatible with the goals and strategy of the Deduction as a whole. Indeed, it makes it much clearer than alternative readings just why Kant divided the proof into two parts.

4

On naturalizing Kant's transcendental psychology

Even though Kant himself never used the term in that way, 'transcendental psychology' has attained wide prominence as a label for what is thought to be most objectionable in Kant's theoretical philosophy, namely, the account of the transcendental activities of the mind. This state of affairs is largely the work of P. F. Strawson, who in his enormously influential study, *The Bounds of Sense*, endeavored to separate what he took to be Kant's "analytic argument" from the concept of experience to "a certain objectivity and a certain unity" as conditions of the possibility of experience from the "imaginary subject of transcendental psychology."[1]

In spite of widespread disagreement regarding the nature and soundness of this analytic argument, the general Strawsonian approach to Kant, and particularly the curt dismissal of Kant's account of the mind and its activities, has been the hallmark of analytic Kant interpretation for approximately a quarter century. Recently, however, things have begun to change, as a new generation of analytical philosophers, trained in naturalized epistemology and cognitive science and distrustful of conceptual analysis, have turned their attention to Kant. Among the forefront of this new breed of Kantians is Patricia Kitcher, who in the very title of her recent book, *Kant's Transcendental Psychology*, issues a bold challenge to Strawson.[2] According to Kitcher, Kant's transcendental psychology, properly, that is, naturalistically, construed, contains an account of mental unity that is demonstrably superior to Hume's, combined with a functionalistic and, therefore, essentially causal account of the content of representations. Thus, far from being an unnecessary appendage that can easily be removed without substantial damage to the body of the work, Kant's transcendental psychology is now seen as the very heart of the enterprise. Indeed, it appears to contain virtually everything that is of interest in the *Critique*.

But herein lies the problem; for in its own way this new reading of Kant is as dismissive of central features of the *Critique* as the analytic reading which it replaces. Accordingly, my concern here is precisely with those aspects of Kant that are dismissed by Kitcher on the grounds that they do not fit into her naturalized picture. I shall argue that her version not only leaves a distorted view of the historical Kant, but also obscures some of his most important insights, specifically, those regarding self-consciousness and spontaneity. This essay is divided into four parts. The first presents a brief sketch of Kitcher's account, including her dismissive treatment of Kant's treatments of self-consciousness and spontaneity. The second and third parts attempt respectively to rehabilitate these notions, arguing for both their coherence and their centrality to Kant's project in the *Critique of Pure Reason*. The fourth deals with the thorny question of the nature of the self or subject of transcendental psychology. It argues against Kitcher and other naturalizers that it cannot be equated with the empirical self, but also that it is not to be identified with some inaccessible noumenal entity.

I

Although she begins with an analysis of Kant's account of spatial perception, the major focus of Kitcher's concern is Kant's transcendental psychology proper, that is, the doctrine of synthesis *cum* apperception, which constitutes the heart of the so-called "subjective deduction." Quite apart from its role in the proof-structure of the deduction, she finds in Kant's treatment of this complex topic an explicit answer to Hume's doubts about mental unity, which can be elucidated in contemporary terms and which when so elucidated makes a significant contribution to the ongoing debate about personal identity.

According to Kitcher's formal definition, "A synthesis is an act, or to be more neutral, a process that produces a representation, by adding or combining diverse elements contained in different cognitive states in a further state that contains elements from these states."[3] The result of a synthesis of "cognitive states" (which is Kitcher's preferred rendering of Kant's *Vorstellungen*,) is thus a further cognitive state, which contains within itself the content embodied or encoded in the preceding states. Representations, on this view, are said to represent, that is, have cognitive content, partly because they are produced by sensory states that are themselves caused by objects affecting the sense organs and partly because they can lead to further representations.[4] Since the cognitive or representative content of a particular representation is thus a function of its place within the system of representations rather than its own intrinsic nature, Kitcher appropriately terms this, "a 'functionalist' theory of the content of representations."[5] Also in the spirit of functionalism, this cognitive system can be analyzed independently of any consideration of the nature of the material or "hardware" in which it is actualized.

Given this analysis, it follows that not merely the content but the very existence of cognitive states or representations is dependent upon previous states (plus initial "input"). Accordingly, Kitcher claims that syntheses produce a "relation of existential dependence on cognitive states."[6] In explaining this choice of terminology, Kitcher remarks that synthesis, so characterized, would appear to be a causal process, but she refrains from calling it such on the grounds that the introduction of the doctrine of synthesis in the Deduction precedes the demonstration of the principle of causality in the Second Analogy and would thus open Kant to a Humean critique. Consequently, the notion of existential dependence is supposed to capture a connection among cognitive states that is stronger than Hume's appeal to association but weaker than the "strong notion of causation" affirmed in the Second Analogy.[7] But since Kitcher neither explains how this relation differs from full-fledged causation nor shows any compunction elsewhere about referring to causal connections between cognitive states, it seems reasonable to take her to be attributing to Kant the view that cognitive states synthetically connected are related as cause and effect.[8]

For Kitcher, this functionalist analysis not only provides the key to explaining how cognitive states can represent and, therefore, in Kantian terms, how judgment is possible, it also accounts for that unity of the mind that proved to be so problematic for Hume and that Kant termed the "transcendental unity of apperception." According to Kitcher, then, "the 'unity of apperception' refers to the *fact* [emphasis mine] that cognitive states are connected to each other through syntheses required for cognition."[9] As such, the doctrine of apperception is the conclusion of Kant's anti-Humean argument rather than, as is usually thought to be the case, the veritable first premise of the Transcendental Deduction.[10] Moreover, as she is quick to point out, apperception, so construed, has nothing to do with the awareness of a self and/or its states or the reflexivity of human experience. Kitcher admits that it often seems as if Kant had something like the latter in mind, but this is glossed as the result of Leibnizian ideas that he was able to neither abandon nor integrate into his essentially functionalist account.[11]

This complete excision of any reference to self-awareness or reflexivity from the authentic Kantian account is also a prominent feature of Kitcher's discussion of synthesis. To be sure, the synthetic processes that produce the unity of the mind and make possible the representation of objects are guided by concepts or rules, but Kitcher is insistent that this not be understood as a matter of conscious rule following. On the contrary, she appeals to Kant's characterization of the imagination as a "*blind* [her emphasis], but indispensable function of the soul" (A78/B103), and suggests that "[R]ules govern syntheses only as the law of gravity governs the movements of the planets."[12]

This view of synthesis is thoroughly in the spirit of contemporary functionalism and provides a reasonably plausible reading of Kant, as long as one confines oneself to the putative activity of the imagination. It is clear from what she says elsewhere, however, that Kitcher does not limit her claim to the operation of the Kantian imagination as distinct from the understanding. On the contrary, appealing to Kant's own emendation of the above cited passage from A78/B103, in which 'understanding' is substituted for 'soul,' she takes the activity of the understanding in conceptualization and judgment to be identical to that of the imagination and, therefore, likewise "blind" or unconscious.[13] Given this identification, it is not surprising that Kitcher consistently denies any proper role for consciousness or awareness with respect to the subject's own mental activity, dismissively characterizing such a putative consciousness as "synthesis watching."[14]

Nevertheless, as in the case of apperception, Kitcher can hardly deny the existence of numerous texts which suggest a quite different reading, since they appear to affirm the conscious nature of synthetic activity (at least to the extent to which this activity is attributed to the understanding). Although she never really deals with this exegetical problem in a direct and detailed fashion, she does adopt a number of tactics intended to defuse its seriousness. One of these is to accuse Kant of a confusion of levels. Accordingly, Kant is judged guilty of confusing what the theorist asserts about the generation of cognitive states with what the subject is aware of in this process of generation.[15] Another is to suggest that Kant was not serious about synthesis watching, since he denies it almost as often as he affirms it.[16] Still another is to blame it on the influence of Tetens' psychology, whom Kant supposedly followed on this point without recognizing its incompatibility with his own best insights.[17] Together, then, these tactics are intended to reinforce the claim that it is safe to ignore the aberration of synthesis watching in an investigation of Kant's account of the cognitive activity of the mind.

Another prominent feature of Kant's account that is notably lacking in Kitcher's reconstruction is the notion of spontaneity. Since Kant characterizes the understanding as the "spontaneity of knowledge" at the very beginning of the Transcendental Analytic (A51/B75) and refers to it on several occasions thereafter (including a characterization of the representation 'I think' as "an act of spontaneity" [B132] and a characterization of apperception as a "consciousness of spontaneity" [B158n]), one would expect an analysis of this central conception to loom large in any account of Kant's views on the nature and activity of the mind. Instead, we find merely a single brief discussion of spontaneity in the text of *Kant's Transcendental Psychology*, which is then expanded upon somewhat in a note attached to that discussion. In the text, Kitcher acknowledges these passages and admits that "taken at face value" they suggest that "a thinker is not a contentually connected system of states, but that which connects cognitive states." And, given the fact that Kant himself links apperception and spontaneity so closely, she admits that "it is tempting to interpret the self, or consciousness, or apperception as something like the power or source of spontaneity itself." Nevertheless, she insists that we must resist this temptation on the grounds that it leads to incoherence. As she puts it:

> The self cannot be identified with acts of spontaneity, since these are distinct events. It could only be the agent that performs these acts. But acts or processes of synthesis could not be performed by agents. They are unconscious activities within agents that

enable them to have cognitive capacities required for agency. In Daniel Dennett's useful terminology, they are 'subpersonal' processes, not acts performed by persons.[18]

Since, as Kitcher herself notes, Kant links spontaneity closely with apperception (the consciousness of the 'I think'), this response simply begs the question against anyone who might try to make sense of Kant's appeal to spontaneity and a consciousness thereof. She goes somewhat beyond the bare reiteration of her position, however, in the attached note, in which she responds to criticisms of her earlier accounts of apperception by Robert Pippin and myself. There she suggests that the real difference between her view and ours is the nature of the spontaneity involved in acts of synthesis. She takes it to be a merely "relative spontaneity," while Pippin and I regard it as absolute. The latter, she maintains, can be ruled out on the grounds that if Kant thought that his doctrine of apperception or synthesis implied absolute spontaneity, he would also have thought that he had a theoretical proof of transcendental freedom, something which the "critical" Kant explicitly denied. Nor, she maintains, is it possible to avoid this implication (as Pippin attempts to do) by claiming that a proof that reason must be assumed spontaneous in one context does not entail that it must likewise be viewed as spontaneous in others. She thinks that this response is too weak, since even though absolute freedom in thinking does not entail a similar freedom in acting, "it would be a giant step in the right direction." And, she adds, "If the universal sway of determinism is once breached, then the plausibility of other exceptions would increase dramatically, as Kant would fully appreciate."[19]

Unfortunately, Kitcher never bothers to explain how she understands the notion of relative spontaneity (which plays a significant role in Kant's "precritical" accounts of agency[20]) or how it relates to her causal-functionalist account of synthesis and mental unity. Accordingly, it seems safe to conclude that for Kitcher's Kant, as for a contemporary functionalist, the mind is nothing but a causally and contentually connected system of mental states, which, as such, allows no room for a consciousness of the I and its activity. Thus, in spite of this rehabilitation of transcendental psychology, Kitcher's Kant, like Strawson's, turns out to be very much a "bowdlerized Kant."[21] Whether this bowdlerization is warranted is the question we must now consider.

II

In dealing with this question, it will be useful to begin with a consideration of a particularly dense passage from the "preparatory" section of the A-Deduction, which contains, either directly or by implication, virtually all the features of Kant's transcendental psychology to which Kitcher objects. The passage follows upon Kant's initial introduction of the notion of transcendental apperception, its distinction from inner sense or empirical apperception, and the affirmation of the unity of apperception as a transcendental condition of the representation of objects. In this context, Kant claims that the unity of consciousness required for cognition "would be impossible if the mind in knowledge of the manifold could not become conscious of the identity of function whereby it synthetically combines it in one cognition" (A108). Apparently, by way of reinforcing this point, Kant adds one sentence later:

For the mind could never think its identity in the manifoldness of its representations, and indeed think this identity *a priori*, if it did not have before its eyes [*vor Augen hätte*] the identity of its act [*Handlung*], whereby it subordinates all synthesis of apprehension (which is empirical) to a transcendental unity, thereby rendering possible their interconnection according to *a priori* rules (A108).

The passage as a whole contains at least three distinct claims which need to be sorted out: (1) The unity of consciousness (equated with the transcendental unity of apperception) is a necessary condition for the mind to perform its basic cognitive task: the representation of objects. (2) This unity is inseparably linked to the mind's capacity to think its own identity in the representation of its manifold, indeed, to think it *a priori* (which Kitcher presumably regards as a level confusion). (3) The mind can think its identity only insofar as it can become conscious of the identity of its function or act (which, for Kitcher, amounts to synthesis watching). Although we shall begin with a consideration of the first claim, since it underlies Kant's whole account of objectivity, the focus will be on the second and third, which are the main targets of the naturalizer's critique. The difficulty, however, concerns not simply the claims themselves, but also the fact that here and in many other places Kant seems to move from one to the other without anything in the way of argument, as if the connections between them were self-evident. Given this state of affairs, it is not surprising that much of the Deduction has remained opaque to many interpreters (including both Strawson and Kitcher).

I do not pretend to be able to remove all of this opacity, and certainly not within the brief confines of this paper. Nevertheless, I do hope to reduce it somewhat by filling in some of the gaps and bringing out the underlying assumptions of Kant's argument. As a first step, it is absolutely essential to keep firmly in mind the normative concern of the Deduction. That the concern of the Deduction is normative is itself hardly controversial, since Kant famously distinguishes the *quid juris* from the *quid facti* and contends that he is concerned only with the former (A84–85/B116–17). What is not always recognized, however, is that even Kant's transcendental psychology or, as it is usually termed, the "subjective deduction," must be understood in light of this normative concern, that is, as part of the project of justifying or establishing the objective validity of the categories.[22]

This normative dimension is made evident by even a brief consideration of the subjective deduction, which can be characterized as an investigation of the subjective conditions of the representation of objects by a mind relevantly like the human (a discursive intelligence with space and time as its forms of sensibility). At the heart of the deduction is an account of the imagination, which has the intent of showing that it is both indispensable and insufficient for cognition. Although rich and suggestive, we can here neglect the details of this account and need consider only the basic reasons for the imagination's indispensability and insufficiency.

Simply put, the indispensability of the imagination stems from its role in unifying the temporally discreet data of inner sense (the manifold of representations). Without this unifying activity, the mind would not have a whole of representations with which to work. As Kant puts it at one point, "since every appearance contains a manifold, and since different perceptions occur in the mind separately and singly, a combination of them, such as they cannot have in sense itself, is demanded" (A120). Of itself, however, imaginative unification is insufficient for cognition, since it yields a merely subjective order of representations, one which reflects the contingencies of the perceptual situation (e.g. the fact that one happens to perceive a before b) rather than an objectively valid connection. It is in order to account for the conditions of the possibility of the latter, which is, after all, the goal of the Transcendental Deduction, that Kant introduces the understanding and its indigenous set of pure concepts.

The argument for the constitutive role of the understanding turns on the familiar, yet crucial, reflection that, since we cannot, as it were, step outside of our representations in order to compare them with an object, objective representation requires that we think our representations as unified in consciousness by means of a rule which requires that they be thought in a determinate way (e.g. as a–b rather than b–a). Such a rule is, of course, a pure concept of the understanding or category; it supposedly accounts for objectivity by imposing a conceptual constraint on the *thought* of the order and connection of the intuitively given representations. In other words, it provides an ordering principle that applies not merely to the connection of representations in a particular consciousness but to their connection in what Kant in the *Prolegomena* terms "consciousness in general." This, in turn, gives to the thought ordering the necessity and universality requisite for objectivity.

Although this line of argument establishes a necessary (rule-governed) unity of consciousness as a condition of objective representation, it says nothing about the mind's thought of its own identity or, indeed, about *self-consciousness* in any form. In order to understand this aspect of Kant's thought (and, therefore, claims two and three), it is necessary to realize that what is required for objective representation is not simply the *de facto* presence of a rule-governed unity of representations in consciousness (something like Kitcher's relation of "contentual dependence"), but the thought or conceptual recognition of this unity. In other words, this unity must not only be *in* a single consciousness, it must be *for* that consciousness in the sense that the mind must be able to represent it to itself or, equivalently, to recognize it as such. This reflexive dimension of cognition follows directly from the normative nature of the claim of objective connection. For unless the mind could think, that is, represent to itself or recognize the rule-governedness of the unification of its representations, it could not affirm the objective validity of this unification. It would remain a merely contingent, causally conditioned connection of mental states without any epistemic significance.

The question thus becomes what is required for the mind to be able to represent to itself such a unity, and Kant's short answer is that it must be able to think its own identity, indeed, think it *a priori*. Even leaving aside for the moment the question of apriority, this response is far from obvious. The preceding analysis clearly entails that the thinking subject must *be* identical (it takes one to know one) and, therefore, that the transcendental philosopher must affirm such identity as a necessary condition of cognition; but this is quite distinct from the claim that the actual thinking subject must have the capacity to think or represent to itself its own identity. Accordingly, it might seem that we have fallen victim to precisely that confusion of levels of which Kitcher accuses Kant.

Nevertheless, further consideration of the reflexivity of objective representation supports this claim and makes it clear that no such confusion is involved. Consider the transitional sentence, omitted in the earlier citation from A108, in which Kant states that "The original and necessary consciousness of the identity of the self [*seiner selbst*] is thus at the same time [*zugleich*] a consciousness of an equally necessary unity of the syntheses of all appearances according to concepts. . . ." This suggests that Kant's view is not that we require a distinct capacity to become conscious of our identity as thinking subject in order to be able to think the necessary unity of appearances; it is rather that to think such a unity is, *at the same time,* to think one's identity. In other words, one cannot unite *a* and *b* in a single consciousness, so as to represent to oneself an objective connection, without also identifying the I that thinks *a* with the I that thinks *b*. And this does follow from the reflexivity of objective representation, for in order to represent to myself an objective connection, I must in the very same act take myself as an identical thinking subject. Otherwise the connection *in* me would not be a connection *for* me. Moreover, since on this account of objective representation, the mind is thinking its identity in light or by means of an *a priori* rule, it can be said to be thinking its identity *a priori*, which is precisely what Kant claims in the passage under discussion.

To be sure, in thinking an objective connection, that is, in judging, the mind need not be explicitly aware that it is also thinking its own identity. In fact, Kant himself readily admits this in the A-Deduction, remarking that it is of no concern whether the "bare representation 'I' in relation to all other representations" (which he terms "transcendental consciousness") is "clear (empirical consciousness) or obscure, or even whether it actually occurs." What is important is rather the principle that the relation of all representations to transcendental consciousness or apperception constitutes the "logical form of all knowledge" (A117n). And from this we can see that Kant's claim about the apperceptive nature of consciousness, the mind's capacity to think its own identity, is not an eliminable feature of his transcendental psychology but an essential ingredient in his account of the subjective conditions of cognition.

As we have already seen, however, Kant maintains not only that the mind must be able to think its identity *a priori*, but also that as a condition of doing so, it must "have before its eyes the identity of its act whereby it subordinates all synthesis of apprehension (which is empirical) to a transcendental unity. . . ." Moreover, this seemingly bizarre claim cannot be dismissed as an aberration on Kant's part, since in the B-Deduction he makes essentially the same point in less metaphorical terms, insisting that apperception, and, therefore, objective representation or judgment, requires not merely a synthesis, but also a consciousness of this synthesis (B133). And this, of course, is precisely the feature of Kant's account that Kitcher dismissively describes as "synthesis watching."

Although this might appear to be a fresh claim, it likewise follows from the reflexivity of objective representation and, therefore, cannot be deleted from an account of Kant's transcendental psychology. Once again, the essential point is that thinking its own identity is not another act that the mind performs in addition to the representation to itself of objective connection. Consequently, it can consist only in the consciousness of the act of representation itself; its recognition of the nature of its own act. And from this it clearly follows that in order to think its identity, the mind must "have before its eyes the identity of its act." Otherwise expressed, a consciousness of the identity of the I that thinks *a* with the I that thinks *b* could only take the form of a consciousness of the identity of the act of thinking them together in one consciousness.

In order to bring out the epistemological significance of this point and, therefore, its connection with the normative project of the Deduction, I have found it useful to analyze judgment or objective representation as an act of "taking as," where the expression is meant to capture the notion of conceptual recognition (recognition in a concept) that is central to the Kantian account.[23] Reducing a long and complex story to its barest essentials, to judge is just to take some intuitively given item or set thereof as a determinate something. In the simplest case, an indeterminate something $= x$ is taken as an F. Apart from or prior to this conceptual determination, there is no content for thought. In more complex judgings or takings, Fx is qualified by further determinations; for example, Fx is G. This schema can easily be expanded to allow for increasing levels of complexity and presumably even to include the notion of quantification that is central to contemporary logic. But leaving all that aside, the main point is that in all cases of taking as, no matter how complex, the mind must not only combine its representations in a single consciousness, it must also be conscious of what it is doing. Moreover, the "must" here is conceptual, for unless I am aware of taking x as F ("recognizing it in a concept" in Kant's locution), I have not in fact taken it as such. In short, conceptual recognition (which is what the objectivating synthesis amounts to for Kant) is an inherently reflexive and, therefore, self-conscious act. I cannot perform it without an awareness of *what* I am doing (a consciousness of the act), although I can certainly do it without reflecting that I (Henry Allison) am doing it.

Kitcher's resistance to any such analysis apparently stems from her view that by "consciousness of synthesis" Kant can mean only introspection.[24] And since an introspective awareness that one knows that p cannot be viewed as a condition of knowing that p without generating an infinite regress, it would seem to follow that "synthesis watching" could not play a substantive role in Kantian epistemology. To argue in this way, however, is to conflate apperception (the consciousness of thinking) with inner sense (the introspective empirical consciousness of one's mental states). Properly construed, apperception or consciousness of synthesis has nothing to do with introspection. This is because it is not another thing that one does when one judges (a kind of second-order knowing that one is knowing); it is rather an essential ingredient in the first-order activity itself.[25]

III

Although the issues are more complex, basically the same considerations also enable us to understand why Kant virtually identifies the understanding with spontaneity and characterizes apperception as "an act of spontaneity" (B132). To begin with, to take x as F is an act of spontaneity in the sense that it is something that the subject does for itself, which, as such, goes beyond the effect that can be produced in the mind by the mere reception of sensory data. Sensibility can present to the mind x's that are F's, but it cannot, not even in collaboration with the imagination, take or recognize them as such. This is the work of the understanding. In this respect, then, Kant's conception of spontaneity is an essential component of his account of the understanding, and particularly its distinction from sensibility.[26]

Admittedly, however, this still does not explain why the spontaneity of the understanding must be thought to involve anything more than the innocuous relative spontaneity to which Kitcher alludes and which Kant dismissively characterizes as that of a turnspit. Presumably, according to this conception of spontaneity, the mind is to be thought of as processing the data given through the senses on the basis of its own internal mechanism rather than merely recording the manner in which it receives the data. Such a conception is clearly in accord with Kitcher's functionalist account of synthesis and would seem to leave the naturalized picture intact.[27] Consequently, if this view of Kant's transcendental psychology is to be rejected, it is obviously essential to show the inadequacy of a merely relative spontaneity for the epistemic function assigned to the understanding.

Although this is a daunting task, I think that it is possible to state the outlines of the Kantian response fairly succinctly. The main point is that this merely relative conception of spontaneity is not sufficient to account for the act of "taking as" or recognition that is an essential ingredient in cognition. In particular, it is incapable of accounting for the normative dimension of this act. The basic Kantian intuition operative here, one which is certainly rejected by most contemporary naturalizers, is that cognition must be conceived as more than an elaborate information processing procedure, one which begins with raw sensible input and ends with the relatively reliable products of the understanding (cognitions). As should be clear from the previous analysis, what is missing in such a picture of cognition (at least from the Kantian perspective) is precisely its self-conscious, apperceptive character. And, not surprisingly, it is also this feature that requires absolute rather than merely relative spontaneity.

In order to illustrate the point, let us consider what is required for the warranted claim that one has understood something, say the proposition that p.[28] Presumably, both Kant and the naturalizer would agree that such understanding involves more than having correct beliefs. These beliefs must also have been arrived at in the correct way; otherwise a successful outcome would be a matter of epistemological luck. The deep difference concerns the manner in which the latter requirement is to be understood. For the naturalizer, the decisive point is that the beliefs be arrived at by the appropriate causal route. On this picture, then, there is neither need nor room for anything like genuine spontaneity. On the contrary, the notion of a merely relative spontaneity (an internal causal connection) nicely captures the requirement.

By contrast, on a Kantian account, the appropriate causal history of one's beliefs (or, alternatively, of the physical states that stand in a relation of token–token identity with these beliefs) is not sufficient for understanding. This is because understanding that p requires not merely arriving at one's belief that p by the correct causal route, that is, having this belief produced by the appropriate set of prior beliefs; it also requires taking or recognizing these prior beliefs as warranting the belief that p. The operative principle here is that reasons can function as reasons only when they are consciously recognized as such. Moreover, this recognition cannot, in turn, be analyzed simply as the possession of a further, second-order belief about the relationship between one's first-order beliefs. It is, after all, one thing to have a belief (even a true belief) that a set of premises entails or otherwise justifies a conclusion and quite another to understand *that* and *how* they do so.

Now, it is precisely because recognition cannot be understood simply as having another belief or, in Kitcher's terms, as being in a "cognitive state," that it is not something that one can coherently take oneself as caused to do, not even by the internal state of "the system" (as the conception of relative spontaneity would have it). Beliefs, cognitive states and the like can easily be thought of in causal terms; thus, as long as cognition is viewed as essentially a matter of being in the appropriate cognitive state, a merely relative spontaneity is all that one need assume. This ceases to be the case, however, once one grants that cognition requires conceptual recognition or taking reasons as reasons. Since this is an act that the subject must perform for itself (self-consciously) rather than a cognitive state in which it finds itself, it follows that we must assume an absolute and not merely a relative spontaneity in order to conceive of its possibility.

It is just at this point, however, that the Kantian position is most open to misunderstanding. Thus, contrary to what one might suppose, the "critical" Kant expressly refrains from drawing any ontological conclusions regarding the absolute spontaneity of the self from his epistemological analysis. The spontaneity-claim concerns rather the way in which the thinking subject must be conceived (or conceive itself) *qua* engaged in cognition. In other words, spontaneity functions in the technical Kantian sense as an idea in light of which the act of thinking must be conceived in order to retain its normative status, but this does not license a metaphysical inference to the absolute spontaneity of the "thing which thinks."

Moreover, far from opening the floodgates for transcendental freedom, as Kitcher seems to fear, this "critical" modesty has its precise parallel in the practical sphere, where Kant insists that we can act only under the idea of freedom, while at the same time denying that this amounts to a theoretical proof of the reality of freedom.[29] Accordingly, Kant grants the epistemic possibility that we might not be genuinely spontaneous beings. What he denies is that we could ever be in a position (say as the result of scientific developments) to deny our spontaneity while still affirming our status as genuine cognizers and agents. In this respect, then, the notion of spontaneity is built into, indeed, constitutive of, the first-person standpoint itself. And, as Kant continually points out, this is perfectly compatible with the possibility of fully naturalized accounts of both thinking and acting considered as event-types in the phenomenal world. From Kant's point of view, it is not that a naturalized account of these activities is either impossible or incoherent; it is rather that it is inherently incomplete, that it lacks the closure which only the idea of spontaneity can give to it.

IV

The preceding reflections bring us to the heart of the problem: the ontological status of the I of apperception, the subject of transcendental psychology. For the naturalizer this can only be the empirical or phenomenal self, and Kitcher is quite explicit on this point. Thus, in a paper devoted to the topic and again in *Kant's Transcendental Psychology*, she insists that it must be the phenomenal self on the apparently reasonable grounds that Kant denies any knowledge of the noumenal, while at the same time claiming to be providing knowledge, albeit of a highly abstract nature, of the self and its cognitive activities. In the same spirit, she also insists that since, for Kant, everything phenomenal is causally determined, this must apply also to the self of transcendental psychology – thus, her short shrift with the concept of spontaneity. Finally, by way of explaining the discrepancy between this result and Kant's official views, she suggests that Kant refused to acknowledge the clear implications of his own views because of their devastating consequences for his moral theory.[30]

Even leaving aside the issues concerning Kant's moral theory, however, it is clear that the phenomenal self cannot serve as the subject of transcendental psychology. Since it is itself an object in the phenomenal world (the object of inner sense), the possibility of cognizing or in any way representing to oneself the phenomenal self can be explained only in terms of transcendental grounds and, therefore, with reference to a transcendental subject. In fact, it should be apparent by now that what is missing from the naturalized account is just the I, the self-conscious thinking subject. Now, there is certainly nothing inherently absurd in the neglect of the I, of the first-person standpoint. From the standpoint of science or what Thomas Nagel has appropriately termed the "objective view of the world" there is no place for the I.[31] Nevertheless, it is deeply problematic to eliminate it from a *transcendental* investigation, the very aim of which is to account for the possibility of such an objective view by a self-conscious thinking subject. And this, I fear, is precisely what the project of naturalizing Kant's transcendental psychology amounts to, particularly insofar as its subject is identified with the phenomenal self.

This does not mean, however, that we must identify it with a separate noumenal self, thereby attributing to Kant the incoherence with which he is so frequently charged. Although the issue is extremely complicated and there are Kantian texts pointing in quite another direction, I believe and have argued in *Kant's Transcendental Idealism* that the question of whether the self of Kant's theoretical philosophy is phenomenal or noumenal is based on the mistaken assumption that it is to be conceived as an object of some sort.[32] Ignoring all details, the essential point is that the phenomenal–noumenal distinction is meant to apply to *objects* of cognition: objects known in accordance with sensible conditions are phenomena, while those (if there are any) cognized in a non-sensible, purely intellectual manner are noumena. Accordingly, to think of a noumenon is just to think of an object *qua* cognized in the latter manner. Moreover, we are perfectly capable of thinking such objects, even though we are lacking the requisite equipment (intellectual intuition) to know them as such. But the distinctive feature of the I of apperception is that it is not an object at all, that is, not an entity capable of being cognized (as opposed to being thought) in either a sensible or purely intellectual fashion. As Kant puts it:

> Now it is, indeed, very evident that I cannot know as an object that which I must presuppose in order to know any object, and that the determining self (the thought) is distinguished from the self that is to be determined (the thinking subject) in the same way as knowledge is distinguished from its object (A402).

And again:

> The subject of the categories cannot by thinking the categories acquire a concept of itself as an object of the categories. For in order to think them, its pure self-consciousness, which is what was to be explained, must itself be presupposed (B422).

Passages such as these naturally give rise to the question of what this mysterious I of apperception or "subject of the categories" is, if it is not an object. The short answer, to which I have already alluded, is simply that it is the subject of thought considered as such. In other words, it is the reference point to which thought must be related in any act of thinking, even if the thinker is not conscious of it as such. In Ryle's helpful terms, this I is "systematically elusive," since any attempt to grasp it comes, as it were, one step too late.[33] For Kant, however, the point goes somewhat deeper. Since the I is already presupposed in the thought of anything whatsoever and not merely of itself, it is not only systematically elusive but also ineliminable. And this, I take it, is why, for better or worse, apperception cannot be naturalized. Indeed, as Kitcher's account shows, the attempt to do so involves reducing the subject of thought to a system of "contentually dependent cognitive states," which, in spite of its allegedly transcendental pedigree, ends up bearing a remarkable family resemblance to "Hume's heap."[34]

5

Gurwitsch's interpretation of Kant: Reflections of a former student

In *Kants Theorie des Verstandes,* we finally have the long awaited, definitive expression of Aron Gurwitsch's interpretation of Kant's theoretical philosophy.[1] The broad outlines of this interpretation were presented in many seminars and lecture courses at the New School for Social Research, and important aspects of it are contained in his seminal study of Leibniz, as well as in the various versions of his article comparing the conceptions of consciousness of Kant and Husserl.[2] But prior to the publication of this monograph, it was not available *in toto* and in detail. Thus, although the work contains few surprises for those of us fortunate enough to have been students of Professor Gurwitsch, its publication is nonetheless welcome, since it should facilitate the dissemination of this highly original and provocative reading of Kant to a wider philosophical public, including the world of Kant scholarship. It is as both a former student and a member of this latter world that I shall attempt to provide an account of this reading, assess its significance, and, as is only proper, offer some criticisms.

Considered simply as interpretation, Gurwitsch's study of Kant is motivated by two distinct but interrelated goals. One is to show that Kant's account of the understanding and its transcendental functions can best be appreciated as a creative adaptation and transformation of the Leibnizian conception of the intellect or "soul-monad." The other, directed largely against Marburg neo-Kantianism, is to show that underlying the Transcendental Deduction, which is the portion of the *Critique* on which he focuses almost exclusively, is a theory of the human mind or consciousness. Common to both is a concern with Kant's doctrine of transcendental apperception. Gurwitsch's concern with the latter is not simply historical, however, since he also endeavors to demonstrate that Husserlian phenomenology, or at least the theory of intentionality, provides the necessary corrective to the inadequacies and limitations of the Kantian theory. In what follows, I shall discuss each of these topics in turn.

I

To claim that Kant was deeply influenced by Leibniz and that he philosophized in an essentially Leibnizian context is, of itself, hardly news. References to Leibniz and to problems posed by the Leibnizian philosophy abound in Kant's works and can be traced from his earliest writings on physical theory to the *Opus Postumum*. Unlike many other students of the Leibniz–Kant connection, however, Gurwitsch directs his attention almost entirely to the Leibniz of the *New Essays*. In other words, for Gurwitsch it is Leibniz the rationalist epistemologist and philosophical psychologist, and not Leibniz the dogmatic metaphysician, or even the quasi-positivistic critic of Newton, who is of decisive importance. Central to this Leibniz is the doctrine of innate ideas and the conceptions of apperception, *"petites perceptions"* and the spontaneity of the mind, all of which, according to Gurwitsch, are taken over in a transformed manner by Kant. And although Gurwitsch's concern is clearly with tracing broad themes and conceptual connections rather than demonstrating actual historical influences, he is careful to point out that the *New Essays* was first published in 1765 and that its appearance almost immediately transformed the philosophical climate in Germany.[3] Thus, the claim is made for a direct historical link and not merely a vague intellectual kinship.

The starting point of Gurwitsch's account is Leibniz's counter-attack to Locke's critique of the doctrine of innate ideas. In response to Locke's view of the human mind as a *tabula rasa* and his adherence to the scholastic principle that there is nothing in the intellect that is not first in the senses, Leibniz retorts famously, "nothing except the intellect itself."[4] It is, then, this conception of the "intellect itself" (*intellectus ipse*) that, according to Gurwitsch, is crucial for interpreting Kant's own theory of the nature and activity of the human understanding. More specifically, three features of this Leibnizian conception turn out to be essential: the doctrine of innate ideas and the conception of necessary truth which it is intended to ground; the conception of apperception, which supposedly accounts for the mind's access to these ideas and truths; and the theory of *petites perceptions*, which performs a number of important tasks for Leibniz, psychological and epistemological as well as metaphysical.

According to Gurwitsch, the distinctive feature of Leibniz's account of innate ideas in the *New Essays* is the suggestion that these ideas reflect the very structure of the intellect. Thus, Leibniz counters the Lockean metaphor for the mind with one of his own: a veined block of marble with a determinate structure, which predisposes it to be shaped one way rather than another.[5] Since at the monadological level, all ideas or contents of the mind must be "innate" for Leibniz (monads have no windows), this serves to distinguish a subset of ideas, which have a special epistemological function and a privileged status, from the remaining ideas, which in Lockean terms are based on experience. Leibniz does not provide an exhaustive inventory of these ideas, but he does note that they include "Being, Unity, Substance, Duration, Change, Action, Perception, Pleasure, and hosts of other objects of our intellectual ideas."[6] This is indeed a mixed bag, which includes some that are recognizable ancestors of Kantian categories, others that Kant will assign to sensibility, and still others that, from a Kantian point of view, play no discernible epistemic role at all. Leaving all that aside, however, the key point is that they are supposed to account for the possibility of *a priori* knowledge, which, since it involves necessity, cannot be based on experience. In fact, as is suggested by Leibniz's metaphor of the veined marble and as Gurwitsch emphasizes, these ideas could be said to structure or condition experience in the sense that they determine what materials are able to gain access to the mind.[7] Correlatively, sense experience, rather than being the source of all knowledge, as it is for Lockean empiricism, serves merely as an occasion for the grasp of the necessary truths which reflect the structure of the mind.

Apperception is the means by which the mind gains access to these truths. Although Leibniz's conception of apperception is a complex topic and there is some doubt that he in fact held a consistent position, Gurwitsch focuses exclusively on that strand of Leibniz's position according to which apperception, identified with self-consciousness or reflection, is the distinctive capacity of rational beings or monads that enables them to make cognitive use of the innate structure of the mind.[8] Thus, whereas the brutes, having only perception and a *"sentiment animal,"* which includes sensible images and memory, must make do with a surrogate or "shadow" of thought involving association based on past experience rather than genuine comprehension, rational beings, with an apperceptive capacity, are able to grasp necessary connections and thereby acquire genuine knowledge. Accordingly, as Gurwitsch emphasizes, in Leibniz we have an assertion of the inseparability of rationality and the capacity for self-consciousness, which is precisely the thesis developed by Kant in his doctrine of transcendental apperception.

Gurwitsch also points out, however, that it is merely the *capacity* for self-consciousness that characterizes rational beings such as ourselves, since this capacity is not, indeed, could not, be actualized at every moment.[9] Moreover, this is one of the many points at which Leibniz's multi-faceted theory of *petites perceptions* comes into play. Very roughly, Leibniz holds that, even apart from explicit reflection, the innate ideas, which determine the structure of our intellect, function in a virtual or implicit manner to guide our judgment. In so doing, they operate in the manner of *petites perceptions*.[10] Accordingly, this theory explains how ideas might be in the mind, and even be cognitively effective, without being explicitly grasped as such. And this, of course, is an essential feature of Leibniz's response to Locke's critique of innate ideas.

Clearly, each of these features has its Kantian counterpart, which, as noted, Gurwitsch seeks to explain as the result of the direct influence of Leibniz. Thus, Leibniz's innate ideas become the Kantian pure concepts or categories, which reflect the very structure of the understanding. Similarly, Leibniz's apperception becomes Kant's transcendental apperception, which in the second edition of the *Critique* is identified with the understanding itself (B 134n).

As one might suspect, the story with respect to the *petites perceptions* is somewhat more complex. Nevertheless, Gurwitsch sees this theory at work in Kant's conception of the analytic judgment (the function of which is to make explicit what is implicitly contained in a given concept), his account of the empirical synthesis of apprehension, and, finally, in some of Kant's obscure remarks about the faintness and sometimes merely implicit nature of apperceptive consciousness.[11]

It is not, however, a matter of Kant simply taking over Leibnizian doctrines. On the contrary, Gurwitsch insists that Kant's appropriation of Leibniz is at the same time a radical transformation. Thus, Kant breaks completely with the notion of innateness and substitutes for Leibniz's fixed concepts embedded in the structure of the mind his own conception of pure concepts, which express the fundamental functions or rules of synthesis that constitute the forms of understanding. As Gurwitsch likes to put it, perhaps echoing Cassirer, Kant "functionalizes" Leibnizian ideas, reconstruing them as "conceptual fixations of the articulating synthesis."[12] In a similar vein, he remarks that, paradoxical as it might seem, Kant has a more activistic conception of the mind than Leibniz.[13] Whereas his great predecessor construed the activity of the monad as the unfolding according to its generative law or complete concept of the contents that are there all along, Kant takes the spontaneity of the understanding to consist in its operation on a manifold given from without. Finally, consistent with this change, the unity of the mind ceases being a metaphysical given to which it has access in reflection (apperception for Leibniz) and becomes instead (in Kant's doctrine of apperception) an achievement, the product of its own synthetic activity.

Moreover, Gurwitsch traces this radical transformation directly to the influence of David Hume, whom he treats as standing in an interesting and complex dialectical relationship to both Leibniz and Kant. On the one hand, Leibniz's account of the mind operating at the level of *"sentiment animal,"* with its contents governed by psychological laws of association rather than rational principles, and the contrast between this and the rational mind governed by its innate principles, both anticipates and provides a critique of Hume.[14] On the other hand, by means of his analysis of the causal relation, Hume demonstrated, at least in Kant's eyes, the untenability of the Leibnizian notion of inner connection, of the implicit analyticity of all truth.[15] Thus, Kant, as Gurwitsch reads him, accepted part of Hume's position, namely, his perceptual atomism or theory of discrete sense data, and endeavored to reestablish unity and connection on a new basis. The basis is, of course, Kant's conception of transcendental apperception.

Although in its broad outlines this account is reminiscent of the familiar picture of Kant as a thinker who was awakened by Hume from his "dogmatic [Leibnizian] slumbers," its sharp focus on the nature of the understanding and its rich and detailed discussions of the precise ways in which Kant transformed the Leibnizian view of the mind sketched in the *New Essays* make it both deeply illuminating and highly original. Certainly, my own reading of Kant has been profoundly influenced by my exposure to Gurwitsch's analyses in his Kant seminar and lectures on the history of modern philosophy.

II

The second major feature of Gurwitch's account is the attribution to Kant of a theory of mind. As noted, this is affirmed in explicit opposition to Marburg neo-Kantianism, which firmly rejected any endeavor to interpret the *Critique* in psychological terms on the grounds that to "psychologize" Kant is to undermine the conception of the *a priori*. Armed with a conception of psychology stemming from Husserlian phenomenology, Gurwitsch sees no danger on this score and, therefore, no obstacles to a genuinely transcendental psychology, which, in Kant's terms, would investigate "the subjective sources which form the *a priori* foundation of the possibility of experience" (A 97).[16]

The natural starting point for such an investigation is Kant's notoriously obscure account of the three-fold synthesis of apprehension, reproduction and recognition. Appropriately enough, Gurwitsch warns against a genetic interpretation of this doctrine, as if Kant were attempting to identify temporally distinct stages in cognition. The analysis of the three syntheses is understood instead to involve a methodological abstraction, a separate consideration of distinct functions involved in the synthetic activity (spontaneity) of the mind.[17] The basic idea is that there are two distinguishable requirements for cognition that must be attributed to the activity of the mind. First, the given manifold of sensible intuition must be grasped as such, that is, as a manifold. This involves its being "run through and held together," which, in turn, requires the capacity to keep before the mind past representations. These are the tasks of apprehension and reproduction, which, taken together, constitute apprehension in a broad sense. Of itself this is insufficient for knowledge, however, since it yields merely a manifold of successively given representations, which happen to exist together in one consciousness, not a set of representations that may be taken as in some sense belonging necessarily together. In Gurwitsch's helpful terms, it accounts for the *Zusammensein* of the data, not their *Zusammengehören*.[18] The latter requires a conceptual as opposed to a merely imaginative unification. This is the task of transcendental apperception and it is accomplished by means of the act of recognition in a concept.

The broad outlines of this account are certainly unobjectionable, but questions can be raised about some of the details. To begin with, there appears to be a certain ambiguity in his account of apprehension (in the broad sense), at least insofar as it is considered apart from the objectifying synthesis of apperception. His treatment of it as a "moment" of cognition, which is separable only in a methodological sense, certainly suggests, if it does not entail, that mere apprehension would not correspond to anything phenomenologically accessible. As I have put it in my own discussion of the Second Analogy, apprehension, understood as a merely subjective synthesis or "play of representations," is what would remain if (*per impossibile*) we could remove the determinate structure or objective order imposed on the sensible manifold by the understanding.[19] From this point of view, there could be no cognitive access to a preconceptualized manifold because the very act of bringing it to consciousness would necessarily subject it to determination by means of the categories. Moreover, Gurwitsch himself apparently endorses such a reading when he remarks that the product (*Leistung*) of apprehension and reproduction, "considered under its objective aspect, does not at all correspond to an effective existence [*effectiven Bestand*] – at least insofar as human mental life is concerned."[20] In fact, he explicitly endorses Cassirer's characterization of it as the "construction of a limiting case."[21]

The problem is that not everything that Gurwitsch says on the topic is easily reconcilable with this view. On the contrary, his commitment to the twin goals of presenting Kant as the heir to Leibniz and of identifying this inheritance with the conception of mind underlying the Transcendental Deduction seems to lead him to a different reading. According to this reading, apprehension and apperception (the Kantian analogues of Leibniz's perception and apperception) constitute two distinct levels of reflection, which he explicitly connects with empirical and transcendental apperception respectively.[22] Given this identification of apprehension and empirical apperception, as well as the fact that he clearly takes 'reflection' in its Leibnizian (or Lockean) sense as designating a mode of self-awareness, it is difficult to avoid the conclusion that Gurwitsch regards apprehension as a phenomenologically accessible level of consciousness (or reflection) after all.

The point can be illustrated by Gurwitsch's use of Kant's important letter to Marcus Herz of May 26, 1789, which appears to have been one of his favorite Kantian texts.[23] In the relevant portion of the letter, Kant is responding to Maimon's charge that he failed to answer the *quid facti* because he has not shown that the data of human sensibility necessarily conform to the categories. Kant replies by noting that apart from the categories the data "would not even reach that unity of consciousness that is necessary for knowledge of myself (as object of inner sense)." And even more emphatically, "I would not even be able to know that I have sense data."[24] This is precisely what one would expect Kant to say, particularly in light of the B-Deduction, which antedates this letter by two years. Gurwitsch's attention is not focused on this, however, but rather on the immediately following lines in which Kant suggests as a *Gedankenexperiment* that we imagine ourselves as animals, which means that we would have a mere play of representations without the possibility of apperception. Not surprisingly, Gurwitsch here detects clear echoes of

Leibniz (*sentiment animal*) and takes it as involving an essentially Humean picture of experience, that is, one in which there would be no necessary unity and, therefore, no experience in Kant's sense.

Up to this point, the analysis is unobjectionable, indeed, illuminating. The problem arises at the next step, where Gurwitsch suggests that, under the terms of the *Gedankenexperiment*, there might still be a distinct empirical consciousness accompanying each of the successive mental states or representations. In support of this reading, he cites a parenthetical clause in which Kant remarks, "assuming [*gesetzt*] that I am even conscious of each individual representation, but not of their relation to the unity of representation of their object, by means of the synthetic unity of their apperception." Apparently ignoring the occurrence of '*gestezt*,' which here could be translated as "even granting that," he takes Kant to be affirming the possibility of an empirical consciousness of each representation taken individually, that is, of a purely empirical apperception. But taking this term and the whole context of the parenthetical remark into consideration, it seems far more reasonable to understand Kant as claiming that, even if for the sake of argument, one were to grant the possibility of such an atomistic consciousness, it could play no role in cognition, not even a cognition of one's mental state. And this is certainly a far cry from affirming the possibility (much less the reality) of such a form of consciousness.

Although this latter example does seem to involve a misreading of the text, I take the pervasive ambiguity in Gurwitsch's account to reflect a deep seated ambiguity in Kant's position rather than a simple confusion on his part. In fact, many of the passages from the A-Deduction to which Gurwitsch repeatedly refers strongly suggest the latter reading. For example, Kant there identifies empirical apperception with inner sense and characterizes it, in contrast to transcendental apperception, as "consciousness of self according to the determinations of our state in inner perception," and he states that it "is merely empirical and always changing" (A107). This certainly suggests that empirical apperception amounts to a form of self-consciousness, which consists in the awareness of the flux of representations in contrast to the abiding I of transcendental apperception. Indeed, such a reading would seem to be demanded by Kant's use of the term '*apperception.*' Moreover, a similar conclusion appears to be warranted by Kant's notorious distinction between "judgments of perception" and "judgments of experience" in the *Prolegomena*, to which Gurwitsch likewise frequently appeals.

None of this is easily reconciled, however, with the main thrust of the B-Deduction. Instead of the contrast between apprehension and apperception, or judgments of perception and judgments of experience, Kant there opposes the objective unity of self-consciousness and the subjective unity of consciousness (B139–40). Although it is impossible to do justice to this complex topic here, the main point is that by a subjective unity of consciousness Kant no longer means anything that can be construed as a form of conscious awareness, judgment or reflection. As I have argued in *Kant's Transcendental Idealism*, a subjective unity of consciousness (not *self*-consciousness) is a unity of representations produced by empirical causal factors (such as association) rather than the spontaneity of the understanding. Since it is produced without the contribution of the understanding, nothing is represented by means of (or intended through) such a unity, not even the subject's own psychological state. In short, such a unity is a possible *object* of awareness, through a judgment of inner sense, but not, like apperception, in any sense a *mode* of awareness.[25]

The upshot of the matter, then, is that we can discern in Kant two distinct views regarding "mere apprehension," "empirical consciousness" or "empirical apperception." According to one, it constitutes a unique form of preconceptual awareness that does not involve the categories. According to the other, it is merely a methodologically distinguishable moment in the cognitive process, since any genuine awareness of one's mental state must involve a judgment of inner sense subject to the categories. Although his phenomenological orientation inclined him toward the former, Gurwitsch was, I think, sensitive to, and attempted to do justice to, both of these views. But since he failed to consider adequately possible differences between Kant's views in the first and second editions of the *Critique,* he ended up simply recapitulating the ambiguity in Kant's own position. As we shall see, similar considerations also apply to Gurwitsch's interpretation of Kant's doctrine of transcendental apperception.

III

Gurwitsch's account of apperception is in many ways the most interesting and important feature of his book. It is particularly significant because he endeavors to do justice both to the transcendental-epistemological and to the psychological dimensions of this central Kantian conception. As such, it consists in a kind of ongoing polemic, not only with Cassirer, but also with Paton, for whom the doctrine of apperception is primarily an attempt to articulate the conditions of objectivity. Gurwitsch acknowledges the possibility of such an interpretation, but he views it as inadequate, since it fails to deal with the questions of how we are to regard the "I" of the "I think" and of the relations between the subjective sources and the achieved objectivity.[26] As he succinctly puts the problem:

What results if, in the higher stage of reflection, we endeavor to grasp the "I" of the "I think"? How do we catch sight of pure transcendental apperception, and as what does it present itself to us? In what way is the belongedness [*Zugehörigkeit*] of all perceptions, appearances, representations to "one universal self-consciousness" revealed, and, what amounts to the same thing, what does this belongedness actually mean?[27]

The key to Gurwitsch's answer to these questions lies in his view of the Kantian conception of transcendental apperception as a "functionalized" reinterpretation of the Leibnizian doctrine. As already indicated, this means an emphasis on the activity of the mind, or, more precisely, the view that its nature is completely expressed in the exercise of its synthesizing functions on the sensibly given manifold. Accordingly, the unity or identity of the "I think," between which Gurwitsch does not distinguish, must be understood in terms of the unity of its act, its synthesizing function.[28] Moreover, against the radically anti-psychological reading of Cassirer, Gurwitsch insists that it is not a matter of abstract, (transcendentally) logical forms, but of an *"activitas formans,"* an "actual intellectual 'spontaneity' " (*wirkliche geistige "Selbsttätigkeit"*), which is operative in every act of thought, and through which it becomes an act of thought.[29]

Interestingly enough, in spite of his emphasis on the activity of the understanding as the source of objectivity, Gurwitsch does not subscribe to what is usually termed an "impositional" view of transcendental synthesis, that is, the view according to which the understanding imposes its own order on an indifferent manifold, thereby "constituting" the objective world of appearance.[30] On the contrary, he maintains that what the conceptual activity of the understanding does is to grasp and make explicit the pre-given spatio-temporal order or *"Vorgeformtheit"* in which the sensible manifold is presented to the mind.[31] In a similar vein, he speaks of the understanding as "respecting" this order, and even of its "ratifying," "sanctioning," "legitimating" and conferring a "title of right" (*Rechtstitel*) upon it.[32] Although this way of characterizing the activity of the understanding seems eminently Kantian, particularly since it makes use of legal metaphors similar to those to which Kant himself was so deeply attached, it nonetheless raises a fundamental problem for Gurwitsch's interpretation, which I shall discuss in the final section of this essay.

For the present, however, we must consider briefly the psychological side of Gurwitsch's account of apperception, that is, his answer to the question: "In what way is the necessary relationship of all sensible data to the identical self of pure transcendental apperception and that which is essentially involved in this relationship experienced [*erlebt*] by us?"[33] At first glance it might seem that the correct answer is not at all, since it is clear that we are usually aware of the products of our conceptual activity and not the activity itself (*das Geleiste, nicht das Leisten*).[34] Nevertheless, Gurwitsch refuses to accept a purely negative answer. Focusing on Kant's claim that "It must be possible for the 'I think' to accompany all my representations" (B131), he aptly characterizes apperception as a *"necessary possibility."*[35] Moreover, he claims that this possibility is to disclose or make explicit the unifying function of the understanding, which is always operative but of which we are seldom explicitly aware. And from this he concludes that, "The self of transcendental apperception is always experienced [*erlebt*], all representations are always given in their belongedness to this self, but not always and above all not necessarily in full explicitness [*Ausdrücklichkeit*]."[36] In short, we are aware of or "experience" the ubiquitous "I think" in a merely implicit manner, which, quite naturally, Gurwitsch interprets in light of the Leibnizian doctrine of *petites perceptions*.[37]

It is this latter feature of Gurwitsch's generally lucid account of Kant's doctrine of apperception that I find most problematic or at least unclear. To be sure, Kant speaks, even in the second edition, of a consciousness of synthesis (B133), which I believe must be taken to refer to the activity as well as its product (the unified, objectified manifold).[38] Nevertheless, it seems highly misleading to characterize this as something *"erlebt"*; certainly it is not *erfahrt* (experienced in Kant's sense), since in an important *Reflexion* Kant explicitly denies that we can experience that we think.[39] And, as he puts it in the Refutation of Idealism, the "consciousness of myself in the representation 'I' is . . . a merely intellectual representation of the spontaneity of a thinking subject," which, as such, has not "the least predicate of intuition" (B278).

Perhaps more to the point, Kant's emphasis on the consciousness of the activity of thinking can be given a purely epistemological sense in terms of his theory of judgment, without introducing a questionable psychological dimension or treating it as a distinct form of consciousness. As I have argued elsewhere, the main point is that although we can perfectly well apprehend or intuit x's that are F's (such a capacity can be attributed even to animals), we cannot conceive or represent to ourselves an x as F without not only doing it, that is, consciously taking it as such, but also without in some sense "knowing what one is doing." Apperception, then, or what amounts to the same thing, the consciousness of synthesis, is not another thing that one does when one judges (second-order knowing that one is knowing); it is rather an ineliminable component of the first-order activity itself.[40] Moreover, if this is correct, it also follows that the difference between the Leibnizian and Kantian views on apperception is greater than Gurwitsch suggests, for it is clear that Leibniz identifies apperception with reflection, which is precisely a second-order knowing.

Since Gurwitsch explicitly denies that the I of the "I think" amounts to an ego or self in the actual sense,[41] and since he is not very clear about the sense in which this identical I or, better, the act of thinking, is "experienced," it is quite possible that he might have agreed with much of the "logical" reading of apperception sketched above. Certainly, as a former student of his, I hope that this is the case. Be that as it may, however, it seems reasonably clear that, just as in the case of apprehension, Gurwitsch's account of apperception is based largely on the A-Deduction rather than on the "depsychologized" B-Deduction. Of itself this is reasonable, even necessary, for a phenomenologically oriented interpretation. Nevertheless, it does result in a failure to consider the senses in which Kant's doctrine might have changed or at least been clarified in the second edition. Moreover, in the case of apperception this failure has important consequences, for Kant there explicitly maintains that the principle of apperception is analytic (B135, 138). Admittedly, this point is either overlooked or dismissed as mistaken by most commentators. But since I have made it the basis of my interpretation of the Transcendental Deduction, I particularly regret the fact that Gurwitsch chose to ignore it in his account of apperception.[42] Certainly, at the very least, it raises questions about the sense in which Kant may be regarded as offering a theory of mind.

IV

Although Gurwitsch's concern in *Kants Theorie des Verstandes* is fundamentally exegetical, he does conclude on a critical note. The basic point of this criticism, which he has also presented elsewhere, is the claim that on the Kantian theory it is impossible to account for repeated perceptions or experiences of the same thing. For example, I take the desk which I am now perceiving to be the same as (numerically identical with) the desk I perceived yesterday. As Gurwitsch construes it, the Kantian story at this point is that this judgment is based on the subsumption of qualitatively similar (but numerically distinct) sensible data under a common concept or rule. The problem is that since the data are different it cannot strictly speaking be claimed that the distinct appearances are of an identical object. This difficulty is then claimed to be resolvable only by appeal to the Husserlian theory of intentionality, more particularly, by means of the conception of a perceptual noema, or object intended as such, which can be grasped by distinct noetic acts. Thus, in spite of the depth and power of its answer to Humean empiricism, in the last analysis Kant's transcendental account founders because of its failure to recognize the intentionality of consciousness.[43]

It is impossible here to address the large issue of the relative merits of Kantian criticism and Husserlian phenomenology or even the smaller question of the extent to which one might find in Kant an anticipation of something like the Husserlian theory of intentionality.[44] What must be noted, however, is that this line of criticism reflects an essentially phenomenalistic reading of Kant, a reading which was already implicit in the account of the objectifying synthesis as consisting in a ratification or legitimation of a pre-given spatio-temporal order. As Gurwitsch sees it, this phenomenalism is the direct result of the fact that Kant took over the Cartesian–Lockean theory of ideas in its final Humean form. In other words, the only contents of the mind are its own representations or sensible data. To be sure, under the influence of Leibniz, Kant came to see that the human mind must be regarded as the active unifier rather than as merely the passive recipient of these data, and it is precisely in this that Kant's achievement consists. Nevertheless, it remains an achievement that is fatally flawed by its erroneous starting point. For, given this starting point, Kant was forced to identify the representations or sensible data of the mind with the properties or states of things.[45] And from this standpoint, there is no possibility of affirming the numerical identity of objects perceived at different times or points of view by a single subject, not to mention by different subjects.[46]

Since the phenomenalistic reading of Kant remains well entrenched in the literature and has so much apparent textual evidence in its favor, Gurwitsch can hardly be condemned for adhering to it. Indeed, the fact that it was expressly affirmed both by Husserl, his philosophical hero, and Paton, his favorite Kant commentator and a usually reliable guide, must have made it virtually irresistible to him. Nevertheless, I believe it to be profoundly mistaken. In fact, it is precisely at this point that my understanding of Kant differs most sharply from that of my teacher.

In order to clarify this difference, let us return for a moment to Gurwitsch's account of objectification in terms of "ratification" or "legitimation." As already indicated, the crucial point here is that what is supposedly ratified is a pre-given spatio-temporal order of representations (actually only a temporal order). Limiting ourselves to the question of objective succession and, therefore, causality, this, in effect, means that an objective succession of the states A–B constituting an event is identified with an appropriately ratified (conceptualized) subjective succession of perceptions a–b. In other words, it is the subjective order, the order of apprehension, that is rendered objective or, what is the same thing, necessary, by being subsumed under a rule (in this case the principle of causality).

Now, once again, it must be admitted that Kant frequently seems to be claiming just this, particularly when he speaks of the rule as a "necessary rule of apprehension" (A191/B236) or of apprehension itself as being "bound down" (A192/B237). Nevertheless, as I have argued in *Kant's Transcendental Idealism,* this cannot be taken as Kant's considered view, at least not if we hope to make any philosophical sense of the argument.[47] Here it must be kept in mind that the objective temporal order for Kant is a *thought* not an intuited order, which means that it is not something pre-given to be "respected" or "ratified." Moreover, as he makes clear in the vitally important third paragraph of the second edition version of the second analogy (B234–36), the problem of objectivity with respect to the temporal order is precisely to explain how it is possible by means of perceptions, which are all that is given us (since time itself cannot be perceived), to represent an objective order that cannot be simply identified with the order of the perceptions themselves. Thus, although objectivity is in Gurwitsch's sense an achievement for Kant, it is not accomplished through the ratification of the subjective order by subjecting *that order* to a rule. On the contrary, the rule is one by means of which we are able to represent to ourselves a distinct objective order *through* these perceptions, not an order *of* them.

Unfortunately, it is impossible to develop this analysis any further here, and

I am certainly not claiming that it is not without difficulties of its own, or even that Kant has an unambiguous position regarding objectivity. My only aim is to suggest the possibility of a non-phenomenalistic interpretation of Kant's argument and to note that Gurwitsch did not seem to have considered such a possibility (apart, of course, from Marburg neo-Kantianism, which is not here in question). In retrospect, however, perhaps I should be grateful that he did not, since if he had, much of my own work might have become redundant.

6

Causality and causal law in Kant: A critique of Michael Friedman

The questions of just what the Second Analogy purports to show and its role in both Kant's overall theory of experience and his philosophy of science remain matters of some controversy. At the heart of the debate is the problem of the connection between the transcendental principle of causality and particular causal laws known through experience. Although Kant consistently denies that ordinary empirical laws can be derived from the transcendental principles alone, he is less clear on the precise relationship between them. On the one hand, he characterizes empirical laws as "special determinations of still higher laws," the highest of which stem from the understanding itself (A126).[1] This suggests a relatively straightforward picture according to which the principles or transcendental laws of themselves guarantee the empirical lawfulness of nature. Experience is required to arrive at particular laws, but the general principle of the empirical lawfulness of nature is sufficiently guaranteed by the transcendental principles. On the other hand, in the Appendix to the Dialectic of the first *Critique* and the two versions of the Introduction to the third *Critique* Kant seems to suggest a more complex story. According to this story, not only the unifiability of particular laws into theories, but also the nomological status of particular uniformities requires an appeal to either reason in its regulative use or reflective judgment.

Gerd Buchdahl, among others, has focused the attention of Kant scholars on this more complex story. At the heart of Buchdahl's interpretation is what he terms the "looseness of fit" between the transcendental and empirical levels. In essence, this means that the Analogies (operating at the transcendental level) perform (and are intended to perform) only the minimal transcendental function of securing an objective temporal order of contingent occurrences, while the actual projection of an empirically lawlike order of nature is seen as the work of reason or reflective judgment.[2] Thus, as far as the Second Analogy is concerned, experience might not reveal any regularities possessing nomological status.[3] Expressed in the language of Lewis White Beck, who opts for a similar reading, this amounts to the claim that Kant's concern is to reply to Hume's challenge to the "every-event-some cause" principle of the *Treatise* rather than to defend the "same-cause-same-effect" principle, which was the target in the *Enquiry*.[4]

Although it undermines the attempt to find in the Second Analogy a comprehensive response to Hume's doubts regarding induction or the uniformity of nature, this approach has at least two significant advantages. First, by weakening the connection between the causal principle and the basic principles of Newtonian physics, it allows for the possibility of finding in the Second Analogy a transcendental argument that is independent of an appeal to the science of Kant's time. Second, it makes it easy to offer a concise and definitive counter to the familiar Lovejoy–Strawson objection that by moving from the determinacy or necessity of the sequence of perceptions in a single instance of event-perception to the existence of a general law covering all sequences of that type, Kant is guilty of a *non sequitur* of colossal proportions.[5] Since on this reading there is no such inference, there is no *non sequitur*.[6]

Recently, however, this "weak" reading of the Second Analogy, a version of which I defended in *Kant's Transcendental Idealism,* has been challenged by Michael Friedman.[7] Central to Friedman's alternative reading is the claim that the Second Analogy, together with the other Analogies, ground both the existence and necessity of empirical laws. Since the laws which they ground turn out to be the basic laws of Newtonian physics (the three laws of motion and universal gravitation), and since the significance of these Analogies consists for Friedman entirely in their grounding function, it follows that they stand or fall with the Newtonian edifice which they ground. Thus, if the aim of Buchdahl's interpretation is to "loosen the fit," the result of Friedman's analysis might be characterized as "tightening the noose," since he attempts to demonstrate the inseparability of Kant's transcendental claims from their connection with Newtonian physics.

Friedman's reconstruction of Kant's philosophy of science, as manifested in the papers produced to date, constitutes a truly impressive achievement. Virtually alone among the commentators, he combines a thorough command of the Kantian texts and a deep knowledge of Newtonian physics with considerable philosophical and scientific sophistication. Nevertheless, I believe that his account of the Second Analogy is not without its difficulties and I would here like to explore some of these difficulties and related problems. This essay is divided into three parts: the first presents an overview of Friedman's position, with particular attention to his analysis of the Second Analogy; the second offers some criticisms of this analysis and reaffirms the main outlines of my earlier position; the third questions his account of the source of the necessity of empirical laws by considering an important passage from the Introduction to the *Critique of Judgment.*

I

Friedman readily acknowledges the *prima facie* plausibility and attractiveness of a reading of the Second Analogy which denies that it entails either the existence or the necessity of empirical laws. In addition to its previously mentioned capacity to deal in a quick and easy fashion with the *non sequitur* objection, such a reading also appears to accord well with Kant's emphasis on the empirical nature of particular laws and his accounts of the regulative function of reason and/or reflective judgment.[8] Moreover, at one time at least, Friedman unequivocally affirmed its superiority to a hybrid reading such as Guyer's, which maintains that the Second Analogy guarantees the existence but not the necessity of empirical causal laws.[9] Since the very concept of a causal law involves necessity (as well as strict universality), the idea that we could have inductively grounded laws lacking necessity is simply a non-starter: "[I]f the universal causal principle asserts the existence of particular causal laws or uniformities, it must also assert their necessity."[10]

Accordingly, the key question is whether the Second Analogy entails the existence of empirical causal laws, and it is here that he takes issue with the weak interpretation. Once again the starting point of his analysis is the concept of causality itself. Since the causal relation for Kant involves strict universality as well as necessity, to say that A is the cause of B is to affirm a universal law to the effect that "*all* events of type A are *necessarily* followed by events of type B." In other words, causal claims involve reference to event-types (not simply singular events), from which it supposedly follows that "[the] universal causal principle must assert the existence of particular causal laws or uniformities as well."[11] Thus, given Kant's conception of causality, if the Second Analogy succeeds in showing that every event must have a cause, it *ipso facto* also shows that every event falls under a causal law possessing more than inductive universality and material necessity.

How, then, are we to understand the connection between the transcendental principle of causality and the particular causal laws, both the existence and necessity of which it supposedly entails? Indeed, how can we attribute necessity at all to such laws, given their empirical character? A key to Friedman's answer to both questions is his insistence that empirical causal laws, insofar as they are genuine laws, are not simply empirical. Rather, they have a peculiar kind of mixed or hybrid status: *qua* empirical they are based on experience (induction), but *qua* law they must have an *a priori* grounding (presumably in the causal principle).[12] In support of this view, Friedman cites a number of Kantian texts, of which the following is representative:

Even natural laws, when they are considered as principles of the empirical employment of the understanding, at the same time carry with themselves an expression of necessity and thus at least the suggestion of a determination from grounds that hold *a priori* and antecedent to all experience. Yet all laws of nature without distinction stand under higher principles of the understanding, in that they merely apply these to particular cases of appearance. These principles alone therefore give the concept that contains the condition, and as it were the exponent, of a rule in general; but experience gives the case that stands under the rule (A159/B198).[13]

In light of texts such as these, Friedman quite naturally sees his central task as explaining how the transcendental principle of causality can supply the *a priori* grounding necessary for empirical laws or, more precisely, how it can elevate inductively observed regularities or uniformities to genuine nomological status by providing them with the material necessity which, *qua* empirical, they lack. His solution, in brief, is that this grounding must be conceived as a two step procedure by means of which empirical regularities are connected first with the metaphysical principles of the *Metaphysical Foundations of Natural Science,* specifically the principles of mechanics corresponding to Newton's three laws of motion, and, ultimately, through these, with the transcendental principles of the *Critique.* In presenting his solution, however, it will be convenient to "begin from above," as it were, that is, with the move from the transcendental to the metaphysical principles.

As Friedman points out, the metaphysical principles are derived from their transcendental counterparts by subsuming the empirical concept of matter (the movable in space possessing impenetrability and weight) under the latter. This secures a synthetic *a priori* status for the metaphysical principles, while at the same time providing them with a significant empirical content, which the transcendental principles lack. Thus, whereas the transcendental principle of causality affirms that every alteration has a cause, the corresponding metaphysical principle maintains that every change of state of matter has an external cause (MAN 4: 543; 104), which is equivalent to the principle of inertia. Correlatively, the First and Third Analogies yield respectively the principles of the conservation of mass or quantity of matter and the equality of action and reaction.[14]

It follows from this that the transcendental principles have a greater scope than the metaphysical principles, since the former apply to all entities in the phenomenal world, including living and thinking beings, while the latter "apply only to the activities and powers of nonliving, nonthinking beings."[15] But while Friedman certainly acknowledges this difference, he effectively denies its significance. This is because the metaphysical principles, on his reading, turn out to be not merely realizations or instantiations of the transcendental principles, but their unique realizations. Moreover, as such, they provide the indispensable means whereby the (dynamical) transcendental principles are constitutive with respect to experience.[16] Although he does not put it in quite this way, I think it fair to say that for Friedman the transcendental principles stand in roughly the same relationship to the metaphysical principles as the categories stand to their schemata. Just as the schemata, as transcendental determinations of time, both realize the categories and restrict the range of their application to what is given in sensible intuition, so the metaphysical principles, by linking their transcendental correlates to the empirical concept of matter, both ensure their applicability to corporeal nature, *qua* merely corporeal, and limit this applicability to the same sphere.

Although such a view raises profound problems regarding the applicability of the categories (including causality) to objects of inner sense and, therefore, for understanding Kant's account of self-knowledge and his psychological determinism, it does have significant textual support. For example, in the "General Note on the System of Principles," added in the second edition of the *Critique,* Kant insists on the need not simply for intuition but for *outer* intuition for the application of the principles (B291–93). And, even more graphically, in the Preface to the *Metaphysical Foundations of Natural Science,* anticipating the language of the Preface to the second edition of the *Critique,* Kant remarks that without the instances taken from "the general doctrine of body, i.e., from the form and principles of external intuition," the understanding "gropes, uncertain and trembling among meaningless concepts" (MAN 4: 478;16).[17] In fact, in the same context Kant claims that the metaphysical principles of corporeal nature make possible the realization of the otherwise empty concepts and principles of transcendental philosophy (including causality) by providing instances from corporeal nature which supply "the conditions under which the concepts of the understanding can alone have objective reality, i.e., meaning and truth" (MAN 4: 478; 16).

These passages are grist for Friedman's mill. Not only do they strongly suggest the inseparability of the transcendental from the metaphysical principles (which links them closely to the Newtonian laws of motion, thereby "tightening the noose"), but in so doing they make it possible to establish the required connection between the transcendental principles and empirical laws. Since the metaphysical principles are the unique realizations of their transcendental counterparts, the latter effectively drop out of the picture. Thus, all that needs to be done is to establish a connection between the metaphysical principles, which provide the content of "pure natural science," and empirical laws. And this Friedman proceeds to do in convincing fashion. This whole process of grounding the empirical in the *a priori* is illustrated by the transformation of Kepler's empirical "laws" of planetary motion, which are at first merely inductive or empirical regularities regarding apparent motions, into a genuine law of nature possessing necessity and strict universality, namely, Newton's law of universal gravitation.

Basing his analysis mainly on the fourth chapter of the *Metaphysical Foundations of Natural Science* ("Metaphysical foundations of phenomenology"), Friedman describes a three step procedure in which the given data (Kepler's observed uniformities) are transformed into the Newtonian law by being subsumed under the modal categories and, more importantly, through the application to the data of the metaphysical principles of mechanics.[18] We cannot here enter into the details of his analysis, but the essential point is that universal gravitation is seen as the paradigm case of a law with a "mixed" status. On the one hand, it is based on observational data, while, on the other hand, it attains its nomological status by being connected in a deductive fashion with the above mentioned synthetic *a priori* metaphysical principles. And since these are the unique instantiations of the Analogies, it follows that this law is itself indirectly grounded in the Analogies.

Friedman further explicates this process of grounding in terms of the notions of "nesting" or "framing." The basic idea is that empirical regularities attain their grounding, which he equates with the achievement of genuine objectivity, only by virtue of being framed or nested in the metaphysical principles and their transcendental counterparts. Properly nested, these regularities follow deductively from the metaphysical principles. This, in turn, accounts for their necessity, which they do not possess considered merely as inductive generalizations.[19] Accordingly, Friedman claims, in opposition to Buchdahl, that the necessity of empirical laws is derived *entirely* from the understanding, without any help from reason's (or reflective judgment's) idea of systematicity. Moreover, in support of this latter point, he appeals to Kant's denial in the Preface of the *Metaphysical Foundations of Natural Science* of scientific status to chemistry in spite of the systematic arrangement of its "laws" (MAN 4: 468–69; 4–5). This, for Friedman, constitutes decisive proof that systematicity alone is not sufficient to account for the necessity attributable to all genuine empirical laws.[20]

Friedman does not, however, deny that reason's or reflective judgment's principle of systematicity has a significant role to play in the Kantian account of science. His point is only that it is not the one Buchdahl and others assign to it. Rather than being the source of the necessity of empirical laws, it provides methodological principles of parsimony, continuity, simplicity and the like, which make possible the unification of empirical concepts and laws into a classificatory system. Moreover, such unification is itself necessary because only by means of it can the overwhelming majority and, indeed, the totality of empirical laws be properly nested so as to receive a transcendental grounding.[21] Accordingly, Friedman claims to find not merely important work for the regulative principle of systematicity, but work that is in accord with his understanding of the relationship between the transcendental principles and empirical laws.

II

In spite of the clarity and persuasiveness of Friedman's overall account, which I have been able only to sketch in the baldest terms, there are some questions raised by his treatment of the Second Analogy. As we have seen, Friedman supports his reading by a direct appeal to the concept of causality itself. Since this concept involves the thought of event-types related by a causal law, rather than merely singular events, and since the law affirms a necessary connection between tokens of these event-types, it follows, according to Friedman, that we cannot apply the concept of causality without presupposing both the existence and the necessity of particular causal laws.

Although undoubtedly correct as far as it goes, this is not sufficient to yield the result Friedman desires. The basic problem is simply that it does not follow from the fact that a causal law affirms a connection between event-types, which I take to be noncontroversial, that there must be more than a single instantiation of each type. After all, the strict universality and necessity of the principle that events of type-A are succeeded by events of type-B is not undermined by a scenario in which there is only a single event of each type. In short, for all that can be inferred from the concept of causality, the possibility remains open that there might be nothing more than what could be termed "instantaneous laws," that is, laws with merely a single instance.[22] As was already noted by Paton, genuine laws require regularity and repeatability.[23] But there is nothing in the argument of the Second Analogy, certainly not the analysis of the concept of causality, that requires the assumption of either.

Friedman's position rests, however, on more than an analysis of the concept of causality. Equally significant, albeit largely implicit in his account, is his apparent adherence to the view that an appeal to causal laws is necessary for judgments of objective succession. In other words, he appears to accept not only the *conceptual* claim that the concept of causality presupposes the existence of particular causal laws but also the quite distinct *epistemological* thesis that the cognitive function supposedly performed by the causal principle can be accomplished only by means of an explicit appeal to such laws. And if this is the case, then, clearly, the Second Analogy must entail the existence of particular causal laws as necessary conditions of the possibility of experience.

An extreme version of this epistemological thesis is held by Guyer, who maintains at one point that "[I]t is only if we are in possession of causal laws which dictate that in the relevant circumstances – that is, not in general, but in the particular circumstances of wind, tide, setting of the sails, and so forth, which are assumed to attain – the ship could only sail downstream that we actually have sufficient evidence to interpret our representations of it to mean it is sailing downstream."[24] Although Friedman, as we have seen, differs from Guyer with respect to the issue of the necessity of empirical laws and would probably put the point differently, he certainly seems to accept the principle that judgments of objective succession require an appeal to specific causal laws.[25] In fact, this lies at the very heart of his view as to how objectivity is grounded.

In response, it can be argued that this claim is implausible on the face of it, since we are obviously able to recognize many instances of objective succession without being able to subsume that succession under a causal law. For example, is it really the case that there can be no "objective experience" of water freezing apart from a knowledge of the causal conditions of this change? Or, alternatively, would we deny that the growth of a living organism is a case of an objective succession of states on the grounds that it cannot, according to Kant, be explicated in terms of mechanistic laws? Moreover, whatever the plausibility of such a doctrine, it simply does not reflect Kant's view. Contrary to what Friedman seems to assume, the Second Analogy does not claim that we must be able to provide the causal ground for an event before we are able to ascertain its objectivity; it claims instead merely that insofar as we experience (or take ourselves to experience) an event, we are constrained to presuppose that it has a cause. This licenses us to look for causal laws, but it hardly guarantees that we shall find them.[26]

Why, then, does Friedman resist this conclusion and instead attribute to Kant the epistemological thesis? Since we are dealing here with an implicit attribution, we can hardly expect to find explicit reasons in support of it. Nevertheless, I believe it possible to isolate two closely related, yet distinguishable, factors underlying Friedman's reading of the Second Analogy. The first is his understanding of the nature of the objective succession supposedly grounded in the causal principle. This can be understood either as a succession of events, e.g., the motion of one body followed, immediately upon impact, by the motion of another, or as the succession of states constituting a single event, e.g., the alteration of water from a liquid state at t_1 to a solid state at t_2. Although he does not concern himself explicitly with this distinction, Friedman consistently takes succession in the former sense, arguing that *this* succession can be grounded, that is, rendered objective, only if it is subsumed under a causal law.[27]

Admittedly, Kant is notoriously slippery on this point, in different contexts characterizing both types of succession simply as *A–B*, which quite naturally leads to a good deal of confusion.[28] Nevertheless, this distinction between the two senses of objective succession is not, as sometimes thought, an unimportant one that has no real relevance to Kant's argument. For Friedman may very well be correct in maintaining that we can judge a succession of events *A–B* to be necessary, that is, more than a contingent sequence, only by subsuming it under a causal law stating that events of type-A are invariably followed by events of type-B. This has absolutely no bearing, however, on the question of what must be presupposed in the judgment of the succession of states *A–B* of an object constituting an event. And, as I have argued elsewhere, it is the latter with which Kant is concerned in the Second Analogy.[29]

The second essential factor is Friedman's tacit identification of the experience for which the *Critique* is to lay the transcendental ground with scientific rather than ordinary experience. As I understand this contrast, the salient difference concerns the manner in which objectivity is construed. Within the scientific framework of Newtonian physics, the problem of objectivity is essentially a matter of distinguishing "real" or "absolute" from merely "apparent" or "relative" motion; this is accomplished only by an appeal to real forces and, therefore, genuine laws of nature. Thus, given *this* conception of experience, it is not only natural but necessary to assume that particular causal (force) laws function as conditions of its possibility. This is not at all the case for ordinary experience, however, where objectivity is understood as that which is public and intersubjectively accessible, that is, distinct from our representation of it. The key point, of course, is that this second and broader conception of objectivity includes what is merely "apparent" for the physicist.

Now, there can be little doubt that it is precisely this scientific picture that Friedman brings to his reading of the *Critique*. This much is clear from the great reliance he places on Kant's account in the *Prolegomena* of how judgments of perception are converted into judgments of experience by being subsumed under the categories (particularly causality) and the complementary discussion in the *Metaphysical Foundations of Natural Science* of how the metaphysical principles serve to transform "mere appearance" into "experience." In his appeal to these texts, Friedman explicitly takes the given empirical regularities with which science proper begins to be analogous to judgments of perception, corresponding to mere appearance, and suggests that they are converted into genuine experience, analogous to judgments of experience, through the application of the metaphysical principles. Only by this means, he argues, is "genuinely objective experience" constituted, or, as he also puts it, "genuinely objective empirical judgments" attained.[30]

As Friedman is well aware, however, Buchdahl has warned us explicitly against being misled in the interpretation of Kant's transcendental claims by the account of the *Prolegomena*, with its explicit reference to empirical causal claims. On Buchdahl's reading, with which I still by and large concur, the concept of causality enters in in at least two different places in Kant's analysis, thereby requiring a distinction of levels to which Kant, unfortunately, does not consistently adhere. On the one hand, it enters as a transcendental presupposition, required for the thought of an objective succession; on the other hand, it functions as a logical or conceptual presupposition of the thought of an explicitly causal sequence.[31] The Second Analogy is concerned with the former and the *Prolegomena* largely with the latter.

Moreover, even granting Friedman's analysis of the grounding of scientific or genuine experience, we still need an account of how the causal principle functions with respect to experience that is less than "genuinely objective." This would include the merely empirical regularities with which science begins and which are converted into genuine experience by being subsumed under causal laws. Presumably, such regularities are objective, if not "genuinely" so, since their component elements are events, that is, tokens of objective succession, which, as such, are distinct from our representations of them. In short, a transcendental account of experience must deal with the conditions of the possibility of what we might term "Kepler-experience," and not simply with the conditions of the transformation of it into "Newton-experience," which appears to be Friedman's sole concern.

Although Friedman neglects this issue, consistency requires him to hold that this succession too is rendered objective by being subsumed under determinate causal laws (rather than the bare schema of causality). But such a view is not without its difficulties. First, it must be explained why it is the case (or at least why Kant thought it to be the case) that we can recognize the occurrence of an event only if we are in possession of the causal law(s) in terms of which it is to be explained. Second, and perhaps more seriously, a way must be found to deal with the apparently vicious circularity of the claim that the empirical laws supposedly required for the experience of events are, *qua* empirical, themselves based (at least in part) on the experience of a regular sequence of such events. Experience (on Friedman's reading) may not be a sufficient condition for the determination of empirical laws, but it is certainly a necessary condition.

Interestingly enough, a similar problem arises for Guyer by virtue of his insistence that empirical laws are necessary for judgments of events. Since the causal principle is *ex hypothesi* a condition of the possibility of experience and since these laws for Guyer are themselves derived inductively from experience, he is forced to explain how experience can provide the conditions of its own possibility. Guyer is fully aware of this problem and deals with it in a direct, albeit in my judgment unsatisfactory, manner by denying that the Analogies are intended to serve as necessary conditions of the possibility of experience in the sense in which this is usually understood. Instead, he asserts that they function merely within the epistemological framework of justification of particular judgments regarding temporal succession and, consequently, that within this context there is no circularity or incoherence in the idea that these same laws might have been inductively derived from previous experiences of objective succession.[32]

Unfortunately, whatever the merits of Guyer's solution to the problem, it is not available to Friedman. Since he rejects Guyer's analysis of the Second Analogy on the grounds that it cannot account for the necessity of empirical laws and wishes, contrary to Guyer, to give the transcendental principle of causality a genuine objectivating function (at least by way of its metaphysical correlate), he can hardly accept an interpretation that denies both of these. Accordingly, the problem of accounting for the conditions of the experience of an event remains.

Moreover, it is precisely at this point that the "weak" reading of the Second Analogy comes into play. For if empirical causal laws are inappropriate candidates to fulfill this transcendental function, then nothing remains except the bare schema of causality. On this reading, then, to which Friedman's is radically opposed, what the Second Analogy purports to show is merely that this schema functions as the rule through which we think a succession of states as objective and, therefore, as constituting an event.[33] But this relatively modest claim, which I take it constitutes the heart of Kant's answer to Hume, does not entail any further claims about the empirical lawlikeness of nature. And if this is correct, then, there is both a certain "looseness of fit" between the transcendental and empirical levels and a distinct and ineliminable transcendental function for the causal principle of the Second Analogy.

III

Up to this point I have accepted Friedman's account of how causal laws are grounded in the transcendental principle of causality and questioned only the claim that the existence of empirical laws is guaranteed by the same principle. Thus, my analysis calls for a sharper distinction between the tasks of grounding and guaranteeing than Friedman seems willing to draw. In this final section, I shall take a brief look at his analysis of the grounding of the material necessity of these laws, which is alleged to be entirely the work of the understanding, without any contribution from reason and/or reflective judgment. In particular, I shall consider a text which strongly suggests the very view that he is attacking. The text in question is from the published introduction to the *Critique of Judgment* where, reflecting on empirical laws, Kant writes:

> These laws, being empirical, may be contingent as far as the light of *our* understanding goes, but still, if they are to be called laws, (as the concept of nature requires,) they must be regarded as necessary on a principle, unknown though it be to us, of the unity of the manifold. – The reflective judgment which is compelled to ascend from the particular in nature to the universal, stands, therefore, in need of a principle. This principle it cannot borrow from experience, because what it has to do is to establish just the unity of all empirical principles under higher, though likewise empirical principles, and thence the possibility of the systematic subordination of higher and lower (KU5: 180; 19).

Not surprisingly, Buchdahl focuses explicitly on this passage in support of his central thesis that the necessity of particular causal laws is entirely a function of their place in a systematic structure of such laws, while this structure, in turn, is seen as a regulative demand of reflective judgment rather than a constitutive requirement of the understanding. Consistent with this view, he also takes the cryptic expression, "a principle, unknown though it be to us, of the unity of the manifold," to refer to reflective judgment's principle of purposiveness.[34]

In the published version of "Kant on Causal Laws and the Foundations of Natural Science," Friedman ignores this passage. Instead, he calls attention to a later passage regarding the necessity of empirical laws, which he claims to be in accord with his interpretation.[35] In a lengthy footnote contained in an earlier version, however, he did refer to the passage in question and directly challenged Buchdahl's reading. As he then viewed the matter, the mysterious unknown principle cannot be the principle of reflective judgment (Buchdahl's view), since *that* principle is perfectly well known to us. Instead, he suggested that what Kant had in mind was a properly grounded mathematical force law, and from this he concluded that the sought-for "principle of the unity of the manifold" must belong to the understanding not reflective judgment.[36]

This is certainly what Friedman wants Kant to say, but it clearly will not do as a reading of the passage in question. The crucial factor to be kept in mind in interpreting this text is that Kant is here engaged in what might be termed the "metaphysical deduction" of the principle of purposiveness; that is, he is endeavoring to formulate the unique principle of reflective judgment, which is then to receive its justification or transcendental deduction in the next section. Thus, this principle is not yet well known to the reader, since it has not yet been formulated; and this, I think, provides decisive confirmation of Buchdahl's interpretation of the passage.

Presumably, Friedman's recognition of this fact explains the deletion of his discussion of this passage from the published version of his paper. But this deletion does not obviate the need to deal with the challenge that the passage poses to his account of the relation between understanding and reflective judgment. Now, apart from the dubious tactic of simply dismissing this text as an anomaly or misstatement, incompatible with Kant's "critical" position, there would seem to be two lines of response open to Friedman. One is to adopt some variant of Guyer's thesis that this account of necessity as grounded in reflective judgment's principle of purposiveness marks a significant departure from the original standpoint of the first *Critique*.[37] In spite of his differences with Guyer regarding the reading of the Second Analogy, he could accept such a result, although it would leave him with the not inconsiderable task of accounting for this shift in Kant's position.

Alternatively, and I think more in the spirit of Friedman's project, he might modify his claim regarding the grounding of necessity, so as to give even more of a role to reflective judgment. Recall that Friedman appeals to Kant's discussion of chemistry in the *Metaphysical Foundations of Natural Science* in support of his view that systematic arrangement is not a *sufficient* condition for the grounding of genuine laws. Clearly, however, this fairly obvious move does not even begin to address the more serious question of whether it might be a *necessary* condition for such grounding. In fact, although I cannot argue for it here, I believe the latter to be the case and to be perfectly compatible with much that Friedman has to say about nesting and the role of regulative principles.[38] Nevertheless, it must be kept in mind that this partial agreement regarding the source of the necessity of whatever empirical laws we may find does not carry over into an agreement regarding the role of the transcendental principle of causality as the ultimate guarantor of the existence of such laws. Thus, it is at this point that the battle lines remain drawn.

7

Kant's refutation of materialism

In the *Critique of Pure Reason*, Kant uses the notion of spontaneity *(Spontaneität* or *Selbsttätigkeit)* to characterize both the ordinary epistemic activity of the understanding and the kind of causal activity required for transcendentally free agency. In spite of the obvious differences between these two conceptions of spontaneity, at one time Kant virtually identified them, since he licensed the inference from the spontaneity of thought manifest in apperception to the transcendental freedom of the thinker.[1] By the mid-1770s, however, he abandoned that view, affirming instead a sharp distinction between "logical freedom," which pertains to acts of thought, and "transcendental freedom," which supposedly pertains to acts of will.[2] This distinction, if not the precise language in which it was originally expressed, remained an integral part of the "critical" philosophy. Moreover, although the topic of freedom is not discussed in the Paralogisms, Kant there insists on the illegitimacy of the attempt to derive any synthetic knowledge regarding the nature of the "thing which thinks" (presumably including its freedom) from the 'I think.'

Both the sharp separation of the two kinds of spontaneity and the negative claims of the *Critique* are grist from the mill of philosophers such as Wilfred Sellars and Patricia Kitcher, who wish to reinterpret Kant in light of contemporary theories of mind. Reduced to its essentials, their basic thesis is that, by disengaging Kant's account of cognition from its attachments with the disreputable features of noumenalistic metaphysics, it becomes possible to combine Kant's important epistemological insights, particularly his anti-empiricist arguments, with a sophisticated contemporary, that is, broadly materialistic, theory of mind. In the same spirit, the argument of the Paralogisms is given a functionalist reading, according to which Kant's attack on rational psychology is reduced to the claim that one cannot infer the "hardware" of the mind from its "software."[3] Indeed, as Sellars maintains on the basis of his Peircean view of the noumenal, it is possible to characterize the "noumenal mechanism" underlying the activity of thinking as the neurophysiological system to be reached by the "ideal science."[4]

Although this reconstructive program has proven to be highly congenial to many philosophers, it either downplays or ignores completely some of the more puzzling yet suggestive aspects of Kant's account of the mind and its cognitive activities. Foremost among these is the claim, which appears to stand in direct contradiction to the whole thrust of the Paralogisms, that the meager resources of the 'I think' suffice to establish "the impossibility of an explanation in *materialist* terms of the constitution of the self as a merely thinking subject" (B420). Closely related to this is the notorious claim in the *Groundwork* concerning the impossibility of conceiving the mind as being causally determined in its judgmental activity, which is frequently regarded as the basis for an indirect argument against determinism. Taken together, these claims and, indeed, the whole account of apperception, suggest the possibility that Kant has a much more complex view of the spontaneity of mind than he is frequently given credit for, one that not only cannot be easily reconciled with contemporary versions of materialism, but that perhaps even constitutes a formidable challenge to that well entrenched position.

In the present essay I propose to explore that possibility. More specifically, I shall try to show that Kant's conception of spontaneity provides the essential materials for a "refutation of materialism" that is relevant to contemporary discussions of the issue. The essay is divided into four parts. The first sketches Kant's account of spontaneity and its relationship to his doctrine of apperception. The second analyzes and shows the inadequacy of his "official" argument for immaterialism, which turns on the unity of consciousness. The third considers the argument from the *Groundwork* and attempts to show that, when buttressed by the account of spontaneity, this argument has force against non-reductive versions of materialism, which treat mental states and activities as supervenient on neurophysiological ones. The fourth extends the argument to meet the challenge of an eliminative materialism that rejects the epistemological assumptions operative up to this point.

I. The preliminaries

A fundamental, yet largely unargued for premise of Kant's "critical" philosophy is that human (indeed all finite) cognition is discursive, that is to say, conceptual. Such knowledge, of course, requires sensible intuition, because it is only through intuition that the object or, better, the material for thinking the object, can be given to the mind. This, in turn, leads to the familiar yet perplexing doctrine that the mind is equipped with *a priori* forms of sensibility (space and time) in terms of which the material for thought is received. For present purposes, however, the essential point is that mere receptivity does not suffice for cognition. In order for an object to be known, it must be conceptualized, that is, "subsumed" under or "recognized" in terms of some general description, which, in principle at least, is applicable to an indefinite number of other objects. According to Kant's theory, all of this is the work of the spontaneity of the understanding. In fact, he goes so far as to identify "the spontaneity of knowledge," defined as "the mind's power of producing representations from itself," with the understanding (A51/B75).

The key to understanding this identification lies in Kant's further identification of discursive thought with judgment. As he puts it, "we can reduce all acts of the understanding to judgments, and the *understanding* may therefore be represented as a *faculty of judgment*" [eine Vermögen zu urteilen] (A69/B94). What judgment "produces" from itself is the representation of objects, that is to say, objectively valid judgments. The understanding is, therefore, spontaneous in the sense that it "constitutes" objectivity or objective reference in and through the act of judgment, and it does this by synthesizing the manifold of sensible intuition in accordance with its own inherent rules (the pure concepts of the understanding).

So construed, the doctrine of the spontaneity of the understanding is an essential and generally recognized feature of Kantian epistemology. What is not so generally recognized is the full nature of the connection between this spontaneity and apperception. Kant explicitly makes this connection at the very beginning of his discussion of apperception in the B-Deduction, when he remarks that the representation 'I think' (which he equates with apperception) "is an act of spontaneity, that is, it cannot be regarded as belonging to sensibility" (B132).

By denying that this thought belongs to sensibility, Kant is anticipating the claim, developed later in the Deduction, that it is necessary to distinguish the "pure" or "intellectual" (non-experiential) consciousness of one's mental activity attainable through apperception from the empirical consciousness of one's mental states attainable through introspection (inner sense).[5] The distinction between these two modes of self-consciousness is reiterated in the Refutation of Idealism, where, by way of contrasting the vacuity of apperception with the determinate knowledge of one's mental state gained through inner sense, Kant states: "The consciousness of myself in this representation 'I' is not an intuition, but a merely *intellectual* representation of the spontaneity [*Selbsttätigkeit*] of a thinking subject" (B278).

Although hardly the focal point of the Refutation of Idealism, the thesis that we are capable of a non-empirical consciousness of our intellectual activity (a consciousness of spontaneity) is a crucial feature of Kant's doctrine of apperception. It is also the one that is most often dismissed as wildly implausible and as not an expression of his considered views on the matter.[6] In reality, however, it is a logical consequence of his conception of knowledge; for this conception commits him not only to the view that judgment involves a synthesizing, unifying activity, exercised upon the given by the understanding, but also that it involves a *consciousness* of this activity. In short, judgment and, therefore, experience (since it necessarily involves judgment) are inherently reflexive, self-referential activities.[7] That is precisely why Kant insists (B134) that apperception involves both the synthesis of the manifold and the consciousness of this synthesis.

The issues raised by this two-fold claim are quite complex and would require a full scale analysis of Kant's conception of apperception to sort out.[8] Nevertheless, the main point can be clarified sufficiently for present purposes by construing judgment as the activity of "taking as." To judge is to take something as a such and such. In the simplest case, an indeterminate something x is taken as an F. In more complex cases, Fx is qualified by further "determinations"; for example, Fx is G (this cat is black). In still more complex cases, distinct "takings" (categorical judgments) are themselves combined in a single, higher-order "taking" (hypothetical and disjunctive judgments). The details are not here important; what matters is merely that in all these cases the mind must not only combine the items (representations or judgments) in a single consciousness, it must also be conscious of what it is doing. Moreover, the "must" involved here is conceptual; the point being simply that unless one is aware of taking x as an F (recognizing it in a concept), one has not in fact taken it as such.

Similar considerations also apply to reasoning. Although Kant characterizes reasoning as "mediate inference," and usually has syllogistic reasoning in mind, the main point is that any genuinely inferential process involves deriving conclusions from premises in such a way that the premises are *taken* to justify the conclusion. In other words, the premises must not only be good or sufficient reasons for asserting the conclusion, they must also be recognized by the reasoner as such. But to recognize one's reasons as good ones requires connecting them with the conclusion in a single consciousness in accordance with a rule or logical ground that functions as an "inference ticket." Indeed, the latter is the crucial factor; for even if the reasons are in fact not good (or the rule of inference is faulty), as long as one links them with the conclusion in this fashion, one is reasoning, albeit badly. Moreover, once again, this "taking" is a spontaneous, inherently self-conscious activity of the subject. Not only is it something the subject does, it is something that it does for itself and, therefore, self-consciously.

It is just at this point, however, that Kant's doctrine is subject to serious misunderstanding. First, the claim that cognitive activities such as judging and reasoning are inherently self-conscious (the heart of Kant's apperception principle) should not be taken as equivalent to the claim that they are analyzable into two distinct activities, namely, a representing and a representing that one is representing. Being conscious of one's activity is not another thing that one does when one judges or reasons; it is rather an ineliminable component of the first-order activity itself.[9]

Second, it should not be objected that, even if the above claim is true, the most that it shows is that I cannot judge, understand, reason etc., without also being conscious *that* I am doing so, but it does not follow that I must be aware that *I* (Henry Allison) am doing so. In Kantian terms, nothing follows from this about my "empirical self-consciousness." Although perfectly correct, this is irrelevant. The self-consciousness at issue here concerns the *activity*, not the empirical subject whose activity it is. This is not to say that the I of the 'I think' is completely idle in the Kantian account; it is simply that the subject for whom there is experience is not as such an ingredient in that experience (I do not experience the world as being experienced by me). To be sure, through a second-order reflective activity, I can make my experiencing into an object, but then this object (me) is always for an I.

The moral of the story is that the I is not only ineliminable, but also, in the language of Gilbert Ryle, "systematically elusive."[10] As with Ryle, the attempt to grasp the I in thought can be compared to the attempt to catch one's own shadow.[11] Moreover, again somewhat in the Wittgensteinean–Rylean mode, this elusiveness can be construed as a consequence of the "logic" of its use. This use is transcendental, not empirical. Rather than naming or referring to a distinct individual, this I functions as a placeholder for the subject of thought, the "I or he or it (the thing) which thinks" (A346/B409). As such, it is not only ineliminable, but also systematically elusive in the sense that it is purely formal, without any empirical content. Both of these poles of the Kantian conception of apperception are captured in the twin claims that "It must be possible for the 'I think' to accompany all my representations" and that it "cannot itself be accompanied by any further representation" (B132).

II. The argument from the unity of consciousness

The elusiveness, emptiness and formality of the I of apperception provide the basis for the critique of rational psychology in the "Paralogisms of pure reason." Kant there maintains that all attempts to establish the substantiality, simplicity, identity and independence of the soul or self on the basis of the 'I think' (which is the "sole text of rational psychology" [A343/B402]) are products of a "transcendental illusion." This illusion takes the form of a conflation of this empty and formal concept with the concept of a real or noumenal (in the positive sense) subject to which non-sensible predicates can be synthetically attached.[12] As we have already seen, however, he also asserts (at least in the second edition) that this suffices to establish the "impossibility of an explanation in *materialist* terms of the constitution of the self as a thinking being."[13] Moreover, this result is claimed to follow from the very simplicity of the 'I think,' which is itself based on the necessary unity of consciousness, and which, in the Second Paralogism, Kant insisted could not be used to establish the simplicity of the thinking subject. Thus, Kant's position seems to be that the unity of consciousness, which the rational psychologist (presumably Leibniz) uses erroneously to establish the positive metaphysical doctrine of the simplicity and hence incorruptibility of the soul, can be used legitimately to establish the weaker thesis of the impossibility of a materialist explanation of the conceptual activities of the mind.[14]

The emphasis on explanation suggests that the kind of materialism that

Kant has in mind here corresponds to what Karl Ameriks (who distinguishes between five different forms of materialism recognized by Kant, each with its corresponding form of immaterialism) characterizes as "scientific materialism."[15] It differs from what he terms "phenomenal" and "noumenal materialism," which are substantive doctrines about the nature or ultimate constitution of the phenomenal and noumenal self respectively, in that it is a claim about the kind of explanation it is possible to provide of the nature of thinking. Put simply, scientific materialism affirms the possibility in principle of a materialistic account of thinking, while the corresponding "immaterialism" denies such a possibility.

As already indicated, the argument in support of this "immaterialism," like that of the Second Paralogism with which it is closely related, turns on the unity of consciousness. Curiously enough, however, Kant's most explicit formulation of the argument is not in the *Critique* (where the emphasis is clearly on the *limitations* of rational psychology), but rather in *On the Progress of Metaphysics*. As he there puts it:

That he [man] is not wholly and purely corporeal may be strictly proven, if this appearance is considered as a thing in itself, from the fact that the unity of consciousness, which must be met with in all cognition (including that of oneself) makes it impossible that representations divided amongst various subjects could constitute a unified thought; therefore materialism can never be used as a principle for explaining the nature of the soul.[16]

What is immediately problematic, both here and in Kant's other formulations of this unity-argument, is the apparent assumption that the materialist is committed to the principle that the distinct representations contained in a single complex thought must somehow be identified with, or assigned to, distinct physical substances. Clearly, the materialist need make no such assumption. On the contrary, the unity of representations in a single complex thought would be explained in terms of the "unity" of the brain (a single complex organ). As Margaret Wilson points out, however, the argument can be reformulated so as to avoid *this* difficulty. Appropriately reformulated, it maintains that since the brain, as a material object, is composed of parts, different components of a single complex thought must be assigned to different parts of the brain. In Wilson's terms, "if a thought were identical with a state of a composite *qua* composite, elements of the thought would be identical with states or elements of the composite."[17] But in that case the different parts of the thought would be distributed among different thinking subjects, which contradicts the assumption of the unity of consciousness.

Unfortunately, as Wilson readily acknowledges, even her improved version seems open to the charge that it is an argument from ignorance, insofar as it appeals to an excessively narrow, essentially eighteenth century conception of scientific explanation.[18] Thus, it would appear that no matter how one tries to shore up the unity-argument, it cannot be saved from the objection that it conflates what is inexplicable within the framework of the science of Kant's time with what is in principle impossible.

III. The *Groundwork*'s argument

The above result makes it clear that, if the Kantian refutation of materialism is to be made even remotely plausible, we need a new argument, one that is independent of any historically conditioned assumptions about the limits of scientific explanation, yet is still somehow connected with the account of apperception. The obvious place to seek such an argument is the well known passage from the *Groundwork* where Kant writes:

> But we cannot possibly conceive of a reason as being consciously directed from outside in regard to its judgments; for in that case the subject would attribute the determination of his power of judgment, not to his reason, but to an impulsion. Reason must look upon itself as the author of its own principles independently of alien influences.[19]

This text has inspired many of the attempts, familiar in the literature, to provide a "transcendental refutation" of determinism (or materialism) on the grounds that, if true, it would be impossible to offer a rational justification for it.[20] Admittedly, this line of argument is usually dismissed contemptuously as unworthy of serious philosophical consideration.[21] Nevertheless, I shall argue that, when considered in light of the view of the understanding and its activity sketched in part one of this essay, the Kantian version does pose a significant challenge to materialist views of mind. Before proceeding with a reconstruction of the argument, however, two provisos are in order. First, since the focus of the argument is on the activity of conceptual thinking, rather than on other aspects of "the mental" such as sensory qualia, it will yield anti-materialistic results only insofar as materialism is taken to entail the availability (at least in principle) of a causal explanation of such activity. Second, in the present section I shall limit my attention to non-reductive forms of materialism, which take "the mental" as in some sense supervenient on the physical and, therefore, as subject to the causal constraints and conditions of the physical system on which it supervenes. In addition to being the most popular on the contemporary philosophical scene, views of this sort (including functionalism in its various forms and "anomalous monism") are the only ones that hold out any hope for some kind of reconciliation of central Kantian epistemological claims with a materialistic theory of mind broadly construed.[22] Accordingly, they would also seem to provide materials for the most obvious and powerful objections to the Kantian anti-materialism argument.

Like many of Kant's arguments, the one presently under consideration is annoyingly cryptic. Moreover, the reference to the notion of reason as "consciously directed from outside" suggests a strawman, since the materialist hardly need accept this picture of a reasoner as conscious of being determined to judge in a certain way by external stimuli.[23] Similarly, it could be claimed that, as formulated, the argument turns on the equation of the causation of mental activity with compulsion, a view which only the crudest sort of causal theory would maintain.[24] The first step, then, is to reformulate the argument so as to avoid these obvious pitfalls.

Up to a point at least, this is relatively easy to do. The key is the claim that "Reason must look upon itself as the author of its own principles independently of alien influences." Elsewhere, Kant makes the point by affirming the necessity of presupposing that the understanding has the capacity to determine judgment according to objectively valid grounds, which is contrasted with the conception of it as governed by the "mechanism of merely subjective determining causes."[25] In both cases, the central claim is that, *qua* thinkers, we must regard our reason (or understanding) as determining itself in accordance with objectively valid normative principles, that is, as autonomous, and that this is incompatible with the conception of our reasoning activity as the conditioned outcome of a causal process. Presumably, the latter is the case because, considered *qua* outcome of such a process, a belief would be something that one is caused to have by the state of one's system (plus input) and that is sufficient for denying it the status of knowledge.

As it stands, of course, this hardly amounts to an argument, since it offers no reason for accepting the conclusion. Moreover, the Kantian texts suggest two distinct ways in which the argument could be developed, each of which has found a contemporary advocate. For reasons that will become obvious, I term these the "epistemological luck" and the "recognition" arguments. Although only the second holds any prospect of success, I shall consider each in turn, together with the anticipated rejoinders. The hope is that this will put us in a position to present Kant's argument in its strongest form and to see whether, in the last analysis, it fares any better than the "unity-argument."

(A) *The epistemological luck argument:* This version of the argument maintains that if materialism were true, then, although we might still have true beliefs, and even good reasons for these beliefs, the contingency of such a state of affairs would be enough to prevent these beliefs from counting as knowledge. The point can be illustrated in terms of the analogy with Kant's conception of moral worth. Appealing to this analogy, one might say that a belief causally dependent on material conditions – or on any conditions for that matter – could be "in accordance with truth" (if it happens to be a true belief), but it would not be "from truth," that is, it would not have a rational grounding. Consequently, the contingency of the accord of such a belief with truth would suffice to deny it "epistemic worth," just as the contingency of the accord with duty of the actions of an agent motivated by either perceived self-interest or immediate inclination suffices to deny to such actions any genuine moral worth.

Expressed in non-Kantian terms, the argument is roughly that if, as materialism assumes, all of our mental states, including belief-states, have causally necessary and sufficient conditions, then it would be merely fortuitous (a matter of epistemological luck) if the reasons which we in fact have for our beliefs were good ones. Moreover, since we would be causally conditioned to have these reasons and beliefs, we could never determine whether or not this was the case. But, so the argument goes, if we could not know whether our reasons are good ones, then we could also never know whether any of our beliefs are true. For all that we could ever know, we might, like badly constructed computers, be wired to churn out false "beliefs" without any possibility of correcting them.[26]

Since this line of argument really reduces to the claim that materialism entails a version of Cartesian skepticism (similar to the familiar brain in the vat variety), it does not stand in any essential connection with the Kantian account of the understanding. Moreover, it suggests two obvious retorts: (1) One could launch a familiar kind of verificationist attack on its main premise, the point being that the assumption that our best evidence or reasoning might somehow be systematically misleading is incoherent or vacuous. This response is, of course, quite independent of materialism, but there is no reason why the materialist could not appeal to it in order to undermine the whole notion of epistemological luck. (2) Alternatively, the materialist could accept the notion of epistemological luck, while denying its allegedly skeptical implications. It is, after all, a contingent matter that, as a species, we have the reasoning powers we do, and the materialist need not deny this contingency. Instead of attributing this to "luck" or to some kind of pre-established harmony, however, the materialist would no doubt prefer to explain it as the outcome of the evolutionary process. On both counts, then, the materialist would find no reason to feel threatened by the argument from epistemological luck.

(B) The recognition argument: As the label indicates, this version of the argument is closely connected with the account of the understanding sketched in the first part of this paper. Again expressed in non-Kantian terms, it turns on two main premises: (1) If, as materialism assumes, there are causally sufficient conditions for my belief that p, then my reasons (whether or not they are good, i.e., justifying, reasons) are not necessary conditions. (2) If my reasons for believing that p are not necessary conditions for my belief, then this belief is not justified and I cannot claim to know that p. The notion of recognition enters the picture because what is claimed to be missing under the materialist scenario is precisely the recognition of the cogency of one's reasons for the belief that p functioning as the ground for the belief. The claim, in other words, is that unless I believe that p *because* I recognize that my reasons for believing that p are good ones, I cannot be said to know that p. It is then further maintained that this epistemological requirement is incom-

patible with the claim that one's neurophysiological state is a causally necessary and sufficient condition.[27]

It is, of course, just this incompatibility that the non-reductive materialist will deny and that is the problematic feature of Kant's own argument. Moreover, it might appear that all that is required to justify this denial is the introduction of supervenience. Put simply, if mental state a is supervenient on neurophysiological state a_1 and the latter is the causally necessary and sufficient condition of mental state b, then mental state a will likewise be a necessary condition of mental state b. By this mode of analysis, then, which turns on the transitivity of the necessary condition relation, it seems easy to reconcile a non-reductive materialism with the epistemological requirement that, in a case of justified belief, one's prior mental state be a necessary condition of the belief-state.[28]

In response, it can be claimed that this misses the main thrust of the recognition-argument. The point of this argument is not merely that one's prior belief-state must be a necessary condition of one's present state, or equivalently, that having reason r be a necessary condition for having the belief that p, it is rather that the *consciousness* of this reason and of its epistemic relevance must be a necessary condition of the belief. In short, reasons cannot function as reasons unless they are consciously recognized as such. Once again, then, the claim is that it is just this moment of recognition that eludes the materialist-causal model.[29]

Although we here at last have a distinctively Kantian move, the non-reductive materialist is not likely to be impressed by it. By appealing to supervenience and a causal theory of belief, it can still be maintained that this presumed recognition must itself be construed as a complex, second-order belief-state, the content of which is a belief about another belief and its epistemic relevance. Since it is obvious that one can be caused to have a belief or, better, be in a belief-state, by the antecedent state of the neurophysiological system and external stimuli, there is no particular reason why recognition-states could not likewise be causally conditioned. Indeed, so the argument goes, it is the denial of this assumption that leads to absurdity.

As a first step in formulating the Kantian response, we can note that one problem with the materialist's rejoinder is its underlying assumption that recognition can be analyzed as a distinct, second-order belief. Moreover, the inadequacy of this analysis can be demonstrated without appealing to any distinctively Kantian doctrines. The key point is simply that I can believe that r is true and that r is a compelling reason for believing that p and still not *recognize* that it is such a reason. Consequently, I can arrive at the true belief that p on the basis of my true beliefs regarding r without actually knowing that p. For example, I can believe a given theorem in Euclidean geometry to be true and believe that the reason why it is true is just that it follows logically from the axioms and postulates etc. Indeed, I can even have correct beliefs about the various steps in the proof and the capacity to reiterate them without *knowing* that the theorem is true. In addition to having a correct belief about the premises and their epistemic relevance, that is, a complex, second-order belief, knowledge also involves understanding how and why these premises license the conclusion. In fact, it is this act of understanding, this grasping of reasons as reasons, that constitutes the required moment of recognition; and this cannot be analyzed as simply having another belief.

Second – and here we return to Kantian soil-recognition, so construed – is equivalent to the act of "taking as," which, as we have seen, is essentially connected with the spontaneity of the understanding. Accordingly, given the earlier analysis, it can be claimed that if the understanding is to take its reasons as reasons and, therefore, as justifying its beliefs, it must connect them with these beliefs in a unitary consciousness in a judgment in accordance with some rule or principle of synthesis, which functions as an "inference ticket." Furthermore, this "taking as" must be conceived as an inherently self-conscious activity, something that the subject does for itself (spontaneously) and is conscious of so doing, rather than as something which it is caused to do and of which it is only conscious as a result.

Otherwise expressed, Kant's fundamental contention is that the act of recognition, through which the understanding takes reasons as justifying beliefs, embodies the structure of apperception; and it is precisely for this reason that it eludes the materialist-causal model. This model can provide a causal account of how one belief-state (or its physical counterpart) can causally determine another belief-state (or its physical counterpart); that is to say, it can account for the production of beliefs and even for self-consciousness construed as a second-order belief. What it cannot account for is the unitary, self-conscious act through which the mind grasps the logical (not causal) connection between its representations. Nor can this failure be remedied by increasing the complexity of the model, for example, by appealing to a still higher-order belief-state, the content of which is the logical ground of the connection between the two beliefs affirmed in the original inference to p. The point here is simply that no degree of iteration can capture the act of grasping (recognition or "taking as") that is the very essence of understanding.

Clearly, our understanding and evaluation of this whole line of argument turns crucially on precisely how we take the claim that the act of recognition, so described, "eludes" the causal-materialist model. Taken in a certain sense, this thesis could easily be admitted by the non-reductive materialist. Here Dennett's familiar contrast between an "intentional" and a "mechanistic stance" and Davidson's "anomalous monism" come immediately to mind. In spite of their considerable differences, all such views admit that a mechanistic account cannot explain thinking, considered as a rational activity based on normative grounds, while also insisting that this is perfectly compatible with the truth of mechanism (broadly construed). Once again, then, we are brought back to the question of why Kant apparently rejected such a compatibilist solution.

The short answer is that the compatibilist views of the kind mentioned above do not "elude" the model in a sufficiently strong sense because, at bottom, they require us to regard conceptual activity as causally conditioned in the same sense as any other natural occurrence. But this is incompatible with the result of the recognition-argument, which shows that taking something as a reason for belief, like adopting an end or deciding on a course of action, is not something that we can consider ourselves caused to do. Consequently, it cannot be regarded as the causal consequence of a set of necessary and sufficient conditions, whether these be construed in neurophysiological or psychological terms. Of course, in deciding on rational grounds we regard ourselves as being led by the reasons, and this has frequently been thought sufficient to ground compatibilist accounts of thought and action. For Kant, however, this will not do, because the reasons for one's belief cannot be regarded as a set of causes producing it; at least they cannot be insofar as one takes oneself to be reasoning. In other words, Kant's position is that, just as we can act only under the idea of freedom, so we can think only under the idea of spontaneity.

Nevertheless, even granting the latter point, one might still wonder whether it amounts to anything more than a gross inflation of the relatively non-controversial principle, accepted by virtually everyone except the die-hard eliminative materialist, that we can and must think about thinking in ways that abstract from or ignore "what is really going on," namely, a neurophysiological process of great complexity, which, considered either directly as such or as a psychological process supervening on it, has its causally necessary and sufficient conditions. Thus, although it is true that in the act of thinking or, alternatively, in the context of epistemic appraisal, one normally does not consider the neurophysiological conditions of one's thought (except in the special case in which one is thinking about these conditions), this hardly entails that our thoughts do not have them and that they are not both necessary and sufficient. Moreover, there is certainly no absurdity or incoherence of any kind involved in considering these conditions in a subsequent act of reflection.

In the endeavor to formulate a possible Kantian response to this line of attack, which comes close to representing the non-reductive materialist's last word on the subject, it is useful to focus on the strangeness of its claim. This strangeness consists in the fact that in the story of "what is really going on" there is no room for the I and its self-conscious activity. As Thomas Nagel has acutely noted, this elimination of the I, of the first-person standpoint, is characteristic of the objective view of the world and, as he also notes, from that viewpoint there is nothing strange or paradoxical in its elimination.[30] But it does not follow from this that it can also be eliminated from an epistemological account, the intent of which is to ground the very possibility of this objective view of the world. Certainly, from within the standpoint of such an account (in Kantian terms "transcendental reflection") it is incoherent to suggest that we can refer meaningfully to the I and its spontaneity only by ignoring "what is really going on."

If we were to stop here, however, we would appear to be open to the retort that the whole dispute can be readily resolved by distinguishing between levels of analysis. The transcendental philosopher, who reflects on the conditions of experience, and the cognitive scientist, who provides an empirically grounded, naturalistic account of how the "mind-brain" actually functions, are operating on radically different levels, telling distinct, but perfectly compatible stories. Although this distinction of level is quite correct, it is not relevant to the point at issue. For the question still remains whether it is coherent for a cognitive subject, engaged in the self-conscious activity of making rationally grounded knowledge claims, to consider this activity (taken under a description that includes its self-conscious, spontaneous nature) to be somehow eliminable from an account of "what is really going on." The clear implications of the recognition-argument, indeed, of Kant's whole account of apperception, is that it is not.

Finally, although it is certainly true that it is possible to reflect in a subsequent act of thinking on the neurophysiological conditions of any given act, this does not help to avoid the difficulty. The crucial point here is that considered as an occurrence in the phenomenal world, which is how it must be taken in an investigation of its causal conditions, any token of the act of thinking is itself something represented, an object for an I, which, considered as such, is not itself an object in the world. In short, we return in the end to the ineliminability and systematic elusiveness of this ubiquitous 'I think.' The former precludes the possibility of simply eliminating it from an analysis of thinking that purports to do justice to its claims to objective validity; the latter precludes the possibility of reducing it to just one more item in the world (whether this item is described in neurophysiological or psychological terms is irrelevant).

IV. A radical alternative

Up to this point, the argument has moved almost entirely within the framework of Kantian epistemology and has been directed primarily against non-reductive versions of materialism, which, by appealing to supervenience, claim to be able to accommodate the basic thrust of this epistemology. As already indicated, this constitutes the main challenge, but it is certainly not the only one. Thus, in order to complete our consideration of the Kantian response to materialism, it is necessary to see whether Kant has anything of interest to say to its most radical version, namely, an eliminative materialism, which would reject out of hand anything like the Kantian conception of knowledge as a relic of a discredited folk psychology or, perhaps worse, a transcendental folk psychology.

Although he does not make any reference to Kant, something very much like this response has been suggested by Paul Churchland against an argument that, in the spirit of the Kantian critique, asserts the incoherence of eliminative materialism. For the purposes of this response, Churchland defines eliminative materialism in bold terms as the doctrine that "the familiar mental states do not really exist." The argument against this doctrine is then sketched in the following terms:

> But that statement is meaningful, runs the argument, only if it is the expression of a certain *belief,* and an *intention* to communicate, and a *knowledge* of the language, and so forth. But if the statement is true, then no such mental states exist, and the statement is therefore a meaningless string of marks or noises, and cannot be true. Evidently, the assumption that eliminative materialism is true entails that it cannot be true.[31]

The gist of Churchland's response to this line of argument is that it is question-begging. In affirming the incoherence of eliminative materialism, it relies on a conception of meaningfulness which the materialist (presumably on the basis of advances in neuroscience) would simply deny. As he succinctly puts it, "If eliminative materialism is true, then meaningfulness must have some different source."[32] Finally, by way of underscoring the absurdity of this line of objection, which he tends to dismiss as a joke, he draws an analogy with a putative defender of vitalism. Supposedly like the defender of the mental against eliminative materialism, the defender of vitalism is made to argue that it is incoherent to deny vitalism because if this denial is correct, then the critic does not possess a vital spirit, from which it allegedly follows that "his statement is just a string of words without meaning or truth."[33]

While there can be little doubt that the defender of vitalism begs the question, there is serious doubt regarding the appropriateness of the analogy to the issue at hand. To begin with, what makes the defense of vitalism question-begging is that it construes vitalism as an empirical theory designed to explain the phenomena of life and meaningfulness. The question is begged because it is assumed, without argument, that it is the only theory capable of doing the job. In the present instance, however (and, indeed, in the argument being rebutted), there is no appeal to an alternative empirical theory designed to account for a realm of phenomena. On the contrary, the appeal is to a non-empirical conception of knowledge (or meaningfulness) with reference to which empirical theories must be validated.

But what about the conception of knowledge? Quite apart from its empirical or non-empirical status, is the eliminative materialist not correct in insisting that it is simply being assumed? And does not this make the argument question-begging? Although there is some justice in this retort, it doesn't get the eliminative materialist as far as one might suppose. The problem stems from what could be called the "Master Analogy" from which the eliminative program derives much of its plausibility. The operative assumption here is that the elimination of the mental, or "subjectivity," is to be conceived as simply one more scientific revolution, perhaps more radical than some others in its effect on our self-understanding, but not qualitatively different. Correlatively, our resistance to it, as it is manifested in charges of paradoxicality, meaninglessness etc., is much like the resistance of our sixteenth- and seventeenth-century ancestors to the Copernican revolution. In short, what is involved here, as in other such revolutions, is a change in our "conceptual framework"; and this will obviously involve changes in how we conceive of "knowing" or what kind of claims we regard as "meaningful."[34]

For our purposes, the main interest of this essentially Quinean response lies in the great weight it places on the notion of a "conceptual framework." While all reference to the "mental" is being excised from the universe of scientific and philosophical discourse, this key notion is itself regarded as unproblematic. Scientific revolutions, including the glorious revolution which will eliminate the I, and which will enable us to conceive of ourselves in new and unexpected ways, are seen as involving changes in our conceptual framework, but this notion itself remains a constant, unaffected by these revolutions. In Kantian terms, it functions as a "transcendental condition," as that with respect to which scientific change becomes intelligible. What, then, one might ask, is a conceptual framework? Is it a set of categories, principles, modes of explanation, canons of evidence etc., that is, a set of ways in terms of which the mind organizes and interprets its experience, or is it a pattern of neural behavior, a way or set of ways in which the brain processes information and computes? Presumably, the defender of the eliminative program will opt for the latter, or at least will contend that this is how the notion is destined to be construed at the time when the physicalistic revolution is complete. But is such a claim really intelligible? Is it not rather that any change in the way in which we think about thinking (or anything else for that matter) is only intelligible in light of the "pre-revolutionary" notion of a conceptual framework sketched above, that is, as a change in the manner in which we conceptualize a certain domain of experience? In short, it seems that the 'I think' must be able to accompany all my representations after all, including the representation of the elimination of the I.[35]

II

Kant's practical philosophy

8

Kant on freedom: A reply to my critics

The first two sections of this reply are devoted respectively to the criticisms of my views raised by Stephen Engstrom and Andrews Reath at a symposium on *Kant's Theory of Freedom*. The third section contains my response to the remarks of Marcia Baron at a second symposium. The fourth section deals with some general criticisms of my treatment of Kant's conception of freedom and its connection with transcendental idealism that have been raised by Karl Ameriks in a review article and by Paul Guyer in his review of my book. The reply as a whole is thus an attempt to clarify and defend some of the central claims of my book in light of the initial critical reaction.

I. Practical and transcendental freedom

Engstrom correctly points out that my primary concern in the first part of *Kant's Theory of Freedom* was to articulate a theory of freedom contained in the first *Critique* that is based on a general account of rational agency rather than on any specific features of moral agency.[1] Central to this account is what I have termed Kant's "Incorporation Thesis," that is, the view that inclinations or desires do not of themselves constitute an incentive or sufficient reason to act but do so only insofar as they are "taken up" or "incorporated" into a maxim.[2] At the same time, however, I also distinguished between practical and transcendental freedom and claimed that the Incorporation Thesis required only the former. This was done, not as Engstrom suggests, in order to provide Kant with a relatively non-controversial conception of freedom, immune from the difficulties of noumenalism (since this conception already involves most of these difficulties), but rather to deal with a thorny textual problem concerning the relationship between the accounts of freedom in the Dialectic and the Canon. Both texts distinguish between practical and transcendental freedom and both construe these notions in essentially the same way: the former being understood negatively as the will's independence of determination by sensuous impulses and positively as the capacity to act on the basis of reason, the latter as absolute spontaneity and complete independence from everything sensible. They differ in that in the Dialectic Kant seems to insist on the dependence of practical upon transcendental freedom, while in the Canon he appears to claim that practical freedom would stand even if there were no transcendental freedom.³

Commentators tend to deal with this problem either by dismissing the Canon account as a pre-critical remnant or by denying that it really does assert the separability of practical from transcendental freedom. Common to both strategies is the assumption that practical freedom, *qua* distinguished from the transcendental variety, must be taken in a compatibilistic, naturalistic sense.⁴ By contrast, I attempted to resolve the problem first by noting that the dependence of practical upon transcendental freedom affirmed in the Dialectic should be understood in a *conceptual* rather than an *ontological* sense and second by challenging this underlying assumption. Thus, I argued that there is evidence to suggest that Kant did, indeed, hold a conception of practical freedom that is distinguishable both from transcendental freedom and from the familiar compatibilistic or naturalistic conception. According to this conception, which is articulated in the metaphysics lectures of the '70s, practical is related to transcendental freedom as human is to divine freedom. More specifically, whereas the defining characteristic of human (practical) freedom is independence from sensuous determination or necessitation, that of divine (transcendental) freedom is independence from sensuous affection.⁵

It is, then, this conception of a practical freedom that is, on the one hand, genuinely indeterministic and, on the other, somehow less than transcendental freedom that is the target of Engstrom's critique. He claims that it is inherently unstable and threatens either to slide back into the Humean compatibilist picture or become inflated into the full blown conception of transcendental freedom. Unfortunately, this reading involves a serious misunderstanding of both my thesis and the reasons for it. Even more unfortunately, it is one for which I am at least partly responsible, since (regrettably) I did say a number of things which suggest his reading and which generate some of his puzzlement. Thus, I am grateful to him for calling attention to these problems and for giving me the opportunity to clarify my position.

Perhaps my major bit of carelessness is that I refer on occasion to "a genuine, albeit limited, spontaneity," thereby suggesting that there might be a continuum of grades of spontaneity and that practical is distinguished from transcendental freedom precisely in involving a lesser grade. Clearly, however, this does not reflect the Kantian view. To be sure, from the '70s on, Kant does distinguish between a merely relative spontaneity (*spontaneitas secundum quid*), which he equates with that of a turnspit, and absolute or genuine spontaneity, which involves full causal independence and is usually associated with transcendental freedom. But, although Kant also frequently distinguishes between transcendental and practical freedom, nowhere to my knowledge does he link practical freedom with a merely relative spontaneity. Moreover, since there is no room for anything like a "quasi-genuine" spontaneity falling between these two, it follows that the difference between the two types of freedom cannot be a matter of their respective degrees of spontaneity.

In what sense, then, is practical freedom limited and distinguishable from full-fledged transcendental freedom? The answer suggested by the metaphysical lectures is that the latter, but not the former, involves independence from all sensuous *affection,* and not simply *determination.* Now, given Kant's view that being subject to such affection is a defining characteristic of finitude, this can hardly be what Kant had in mind when, in the second *Critique,* he insists that freedom in the "strictest, i.e., transcendental, sense" is the condition of morality (KprV5: 29; 28). Nevertheless, there is a related, successor concept to this notion of divine freedom, one that is applicable to the human will, namely, autonomy.

I have tried to clarify the difference between the two conceptions of freedom by contrasting the different senses of independence connected with each.[6] Spontaneity involves causal independence or, in Kantian terms, "independence of the causality of nature." By contrast, autonomy involves what I have called "motivational independence," by which I mean the capacity to determine oneself to act on the basis of considerations that are completely independent of one's needs as a sensuous being.[7] The divine will possesses such independence *ex hypothesi,* since it does not receive any sensuous input. Although this is not true of the human will, it is the case, according to Kant, that we have what amounts to a genuine motivational independence insofar as we have the capacity to disregard all claims of inclination and act solely from respect for the moral law.

Given this distinction, it follows that we must allow at least conceptual space for the notion of an agent that possesses genuine spontaneity but not autonomy, that is, one that is both free in an indeterminist sense and heteronomous. In *Kant's Theory of Freedom,* I used this notion for two distinct purposes: (1) to characterize the conception of freedom underlying Kant's moral theory circa 1781 (what I have termed his "semi-critical ethics"); and (2) to underscore the significant difference that the introduction of the conception of autonomy makes to his moral theory.

Unfortunately, I muddied the waters in my book by suggesting that such an agent might regard its ends as implanted by nature. This is seriously misleading, since, as Engstrom notes, it seems to conflict with the conception of a rational agent as a genuine framer of ends. What I should have said is rather that such an ineluctably heteronomous agent would require a sensuous inclination in order to have a *sufficient* reason to adopt an end (or to act at all). In this sense the ends of such an agent might be said to be "set by nature," albeit not in a way that obviates an ineliminable role for practical reason and genuine spontaneity. After all, it is one thing for an agent to regard its ends as "good" in the sense of being endorsed by practical reason rather than as simply being given to it by instinct or some other mechanism, and quite another for such an agent to adopt ends on purely rational grounds, independent of any input from inclination.

Finally, I must point out that, contrary to Engstrom's suggestion, I never did claim that such a putatively spontaneous yet heteronomous agent was able to act *only* on the basis of hypothetical imperatives. The claim was rather that Kant analyzed freedom in the first *Critique* in terms of the general capacity to act on the basis of imperatives, whether they be principles of morality or prudence. And this was because he then viewed the conditions of agency as identical with respect to the two types of imperative. This entails that some extra-moral incentive is required to provide a reason for adopting the moral imperative, which, from Kant's later standpoint, amounts to heteronomy. I have tried to show, however, that the Kant of 1781 did not see things in quite this way. Otherwise, he could not have claimed, as he does in the *Critique of Pure Reason,* that "without a God and a world invisible to us now but hoped for, the glorious ideas of morality are indeed objects of approval and admiration, but not springs of purpose and action" (A813/B841).[8]

In light of these clarifications, let us now turn to Engstrom's basic objection. Appropriately reformulated, it amounts to the claim that the conception of a (genuinely) spontaneous yet heteronomous agent is incoherent or at least unstable, and this is to be shown by means of an analysis of what it would mean for such an agent to act on the basis of a hypothetical imperative. (How such an agent might act on the basis of the categorical imperative is simply not brought into consideration.) In essence, I am confronted with a dilemma: either I construe such an imperative in a purely "formal" sense, in which case I must both deny its genuinely hypothetical character and admit that action governed by it can be accounted for in standard Humean terms as action based on the strongest desire; or I take it in a "material" sense, in which case I must assume autonomy as a condition of the possibility of acting on the basis of it.

To begin with, I have some difficulties with this distinction between two interpretations of the hypothetical imperative. In discussing the hypothetical as well as the categorical imperative, it is important to distinguish between a first-order principle, which would count as "material" in Engstrom's terms, and a purely "formal" second-order principle. In the case of the hypothetical imperative, the second-order formal principle is: "either will the means or abandon the end." As Engstrom correctly notes, the latter is not itself hypothetical, but is rather a categorical or "unconditioned" requirement in disjunctive form. Nevertheless, it does generate hypothetical imperatives, since it entails that *if* you will the end, then you are rationally constrained to will the "indispensably necessary" means.[9]

I also take issue with Engstrom's account of how, on the "formal interpretation" of the hypothetical imperative, the Kantian view of agency slides inevitably into the Humean one. According to Engstrom,

> The source of the difficulty . . . lies in the fact that our very conception of a desire or inclination of a rational agent has a consistency requirement built into it. We cannot make sense of the idea of a rational agent's having a desire except insofar as we suppose that to that extent the agent has an aversion to choices of action the agent knows to be incompatible with the satisfaction of that desire. This means that the very idea of a rational agent's having a desire involves the supposition that the agent has an interest in making choices in a manner consistent with the satisfaction of that desire.[10]

I think that this claim is false on the face of it; but, in any event, it certainly is denied by Kant. The Incorporation Thesis of itself entails that desires do not come with pre-assigned weights. On the contrary, it is the value placed on a desire or inclination by an agent that gives it its "motivational force," its status as a reason to act. Granted, this evaluation rests on an appeal to practical reason (some sense of the good), but not necessarily to *morally* practical reason.

Moreover, fundamental to Kant's conception of agency (and not merely moral agency) is the distinction between willing and wishing. Accordingly, hypothetical imperatives (and their formal principle) have nothing whatsoever to say about what can be consistently desired (or wished for); they concern only what can be consistently *willed.* Thus, I can perfectly well really desire to be healthy and at the same time also really desire to eat fattening foods, drink to excess and lounge about rather than exercise. There is no inconsistency in this at all, nor is there any sense to the claim that I ought not to wish for or desire a scenario in which I could become healthy while still maintaining these habits. What I cannot do is *will* to be healthy, or, more properly, will to attempt to become healthy, while also refusing to change my behavior.

Finally, this brings us to Engstrom's account of the hypothetical imperative on the so-called "material interpretation." His argument, as I understand it, takes the form of a *reductio* of the view that a rational agent might be bound only by hypothetical imperatives. Since I have already denied that this represents my view, I shall turn directly to the argument itself, which seems to consist of the following six steps: (1) As free and rational, the agent must be thought of as framing its ends for itself. (2) This requires that the ends be regarded as in some sense good, that is, as endorsed by practical reason. (3) But the ultimate end in question here is *ex hypothesi* happiness, so the goodness of the means must be regarded as a function of the goodness of this end. (4) But there must be some rational ground for regarding happiness as a good. (5) Such a ground can only be provided by the moral law, as is shown by the argument for the highest good in the Canon. (6) Consequently, an agent seeking its own happiness could not consistently regard itself as subject to hypothetical imperatives without also acknowledging being bound by the categorical imperative.[11]

The fallacies of this line of argument are not hard to locate. First, happiness for Kant is not so much a determinate end as a place-holder for the sum-total of private or subjective ends.[12] That is why Kant insists that, strictly speaking, there are no imperatives of happiness but merely counsels of prudence.[13] Second, insofar as happiness is considered an end, it is of a unique sort, since it is one which we necessarily have as sentient beings and, therefore, cannot help but pursue.[14] Accordingly, there is no need to appeal to a rational ground in order to certify it as good. Admittedly, this creates a certain tension between Kant's conception of happiness and his doctrine of ends as set through free choice rather than nature, but I think that this can be resolved by focusing on the status of happiness as a mere place-holder. The point is that although as finite beings with needs we cannot help but pursue what we take to be in our self-interest, it is we who determine how this interest is to be defined.[15]

The main point, however, is that the moral law cannot function in the manner in which Engstrom suggests: as the source of the goodness of happiness in the sense of providing the reason to pursue it. (If it did, we would have a duty to promote our own happiness, which Kant explicitly denies.) The law rather functions to determine the conditions under which one may be considered worthy of happiness in the eyes of an impartial judge. In effect, then, Engstrom conflates the desirability of happiness to an agent with the conditions of its being deserved by that agent. The moral law governs the latter, but it has nothing to do with the former. For these reasons, then, I cannot accept his conclusion that "for Kant there is an important sense in which we would not be bound by imperatives at all if we were not bound by the categorical imperative."[16] Instrumental rationality has its own sphere and its own logic – I am almost tempted to say its own autonomy – which holds independent of any moral considerations.

II. Kant's reciprocity thesis

Reath provides a lucid and accurate overview of my project in *Kant's Theory of Freedom*, but focuses his critical remarks exclusively on the Reciprocity Thesis, that is, the claim that freedom and the moral law reciprocally imply one another.[17] Moreover, as a good critic, he does not simply raise problems but also proposes at least the outline of a solution. Accordingly, I shall discuss both the problems which he raises and his proposed solution, which, I shall argue, lends itself to the very same kind of objection that he raises against me.

According to Reath, the two fundamental problems posed by my defense of the Reciprocity Thesis are: (1) that it fails to deal adequately with the question of how fundamental principles may be thought subject to a justification requirement – a line of argument used to great effect by Bernard Williams (among others) in his critique of Kantianism; and (2) that, even if this be granted, it remains unclear why the moral law must be viewed as uniquely authoritative. As Reath puts it, what is wrong with taking personal happiness as one's ultimate norm? Why should the assumption of transcendental freedom make a difference here?[18]

Our first question then is: how is a reasoned choice of fundamental principles possible? Since I assume that no general problem about the reasoned choice of principles is being raised, the difficulty must stem from the presumed fundamental status of the principles. Although Reath does not bother to provide an actual argument showing just why this is a problem, from his brief remarks I suspect that he has something like the following in mind. Since, *ex hypothesi*, there are no higher principles to which one can appeal and, therefore, no further considerations on which to base the choice, it follows either that the very notion of choice is out of place or that this choice must be seen as a kind of Sartrean brute *choix* or *projet fondamental*, a leap "by virtue of the absurd," made without any pretense of justifying grounds.

This objection presupposes that the considerations to which one must appeal in order to justify the choice of a putatively highest principle are of the same order or type as the principle which they supposedly justify. And given this presupposition, the objection does, indeed, seem cogent. Clearly, however, Kant would not accept this assumption. On the contrary, at the very heart of his account of practical reason is the contrast between subjective and objective practical principles: maxims and laws. The former are the first-order principles on which rational agents actually act. The latter are the second-order principles or norms which dictate how such agents ought to act and which, therefore, govern the choice of maxims.

In his later writings, Kant fleshed out this distinction between first- and second-order practical principles by connecting it with the distinction between *Wille* and *Willkür*, or legislative and executive will, conceived as two poles of a unified faculty of volition (*Wille* in the broad sense).[19] Maxims, on this later account, are linked specifically with *Willkür* and objective practical principles or laws with *Wille*. This means that only maxims can be said to be chosen, a point which Kant makes in the *Metaphysic of Morals* by insisting that only *Willkür* can be regarded as free, and that *Wille* (identified with practical reason) is neither free nor unfree.[20] Accordingly, if we are to talk within a Kantian framework about the choice of ultimate principles, these must be maxims or subjective principles, which for Kant are all self-imposed. But, if that is the case (and Reath seems to acknowledge as much), then there would indeed be higher-order principles that could be brought to bear on our most fundamental maxims or subjective principles: the dictates of *Wille* or practical reason.

This response leads directly to Reath's second worry, which concerns the authority of the dictates of *Wille*. Although not themselves chosen, it might still seem to be the case that we (or *Willkür* within us) freely choose to either recognize or deny this authority, which reopens the whole problem. Before turning to this problem, however, we must consider another objection that might be raised against the previous analysis. I don't know whether Reath has something like this in mind, but the objection would be that, even granting the *Wille–Willkür* distinction, serious questions arise concerning the intelligibility of the idea of a choice of a highest or most fundamental maxim. This is because the choice of a maxim would seem to presuppose a higher maxim on which this choice is based as well as objective principles of practical reason, and this suggests the danger of an infinite regress, which could be broken only by an appeal to some timeless noumenal choice.

Although this calls to mind Kant's doctrine of radical evil and the choice of *Gesinnung*, it is, fortunately, not really necessary to delve here into those murky waters in order to deal with the present objection.[21] The basic point is simply that it reflects an erroneous picture of the relationship between a fundamental maxim and the subordinate maxims which an agent adopts in light of it.[22] It is not that one first adopts a fundamental maxim, say to maximize happiness, and then selects the more specific, lower-order maxims in terms of which this project is defined. It is rather that one finds on reflection that one has been committed to this principle all along, perhaps even without a prior awareness of this fact, and certainly without any need to assume that it was explicitly chosen at a given point in (or outside of) time. All that is required is that this principle be recognized as presupposed by one's more specific maxims as their ultimate explanatory ground. This suffices both to certify the maxim as the ultimate subjective determining ground of *Willkür* and to make it eligible for critical evaluation in light of the objective norms of *Wille*.

But why must *Willkür* accept the authority of *Wille*, particularly with respect to its basic, life-defining projects? This is Reath's second and more fundamental question, which he puts largely in terms of a challenge regarding the principle of personal happiness. Although I am afraid that my response amounts to little more than a reformulation of the main points that I have already made in previous discussions of the topic, I hope that this reformulation will help to clarify my position. To begin with, let us take this principle of personal happiness to claim that it is reasonable and, therefore, legitimate for everyone to seek to maximize their own happiness, regardless of the consequences to others (or even themselves). The question that arises immediately is: what could make this choice either reasonable or unreasonable? More precisely, what norm could justify or condemn the adoption of such a principle by a transcendentally free agent? Since, as we have seen, the justification requirement is still in place, such a norm must be provided.

Now, clearly, the claim that such a principle is universalizable in the weak sense that it would be reasonable for anyone to act on the basis of it cannot suffice, since this does nothing more than to restate the original claim of reasonableness. One still needs to know the ground of this reasonableness. Equally clearly, it does not suffice to point to a psychological fact regarding the strength of one's desire. Given transcendental freedom, it follows that the mere presence or strength of a desire does not constitute a sufficient reason to act. A transcendentally free agent requires a desire-independent warrant for acting on the basis of desire. But such a warrant could stem only from a principle that applies to all agents independently of their desires, that is, in Kant's terms, from an "unconditional practical law," which, with further argumentation that cannot be supplied here, can be identified with the moral law or categorical imperative.[23] Thus, assuming transcendental freedom, the principle of personal happiness (or any subjective principle) could be evaluated only by appeal to the moral law; and, as we all know, this law would not justify such a principle.

At this point it might be objected that even if the argument sketched above establishes the *validity* of the moral law, it still does not account for its supreme legislative *authority*. After all, not only is it the case that a transcendentally free agent can disobey this law, but Kant himself insists that there is a universal propensity to subordinate its dictates to the claims of personal happiness, which would seem to involve a denial of its authoritative status.

The short answer is that the legislative authority of the moral law is a function of its justificatory force. In other words, a transcendentally free agent must grant supreme authority to this law insofar as the agent recognizes that it provides the ultimate ground for the justification of its maxims. Moreover, such justification matters precisely because a transcendentally free agent is also a rational agent, that is, one who acts on the basis of principles or "the conception of law."[24] This is also why Kant insists that even in disobeying the law we respect its normative status, since we attempt (albeit without success) to justify our deviant policies as legitimate exceptions to what generally holds.[25]

Let us now turn briefly to Reath's version of the argument in support of the Reciprocity Thesis. In essence, it seems to differ from my approach in its further thickening of the conception of transcendentally free agency to include the positive aspect of autonomy: the notion of a will that is essentially legislative, that gives law through its very nature, independently of any external authority. This, in turn, leads to the apt analogy between a will, so conceived, and a sovereign. This conception, Reath argues, makes it possible to explain what my own relatively thin conception of motivational independence could not: why such a will would have a reason to adopt as its fundamental maxim the principle of acting from reasons that are universally valid. The reason is that only by acting in this way can the will retain its sovereign status.[26]

Apart from some minor quibbles, which need not concern us here, I have nothing to object to in Reath's suggestive account. Nevertheless, it is still not clear to me what has been gained with regard to the particular point at issue. We are told that a will which opted for the principle of happiness would be undermining its own sovereignty, and this is supposed to provide the reason for rejecting this principle. But, echoing Reath's own question, why can't an autonomous will subordinate its own sovereignty to considerations of personal happiness? What is wrong with opting for happiness over sovereignty? Reath states that "An autonomous agent has reason to choose in ways that maintain its sovereign status."[27] Unfortunately, he does not tell us what that reason is or why sovereignty matters at all, much less why it overrides all other considerations. Instead, he seems content to point out that opting for any norm other than the categorical imperative would entail a loss of sovereignty. This may be true, but it hardly answers the question.

This also helps to bring out what distinguishes my interpretation of Kant from that of many others, including Reath's. These interpretations all tend to regard Kantian ethics as at bottom one of self-realization or perfection. According to this view, the reason for respecting the dictates of the moral law is that only by doing so can one realize one's true nature, autonomy, "supersensible vocation," or, in Reath's terms, one's sovereignty. On this reading, then, Kant's ethics remains deeply teleological in spite of its rejection of eudaemonism. I readily acknowledge the presence of this strand in Kant's thought, but I also believe that there is a somewhat different strand, yielding what might be termed an ethic of self-justification. According to this strand, on which my own interpretation is largely based, the ultimate question is always how a maxim is to be justified rationally. Once again, justification matters because as long as we take ourselves as rational agents, we cannot abandon it as a requirement. The principles on which we act must be justified, at least to ourselves, if not to others.[28] And, of course, if we abandon the conception of ourselves as rational agents, then there is no longer any place for talk of principles and their evaluation.

III. The Incorporation Thesis

In her contribution, Marcia Baron raises a number of interesting criticisms and puzzles regarding the Incorporation Thesis and my interpretation of it.[29] Although this topic has already been touched upon briefly in connection with the response to Engstrom, I would like to begin here by trying to clarify just what kind of thesis I take it to be.

First of all, the thesis is not an empirical claim. It is not based on introspection of what goes on in our heads when we decide; so we cannot, as it were, catch ourselves in the act of incorporating. Nor, on my reading, is it a straightforward metaphysical thesis about what is really going on in the noumenal world. Like the account of freedom with which it is inseparably connected, it is rather a conceptual claim. More precisely, it is a claim about the model we are constrained to adopt insofar as we regard our reason as practical, that is, insofar as we take ourselves as genuine agents rather than automata. As already indicated, the major consequence of this thesis is that an inclination or desire does not *of itself* constitute a reason to act, as it does on the standard Humean model and its variants. On the contrary, an inclination or desire becomes a reason to act only with reference to a principle of action that stipulates a policy of acting in such a way as to satisfy it, that is to say, a maxim. Accordingly, the Incorporation Thesis is inseparable from Kant's conception of action as based on maxims, which are themselves products of the practical spontaneity of the agent.

This puts us in a position to consider Baron's initial worry, which concerns the possibility of refraining from acting on an inclination without refusing to act as the inclination directs. Apparently, she takes the Incorporation Thesis to maintain not merely that we can refuse to act on the basis of an inclination (which she grants), but also that we can "act as the inclination directs, but not from that inclination – for we do not incorporate that inclination into our maxim."[30] The latter suggests that we are somehow able to choose not to incorporate an inclination into a maxim without abandoning the maxim, and it is this that she finds problematic. As an example, she cites the case of someone who desires to cause someone else pain by telling her something that is, in fact, true and that she ought to know. According to Baron, given the malicious desire, the only way one could refrain from acting on that desire would be to forgo the course of action stemming from it. It does not seem plausible to assume that one could perform the act one desires to perform, yet not from that very desire.

As formulated, this worry suggests a picture of rational choice as involving two distinct decisions: one to act in a certain way or to adopt a maxim to perform actions of that type; then a second to choose the reason for performing the act or adopting the maxim in question. Now, admittedly, if this is the picture to which the Incorporation Thesis commits us, it would not be particularly attractive. Fortunately, however, I do not think that this is the case. What is misleading in this scenario is the implicit separation of the incorporation of an inclination into a maxim from the adoption of the maxim itself. Otherwise expressed, it is not that one first adopts maxims and then casts about for the appropriate incentive to incorporate into them; it is rather that in adopting a maxim, one is at the same time incorporating an incentive, since an incentive to act in a certain way is part of the structure of every maxim, even if it is not always made explicit.[31]

The point can be clarified by a comparison of Kant's notorious shopkeeper who treats his customers honestly out of prudential considerations and a truly virtuous shopkeeper who acts in the same way on purely moral grounds. Although the two shopkeepers behave in essentially the same way, they act on the basis of quite different maxims embodying distinct interests. In the first case, it is roughly: treat your customers in such a way as to ensure that they will continue doing business with you, thereby maximizing profits. In the second, it is: treat your customers as persons or ends in themselves, who are not to be used merely as means. Does it seem counter-intuitive to suggest that the first shopkeeper should abandon his maxim and adopt that of the second? I think not.

Let us, then, take a second look at Baron's example. Properly construed, the issue is not which reason is to be chosen for adopting the course of action antecedently decided upon (revealing the painful news); it is rather on which maxim the agent is to act. In other words, does the agent intend to cause pain and use the conveying of the information as a means to that end; or, alternatively, does she convey it because she realizes that the other person has a right to the information and, in fact, would prefer to know the truth, no matter how unpleasant? Although, objectively speaking, there is only one course of action envisaged (just as in the case of the shopkeepers), there are clearly two quite different intentions and, therefore, distinct maxims. Granted, as Baron, following Kant, notes, there is still plenty of room here for mistake or self-deception (one might believe oneself performing a dutiful act, whereas in fact one acted from a desire to cause pain), but this does not affect either the coherence of the picture or its compatibility with the Incorporation Thesis.[32]

Baron's second worry concerns the question of moral weakness or frailty [*Gebrechlichkeit*] and its reconcilability with the Incorporation Thesis. As she correctly notes, there seems to be a dilemma here, since, on the one hand, the thesis appears to be incompatible with the admission of moral weakness, while, on the other hand, Kant clearly and unambiguously affirms the existence of such weakness, characterizing it as the first of three successive stages of the propensity to evil that is supposedly inherent in all members of the human race. In light of this genuine problem, she criticizes me for providing a solution that really changes its terms, substituting something else for what Kant appears to describe as a straightforward case of weakness and, in the process, blurring the distinction Kant draws between it and the subsequent stages of impurity and wickedness.[33]

With regard to the first part of the objection, Baron certainly has a point. I do in a sense change the subject, but I believe that such a change is thoroughly in the spirit of the argumentation of *Religion* and provides a reasonable interpretation of Kant's intent in that work. My basic hermeneutical assumption is that Kant's entire account of evil, including the brief discussion of frailty, must be understood in light of the governing principle that "Man *himself* must make or have made himself into whatever, in a moral sense, whether good or evil, he is or is to become" (Rel 6: 44; 40). If this is the case, then weakness itself must somehow be something for which one is responsible; that is to say, we cannot appeal to any form of constitutive moral luck in order to excuse our failings. But a weakness for which one is responsible is no longer a simple weakness; it is rather a self-imposed or, as Kierkegaard might have put it, a "dialectically qualified" weakness.

Accordingly, the question becomes how is such "weakness" to be conceived, and I attempted to answer it by identifying it with the bare propensity to evil, understood as the ineliminable tendency of even the best of us to subordinate the incentive of morality to that of self-love. More fully explicated, it can be characterized as an openness to temptation, which amounts to a susceptibility to just such a subordination. This openness or susceptibility, in turn, is the condition of the possibility of such a thing as weakness, which is self-deceptively taken by the agent as a brute given, part of his nature, which he laments but for which he does not hold himself responsible. Granted, this hardly sounds like the equivalent of the words of the Apostle, which Kant cites in this context. Nevertheless, it is, I suggest, how these words must be interpreted for the purposes of a "religion within the limits of reason alone," that is, a rational reconstruction of Christian doctrine in light of Kant's conceptions of freedom and morality. On any other understanding of them, moral weakness is, as Baron suspects, incompatible with the Incorporation Thesis.

This identification of moral weakness with the bare propensity to evil also provides the key to distinguishing it from the subsequent stages of impurity and wickedness. These involve a further development of this propensity, that is, a further compromise with the principle of self-love, combined with an increased level of self-deception. Against this reading Baron insists that, in contrast to the subsequent stages, frailty involves a "real commitment to the moral law."[34] I believe that this is true but insufficient, since it fails to grasp the dialectical nature of Kant's analysis. The genuineness of the commitment to morality is reflected in the lament, which is totally lacking in the moral reflection of both the impure and wicked person. Here we find moral regret, self-chastisement and the like, which is, I believe, why Kant suggests that frailty is compatible with a good will. At the same time, however, the commitment cannot be *fully* genuine. If it were, frailty could not be considered a level of evil, but merely an inescapable limitation due to finitude.

Baron's third worry concerns my attempt to make sense out of Kant's puzzling claim in *The Doctrine of Virtue* that we have an indirect duty to cultivate our sympathetic feelings (which supposedly involves an obligation to visit scenes of human misery such as hospitals and debtor's prisons) "and to make use of them as so many means to sympathy based on moral principles and the feeling appropriate to them" (MS 6: 457; 251). This is puzzling enough of itself, but the real problem stems from Kant's ensuing claim that this feeling of sympathy is "one of the impulses that nature has implanted in us to do what the representation of duty alone would not accomplish" (MS 6: 457; 251). This clearly appears to conflict with Kant's notorious insistence on the sufficiency of the duty motive or, as Baron puts it, it seems to yield a very un-Kantian injunction to develop an impure will.[35]

IDEALISM AND FREEDOM

My initial explanation of this in *Kant's Theory of Freedom* was that this is required of us as a means for increasing our awareness of (and sensitivity to) the true suffering of others, which, in turn, will enable us better to fulfill the duty of beneficence. Baron accepts this analysis but disagrees with what I took to be its further explication or fleshing out in connection with the doctrine of radical evil: we ought to cultivate feelings such as sympathy not as surrogates for the duty motive, but rather as weapons in the struggle against the propensity to evil. Against this, she objects first, that I fail to side-step successfully the impurity problem; second, that my account of the virtuous person as one committed to doing as much as possible to help others, consistent with other moral requirements, does not represent Kant's view; and third, that when my analysis is corrected on this score, it falls prey again to the impurity problem. At bottom, however, her main point seems to be that my analysis of the indirect duty as a requirement to cultivate a counterweight is difficult to reconcile with Kant's conception of freedom.

I believe that all of this points to some real inadequacies in my analysis, which, clearly, was not sufficiently worked out. To begin with, even though Kant himself uses it, my choice of the term "counterweight" to characterize the role of the cultivated feelings was less than felicitous, particularly given my emphasis on the Incorporation Thesis and rejection of a "conflict of forces" picture of motivation. Moreover, I did at one point refer to the feelings as a "counterweight to the self-regarding inclinations," which suggests that one inclination is being used to balance out or check another. Finally, although I am not so sure on this point, I may have been wrong in attributing to Kant the view that a virtuous person will strive to do all that is possible, consistent with other moral obligations, to help those in need.

Even granting this, however, I believe that the main thrust of my analysis remains intact. The most important point here is that a counterweight is needed not to the inclinations but to the propensity to evil. More precisely, we need a counterweight to our tendency to quibble with the strict requirements of duty, to moderate them so that they no longer conflict with what we take to be in our self-interest. Such a counterweight is required, particularly in the case of wide duties such as beneficence, precisely because this propensity is deemed inextirpable. It can (and should) be struggled against, but it can never be completely vanquished. Otherwise expressed, the need for a counterweight reflects the dialectical nature of the moral struggle, which, as a struggle against the propensity to evil, is really a struggle of freedom with itself rather than simply with nature under the guise of the inclinations.

This also enables us to understand how the counterweight can be conceived to operate in a way which is compatible with Kant's conception of freedom and the requirement of moral purity. It does so not by providing a countervailing feeling that somehow "outweighs" the self-directed inclinations, but rather by serving as a source of reasons to act as duty requires. Moreover, this is the function of the increased sensitivity to the needs of others that is produced by visiting the sick and the like. Although of itself the feeling of sympathy or compassion is "aesthetic" rather than "practical," by attuning one to both the extent and depth of human suffering, it arms us with powerful reasons to resist the omnipresent temptation to self-indulgence or moral compromise. In this sense it does, indeed, what the thought of duty alone cannot accomplish, since this thought requires only the adoption of the indeterminate end of the happiness of others, leaving it up to us when, how, and to what extent we are to exercise our beneficence. And this, in turn, leaves us still open to temptation at virtually every occasion at which beneficent action might be called for. Thus, even if it is not the case that one is required to do as much as possible to promote the happiness of others, the virtuous person will certainly endeavor to do more than the minimum, and this, of itself, creates the need for a counterweight to possible temptation.

In *Kant's Theory of Freedom,* I suggested an analogy between the requirement to cultivate one's sympathetic feelings and the instrumental value with regard to the development of a moral disposition that Kant attributes to a sensitivity to the beautiful (in nature) and the sublime in the *Critique of Judgment.*[36] Perhaps a more pertinent comparison, however, is with that other major indirect duty in the Kantian moral scheme: the duty to cultivate one's own happiness. In spite of his unqualified attack on eudaemonism, it is noteworthy that, in all three of his major writings in moral theory, Kant not only insists that we have such an indirect duty, but he connects it with the need to ward off temptation.[37] The basic idea seems to be that insofar as we are ourselves miserable, we will have a greater temptation to focus exclusively on one's own situation, thereby ignoring the situation of others. Our own happiness, or at least moderate well-being, thus seems to function as a kind of facilitator of morality, so the virtuous person will have moral (as well as natural) grounds for not neglecting completely his or her own well-being. If I am correct, this must likewise be understood against the backdrop of radical evil. Indeed, although this goes beyond the direct textual evidence, perhaps we can even say that the whole puzzling notion of an indirect duty must be understood in light of an overriding obligation to minimize the ineliminable temptation to ignore our direct obligations. In short, only a radically evil agent could have indirect duties.

IV. Kant's incompatibilist conception of freedom

Whereas Engstrom's critique is directed mainly at my attempt to distinguish the conception of freedom to which Kant adheres in the *Critique of Pure Reason* from that of his later works in moral philosophy, Reath focuses on my defense of the Reciprocity Thesis. While Baron questions some of the details of my interpretation of Kant's moral psychology, other critics have directly attacked the metaphysical underpinnings of my view: the incompatibilist or indeterminist conception of freedom which I attribute to Kant and attempt, in a limited way, to defend against the standard objections.[38] The complaint is not so much that I am wrong in attributing such a conception to Kant; it is rather that I am wrong in thinking it necessary – at least for a general account of rational agency. All that Kant wants to say about agency, it is argued, including the whole of his moral psychology, is perfectly compatible with a naturalistic account, according to which the ascription of freedom does not carry with it any assumptions about a "contracausal power" or a non-empirical subject. It is also argued that my attempt to defend Kant's conception by linking it closely to my "double-aspect" interpretation of transcendental idealism fails both as a reading of Kant and as a response to the objections. In spite of many differences in detail and in the spirit in which they approach my project, this line of criticism has been expressed by both Karl Ameriks and Paul Guyer.[39] Accordingly, in what follows, I shall for the most part attempt to respond to their common challenge rather than to consider each critique separately. Before doing so, however, I must say a word regarding the misrepresentation of some of my views in Guyer's critique.

At the heart of Guyer's account is the claim that I attempt to find and defend a *theoretical* proof of the *reality* of transcendental freedom in the *Critique of Pure Reason*.[40] He further contends that I proceed to interpret Kant's moral theory of freedom exclusively in light of this one idea.[41] And, given this, he also charges that I "attempt to prove that Kant thought that our possession of rational agency in general, which suffices to prove our transcendental freedom, also entails our recognition of the moral law in particular."[42] Finally, although he does not state it explicitly, he certainly intimates that I (in contrast to him) fail to recognize any significant development or shift in Kant's thought, but instead naively adhere to the idea that the three *Critiques* constitute a profound and unproblematic unity.[43]

Whatever one's views of the merits (or lack thereof) of my book, I hope that any reasonably attentive reader would recognize that I am guilty of none of these offenses. To begin with, I nowhere claim or even suggest that Kant proved or attempted to prove the *reality* of transcendental freedom in the first *Critique*, much less that the grounds of this so-called proof were theoretical rather than practical. In fact, such a claim would be truly astonishing, since Kant himself explicitly denies that it was his intention to establish either the reality or even the real possibility of such freedom (A557–58/B585–86). On the contrary, as I believe I made reasonably clear, my claim was that the transcendental idea of freedom plays a necessary regulative or modeling function with respect to our conception of ourselves as rational agents. And, as I also noted at some length, not only is this perfectly compatible with the (epistemic) possibility that we are merely complex mechanisms rather than genuine (spontaneous) rational agents, but this was clearly recognized by Kant.

KANT ON FREEDOM: A REPLY TO MY CRITICS

Second, it is manifestly false to claim that I interpret Kant's moral theory exclusively (or even primarily) in light of this general conception of rational agency, and it is a complete misrepresentation of my view to suggest that I attempt to derive the bindingness of the moral law from this conception. As should be clear from my dispute with Engstrom (if not from my book itself), the main thrust of my account is precisely to emphasize the *insufficiency* of the conception of freedom required for rational agency for the purposes of morality, including that of establishing the validity of the moral law. Once again, practical freedom (spontaneity) is one thing and autonomy quite another. Thus, far from affirming the continuity of Kant's thought, I insist upon a significant discontinuity, with the great divide marked by the introduction of the principle of autonomy in the *Groundwork*.

Having disposed of these misrepresentations, let us now proceed to the genuine problems. The fundamental objection to my analysis concerns the claim that an incompatibilist conception of freedom is a general requirement of rational agency, as opposed to a condition of the possibility of acting from duty. Thus, Guyer questions the claim that "the incorporation thesis implies the spontaneity thesis, that is, that action on principles and never merely *per stimulos* alone requires transcendental freedom."[44] Similarly, Ameriks wonders whether the mere capacity to act in accordance with self-imposed maxims and on the basis of rational norms, which presumably is what is meant by rational agency, "already defines us as having agency in an incompatibilist sense."[45]

This is certainly a reasonable, albeit hardly unexpected, response to the very unfashionable position I have attributed to Kant and tried to defend. And given the near total dominance of compatibilist views in contemporary thought, the burden of proof is surely on one who argues for their inadequacy.[46] Moreover, I do not pretend to claim that I can fully meet this burden, particularly within the confines of the present limited discussion. Nevertheless, I do hope at least to clarify the issues somewhat by underscoring what I take to be the essential features of Kant's position, which have not been given adequate weight by my critics.

To begin with, it must be insisted that if the general argument from the presuppositions of rational agency fails to provide adequate support for an incompatibilist conception of freedom, then no subsequent appeals to specifically moral requirements or "facts" could conceivably do the job. Basically, this is because any claim to the effect that our general capacity to act on the basis of principles, frame ends or incorporate incentives etc. can be adequately accounted for in a naturalistic, causal fashion could easily be extended to our presumed capacity to act from duty alone.

Moreover, it is not only within the context of questions of moral responsibility that the familiar issue concerning the capacity to do otherwise arises. Precisely the same problem comes up in purely prudential contexts, where we blame ourselves or others for acts and omissions that we do not regard as morally blameworthy. Ought implies can (in the relevant counterfactual sense) either in both cases or in neither. In that sense, then, there is nothing special about *moral* responsibility.

It follows from this that if an incompatibilist conception of freedom is to have any function, it must be as a general condition of rational agency, but it obviously does not follow that it in fact has such a function. Indeed, this line of argument would seem to play into the hands of the compatibilist, who can simply deny the necessity of appealing at all to a contracausal freedom. Underlying this denial, however, is an assumption which is shared by Ameriks and Guyer but I believe rejected by Kant. I further believe that his rejection of this assumption is the key to understanding both Kant's distinctively "critical" treatment of freedom and its connection with transcendental idealism. The assumption in question is that the appeal to freedom is introduced in an attempt to provide something like the best explanation for the "phenomenon" of rational agency, that is, of our capacity to deliberate, choose, adopt maxims and the like. Given this assumption, it is then easy to dismiss the move on the dual grounds that the forthcoming "explanation" in terms of noumenal capacities is either vacuous or incoherent and that it neglects sophisticated forms of compatibilism, which are allegedly capable of reconciling everything we view as essential to rational agency with a broadly naturalistic account.

According to my reading of Kant, however, the insistence on the connection between rational agency and freedom is to be understood as a conceptual claim rather than a putative metaphysical explanation. The appeal to freedom cannot function in an explanatory manner because (theoretically speaking) freedom cannot explain anything. Otherwise expressed, freedom is not something that we need to add to our conception of ourselves as rational agents in order to make some kind of metaphysical sense out of it; it is rather the defining feature of this very conception. It is precisely this idea which I attempted to express in my book by emphasizing the modeling function of the transcendental idea with respect to our conception of ourselves as rational agents.[47]

Reduced to its bare essentials, Kant's conceptual claim has roughly the following form: (1) To think of oneself as a rational agent requires presupposing that one is capable of projecting ends, acting on the basis of self-imposed general principles (maxims) and in light of objectively valid rational norms. (2) But to think of oneself as having these capacities requires the assumption of an independence from determination by antecedent causes, including one's desires. It is not that one's desires are irrelevant to the determination of what one chooses to do (they are obviously the source of reasons to act); it is rather that they are not *sufficient* reasons. (This is where the Incorporation Thesis comes into play.) (3) To attribute such independence to oneself is to conceive oneself in light of the idea of spontaneity (transcendental freedom). (4) Consequently, I cannot coherently think of myself as a rational agent without also attributing to myself such spontaneity. Clearly, it does not follow from the fact that we are constrained to think of ourselves in this way as agents that we really are such, but the "critical" Kant cannot be accused of making any such mistake.

The key step is obviously the second, and it is here that the compatibilist's objections will arise. Why, after all, should the capacity to project ends, act on the basis of reasons, or even independently of desire, require the assumption of a mysterious contracausal faculty? Could it not rather be the outcome of a cognitive process that is completely explicable in naturalistic terms?[48]

The short Kantian answer is that it very well could be the outcome of such a process, but that it cannot be regarded by the agent as such, at least not without the loss of the thought of agency. Insofar as we take ourselves as rational agents, we necessarily regard our decisions and the actions ensuant upon them as "up to us," not simply in the sense of being arrived at independently of any extrinsic causal factors such as passions or overwhelming urges, but also in the sense of not being merely causal consequences of our antecedent states. If the latter were the case, we would have to think of ourselves as automata or turnspits possessing a merely relative spontaneity, whereas the thought of agency necessarily involves the idea of genuine (absolute) spontaneity.[49] This is not, of course, to deny that there is any connection between an agent's antecedent condition or underlying character and the ensuing action, but it is to deny that the connection can be understood in strictly causal terms. As Kant himself put it, the cause is not "so determining that it excludes a causality of our will – a causality which, independent of those natural causes, and even contrary to their force and influence, can produce something that is determined in the time order . . . , and which can begin a series of events entirely of itself" (A534/B562).

As the above account indicates, this conception of ourselves as agents, which presupposes the idea of spontaneity, is itself closely linked with, if not identical to, the conception of ourselves as persons, selves or egos (centers of thought and action). If an action is viewed as the mere causal consequence of my past state, then it is not, properly speaking, viewed as "mine," that is, it is not imputable. Accordingly, the idea of spontaneity is inseparable from the first-person standpoint. Indeed, Kant expressed himself with notable clarity on this very point in the metaphysics lectures from the '70s where he stated:

If I say I think, I act, etc., then either the word "I" is used falsely or I am free. Were I not free, I could not say: I do it, but must rather say: I feel in myself an impulse to do it, which something has incited in me. If, however, I say: I do it, this signifies a spontaneity in the transcendental sense (ML, 28: 269).

To be sure, the critical Kant could no longer license the inference from the capacity to say I or apperception to the *reality* of transcendental freedom or spontaneity. That move went the way of all rational psychology. On my reading, however, he kept the purely conceptual connection between them, from which it follows that the denial of spontaneity entails the elimination of the I. Moreover, from a Kantian standpoint the elimination of the I is not only pragmatically impossible (since the I must do the eliminating) but also incoherent on a deeper level, for the broadly mechanistic world in which the I is dissolved in the thoroughly naturalistic story is itself only for the I. And this, I take it, is at least part of what Kant meant when he claimed in the *Critique* that, "Were we to yield to the illusion of transcendental realism, neither nature nor freedom would remain" (A543/B571).

At the same time, however, the naturalistic story retains its truth and the knowing and acting subject is included in it, as the compatibilist rightly insists. Thus, Kant's task as a philosopher is to show how the thought of the I and its spontaneity can be reconciled with this naturalistic story or, as Allen Wood has aptly put it, it is to show the "compatibility of compatibilism and incompatibilism."[50]

Transcendental idealism, construed in terms of a contrast between two "points of view" or "ways of considering," as opposed to two "worlds" or sets of entities, is the key to Kant's solution to this problem. It accomplishes this goal by providing a conceptual space in which the thought of freedom can be held alongside of the thought of nature, not by the positive assignment of freedom to an inaccessible noumenal world. Admittedly, we find a good deal of talk about a noumenal or "intelligible world," but, as Kant reminds us in the *Groundwork*, "The concept of the intelligible world is thus only a *point of view* which reason finds itself constrained to adopt outside appearances *in order to conceive itself as practical*" (Gr 4: 458; 126).

In addition to the light it sheds on how Kant conceives of the intelligible world, this passage is noteworthy for its clear statement of the conceptual nature of his basic claim. Reason's problem is precisely "to conceive itself as practical," and this requires the adoption of a standpoint "outside appearances," that is, a non-naturalistic standpoint. I have tried here and, in more detail in *Kant's Theory of Freedom*, not only to show why Kant thought this to be the case, but also to defend this claim. To this I would now only add that Kant could have, indeed, should have also said that the adoption of a non-naturalistic standpoint is necessary in order for reason to conceive itself as reason (whether theoretical or practical).[51]

9

Autonomy and spontaneity in Kant's conception of the self

Although Kant never developed what one might call a theory of the self, his virtual identification of selfhood with freedom provided much of the material used by his idealistic successors to develop their own theories. At the same time, however, Kant's actual account of freedom remains among the most perplexing features of his philosophy. One of the major problems is the bewildering variety of ways in which freedom is characterized in different Kantian texts. Thus, Lewis White Beck has distinguished between five different conceptions of freedom in Kant: empirical freedom, moral freedom or autonomy, spontaneity, transcendental freedom and postulated freedom.[1] Since empirical freedom is non-problematic, while postulated freedom turns out to characterize the status of the non-empirical freedom that we supposedly possess rather than a distinct kind of freedom, and finally, since transcendental freedom (as applied to humans) is identified with the absolute spontaneity of the will, this list can be shortened somewhat. Nevertheless, this still leaves us with spontaneity and autonomy as distinct species of freedom: the former concerns rational agency in general, that is, the capacity to determine oneself to act on the basis of general principles (whether moral or prudential); the latter concerns moral agency in particular, that is, the capacity of pure reason to be practical (to determine the will independently of inclination or desire.)

It is sometimes claimed that the *Wille–Willkür* distinction, drawn in the Introduction to the *Metaphysic of Morals*, constitutes Kant's attempt to explain the connection between these two conceptions of freedom.[2] And there is certainly some truth to this, although the latter distinction, which amounts to the contrast between the legislative and executive functions of the will, cannot simply be equated with that between autonomy and spontaneity. For one thing, Kant there denies that *Wille*, properly speaking, can be regarded as either free or unfree (MS 6: 226; 52). For another, autonomy applies only to *Wille* taken in the broad sense as the whole faculty of volition, not to *Wille* in the narrow sense in which it is contrasted with *Willkür*.[3] Accordingly, the question of the relation between spontaneity and autonomy remains even after this distinction is introduced. Moreover, this question is itself a reflection of a larger issue: whether the foundations of Kant's conception of freedom (and, therefore, selfhood) are to be located in his general views on rational agency or in the specifics of his moral theory.

IDEALISM AND FREEDOM

My concern here is with this larger issue, and although much of what Kant says from 1788 on suggests the latter view, I shall argue for the former. In other words, I shall try to show that it is only in light of the conception of spontaneity that Kant's account of autonomy and the claims that he makes for it become intelligible. The analysis is a development of the account offered in *Kant's Theory of Freedom*. As in the book, I shall be concerned with two theses, the Incorporation Thesis and the Reciprocity Thesis, which I link with spontaneity and autonomy respectively. In contrast to the book, however, I shall here focus directly on the question of the relation between these two theses and their underlying conceptions of freedom. The discussion thus falls naturally into three parts. In the first two I discuss the two theses separately and in the third their connection in the full Kantian conception of freedom.

I

The conception of freedom as spontaneity is clearly expressed in the Incorporation Thesis. Kant's canonical formulation of this thesis is contained in *Religion within the Limits of Reason Alone*, where he writes:

[F]reedom of the will [*Willkür*] is of a wholly unique nature in that an incentive [*Triebfeder*] can determine the will to an action *only so far as the individual has incorporated it* [*aufgenommen hat*] *into his maxim* (has made it the general rule in accordance with which he will conduct himself); only thus can an incentive, whatever it may be, coexist with the absolute spontaneity of the will [*Willkür*] (i.e., freedom) (Rel 6: 24; 19).

There are at least three aspects of this thesis that need to be emphasized. First, although Kant introduces it in connection with the explication of his "rigorism" (the claim that every action and agent must be judged either good or evil – the doctrine of moral bivalence) and suggests that it is of great significance to morality, it actually amounts to a claim about rational agency in general. Kant himself indicates this by stating that it applies to every incentive, "whatever it may be," implying thereby that it covers actions motivated by inclination as well as purely moral considerations.

In fact, the Incorporation Thesis is best seen as a general thesis about how motives function in the case of finite rational agents or an *arbitrium liberum*, as contrasted with an *arbitrium brutum*. The latter, as Kant indicates in numerous places, is not merely sensuously affected, but also sensuously determined or necessitated. In other words, a subject with an *arbitium brutum* is causally conditioned to respond to the strongest stimulus or desire, with this strength being determined by physiological factors, independently of any valuation placed upon it by the subject. Such a subject is, therefore, more properly characterized as a patient rather than an agent. By contrast, although a finite rational agent is still sensuously or "pathologically" affected, that is to say, it finds itself with a set of given inclinations and desires, which provide possible motives or reasons to act, it is not causally necessitated to act on the basis of any of them. For such an agent, then, one can no longer speak simply of being moved to act by the strongest desire, as if desires came with pre-given strengths, independently of the significance assigned to them by the rational agent by virtue of its freely chosen projects. Instead, the Incorporation Thesis requires us to regard the agent as acquiescing to the desire, granting it, as it were, honorific status as a sufficient reason to act. As the text indicates, this status is attained by incorporating the desire into one's maxim or principle of action. For example, I may have a strong desire to indulge myself in an ice cream cone, but the mere presence of such a desire or craving does not provide me with a sufficient reason for doing so. It can only become such in light of a rule permitting such indulgence under certain conditions. Consequently, in acting on the desire, I am also committing myself to that rule, and such a committment must be viewed as an act of spontaneity on my part (of self-determination, if you will), which is not reducible to the mere having of the desire. It is, then, in this commitment and incorporation, which is inseparable from the practical use of reason, that we find the locus of agency.

The second point to be made with respect to the Incorporation Thesis is that it is by no means unique to *Religion within the Limits of Reason Alone*. On the contrary, as the reference to the necessity of taking up or incorporating an incentive into a maxim indicates, this thesis is nothing more than an explication of what is already implicit in the familiar account of rational agency as based on the "conception of law" or principles in the *Groundwork* (Gr 4: 412). Since maxims are the first-order, subjective principles on which rational agents act, and since they are self-imposed (we do not simply have maxims, we *make* something our maxim), maxim-based action involves self-determination and, therefore, an exercise of spontaneity. Moreover, if in the *Groundwork* the Incorporation Thesis is used without being mentioned, in other texts it is expressly affirmed, albeit not in the precise terms of *Religion within the Limits of Reason Alone*. A good example of this is *Reflexion* 5611, which belongs to a set of *Reflexionen* that illuminate the discussion of freedom in the *Critique of Pure Reason*.[4] As Kant there puts the matter, actions are to a large part induced [*veranlasst*], but not entirely determined through sensibility, for reason must provide a "complement of sufficiency" [*Complement der Zulänglichkeit*] (18: 252). This idea of a complement of sufficiency clearly corresponds to the incorporation of incentives into a maxim. In both cases the essential point is that reason somehow intervenes even in actions based on sensuous motives. Similarly, in *Metaphysik K3*, dated 1794–95, Kant maintains that, in addition to sensible stimuli, the "concurrence of the understanding" [*concurrenz des Verstandes*] is necessary to determine a rational agent to act (MK3 29: 1015). As Karl Ameriks has noted in his discussion of this text, "What Kant has in mind here is ... a model where the self 'goes along' with what is proposed to it without being compelled by this proposal. . . . "[5] Ameriks is perfectly correct in referring to this as a "model," and he is likewise correct in emphasizing that the point of this model is to articulate the key Kantian principle that sensibility of itself, apart from the contribution of the understanding or reason, is insufficient to account for either agency or cognition. To this I would only add that this doctrine of concurrence is nothing new, but merely a fresh expression of the view to which Kant had been committed at least since the beginning of the "critical" period.

The third and for present purposes most important point is that this incorporation is based on what Kant terms the "absolute spontaneity of the will." Although Kant does not discuss the matter in *Religion within the Limits of Reason Alone*, this is presumably to be contrasted with relative spontaneity, which he sometimes describes as "*spontaneitas secundum quid.*" In his precritical metaphysical lectures, Kant compares the latter mode of spontaneity to that of a turnspit because its exercise depends upon a prior determination by an external force and contrasts it with the absolute spontaneity required for genuine agency (ML, 1 28: 267).[6] Moreover, in a famous passage in the second *Critique* Kant uses precisely the same expression to characterize the "psychological" or "comparative" conception of freedom affirmed by Leibniz, which, in Kant's eyes, effectively reduces the soul to an "automaton *spirituale*" (KprV 5: 97; 100). And from this, together with the accounts in the first *Critique*, the *Groundwork* and the other texts mentioned above, it seems reasonable to conclude that Kant held that the act of incorporation that is supposedly constitutive of rational agency requires more than a merely comparative freedom. More precisely, it requires a capacity to determine oneself to act independently of the "causality of nature," a capacity which can be thought only in light of the transcendental idea of freedom.

As has been frequently pointed out, this account of spontaneity has a parallel in the theoretical sphere, where Kant contrasts the spontaneity of the understanding with the receptivity of sense. Although the issues involved are quite complex, the case for epistemic spontaneity can be expressed fairly succinctly and in a way that helps to highlight the comparison with the practical variety. The main point is that the reception of sensible data is no more capable of accounting for cognition than being sensibly affected is sufficient to account for rational choice. As Kant avers in many places in the first *Critique*, sensibility and the imagination (in its empirical, reproductive function) can present to the mind merely a subjective order of representations (a–b), which reflects the contingencies of one's perceptual situation (the fact that one happened to perceive a before b). But such a subjective order does not of itself possess any cognitive worth, that is, it does not amount to the cognition of an objective connection or order. The latter requires that the understanding subject the given representations to an ordering principle or rule (pure concept of the understanding), by means of which the order is determined as objective. Kant characterizes this as an act of spontaneity of the subject, since it is not determined by the sensible data, and it constitutes the epistemic analogue to the act of incorporation or concurrence. In both domains, then, we might say that the mind is "undetermined by the data," and that complete determination requires a contribution on the part of the subject. In the cognitive domain, this contribution (the act of spontaneity) amounts to a determination of the object, whereas in the practical domain it is a matter of self-determination.

Given this parallelism, it is not surprising to find Kant occasionally appealing to a linkage between these two kinds of spontaneity. The best known of these places is in *Groundwork III*, where he appears to move from the epistemic spontaneity of rational beings to their practical spontaneity or freedom, only to draw back from the conclusion that his premises seem to warrant. As Kant there puts it:

Reason must look upon itself as the author of its own principles independently of alien influences. Therefore as practical reason or as the will of a rational being, it must be regarded by itself as free; that is, the will of a rational being can be a will of his own [*ein eigener Wille sein*] only under the idea of freedom, and such a will must therefore – from a practical point of view – be attributed to all rational beings (Gr 4: 448; 116).[7]

Since I have dealt with this text and the complex line of argument it involves at length elsewhere,[8] I shall here limit myself to pointing out that Kant's refusal to draw the expected conclusion (that we are warranted in regarding ourselves as free in the practical sense) stems from a significant disanalogy between epistemic and practical spontaneity. This disanalogy does not concern the type of spontaneity (as if cognition requires merely relative and agency absolute spontaneity), but rather the kind of certainty possible with respect to each. Although Kant, to my knowledge, never expresses himself in this way, it seems reasonable to attribute to him the view that the spontaneity of the understanding (or reason in its theoretical capacity) is self-certifying somewhat in the manner of the Cartesian *cogito*. To doubt one's spontaneity in this sense would be to doubt that one is a thinking being; but this, of course, would itself require an act of thought. The 'I think' must be able to accompany all my representations, even the thought that I am not really thinking.

By contrast, in the practical domain, not even this degree of self-certification is available. Here, then, we must conclude that reflection on the ineliminable moment of spontaneity can yield only the conditional result: if I take myself to be a rational agent, that is, if I take myself to be acting on the basis of reasons and a reflective evaluation of my situation rather than merely responding to stimuli, I must necessarily regard myself as free. In the terms of the *Groundwork*, I can act only under the idea of freedom (Gr 4: 448; 116). Or, as Kant is quoted as claiming in a metaphysics lecture, "Freedom is practically necessary – man must therefore act according to an idea of freedom, otherwise he cannot act [*anders kann er nicht*]. That does not, however, prove freedom in the theoretical sense" (MM 29: 898). As the latter remark indicates, the practical necessity of acting under the idea of freedom leaves in place the epistemic possibility that I am deluded in believing that I am acting or, as Kant sometimes puts it, that my "reason has causality." Here the Cartesian demon is more difficult to dislodge. In fact, it cannot be exorcized by any theoretical means, although it can be safely ignored from the practical point of view.

Finally, in light of these considerations, we are in a better position to appreciate the status of the Incorporation Thesis as the expression of a non-empirical, normative model of agency, which constitutes the Kantian alternative to the familiar Humean, belief-desire model. First, the model is non-empirical because the thought is just that, a thought or idea, rather than an object of possible experience. We cannot, as it were, introspectively catch ourselves incorporating incentives into our maxims any more than we can introspect the act of thinking itself.[9] Accordingly, this act is something "merely intelligible," which cannot be assigned to the self as phenomenon. Second, the model is normative because it is only in light of it that we regard ourselves as acting on the basis of reasons and, therefore, as subject to evaluative norms (whether moral or prudential).

II

Whereas the conception of freedom as spontaneity and the Incorporation Thesis in which it is expressed have pre-critical roots, the characterization of freedom as autonomy and the associated Reciprocity Thesis are first explicitly formulated in the *Groundwork*. Autonomy is introduced in *Groundwork II* as the culmination of a regressive account of the conditions of the possibility of a categorical imperative. Although Kant confounds matters by referring to a "formula of autonomy," supposedly on a par with the other formulas of the categorical imperative, his major claim is that autonomy is the "supreme principle of morality" in the sense of being the condition of the possibility of action on the basis of this imperative. Autonomy, so construed, is defined as "the property the will has of being a law to itself (independently of every property belonging to objects of volition)" (Gr 4: 440; 108). This is contrasted with heteronomy, according to which "the will does not give itself the law, but the object does in virtue of its relation to the will" (Gr 4: 441; 108).

If one is to understand fully the significance of this conception, it is necessary to focus on the parenthetical clause. This is because, of itself, the conception of the will as having the property of "being a law to itself" need not take us beyond the Incorporation Thesis. Maxims, after all, are described by Kant as "subjective laws" and they are by their very nature self-imposed or self-legislated. Consequently, it is sometimes argued that the will exercises its "autonomy" (in the sense of being a "law to itself") in all cases of rational choice, even when it involves immoral behavior.[10] And if this is the case, then we cannot regard autonomy as a new conception of freedom, one explicitly tied to the capacity to act on the basis of the categorical imperative. Moreover, on this reading, heteronomy would not be a contrasting form of agency, but rather a simple lack of agency, a complete subjection of the will to the "causality of nature." Although the latter is precisely how the conception of heteronomy is frequently understood, such a reading makes nonsense of Kant's critique of alternative moral theories as based on the *principle* of heteronomy. As we shall see, this critique turns on the claim that all such theories embody an inadequate account of moral motivation (one which ultimately revolves around the principle of self-love), but this presupposes that the subjects of morality are regarded as agents, who act on the basis of principles rather than merely respond to stimuli.

The parenthetical clause offers the prospect of a way out of these difficulties because it suggests that autonomy involves not simply the capacity of the will to determine itself to act on the basis of self-imposed principles (which would include heteronomous principles), but the capacity to do so in a particular way: "independently of every property belonging to the objects of volition." Accordingly, the task is to determine just what this independence condition involves, and this can best be accomplished by considering a mode of volition which lacks it, that is, one in which "the will does not give itself the law, but the object does so in virtue of its relation to the will" (Gr 4: 441; 108).

If the latter is to be understood as a form of agency, it must be one in which all the agent's maxims reflect its needs (directly or indirectly) as a sensous being, needs which are themselves explicable in terms of the laws of nature. In short, it is not that the agent is causally conditioned to act as a result of these needs (in which case it would not even have an *arbitrium liberum*); it is rather that these needs (including psychological or "ego needs") provide the only available sources of reasons to act. Although this is quite far from the picture of agency presented in Kant's major writings in moral theory, it is arguably the view to which he adhered, at least implicitly, prior to the *Groundwork*.[11] Conversely, an agent with the property of autonomy would not be subject to this limiting condition, and this means that it would have the capacity to recognize sufficient reasons to act that do not stem (even indirectly) from its needs as a sensuous being. Since such reasons can stem only from pure practical reason, the will (as practical reason) would be self-legislative in the fullest sense and pure reason would be practical.

In light of this conception of autonomy, it is easy to see both why Kant regards autonomy as the supreme principle of morality and denies that any view of agency that does not acknowledge autonomy in this sense is capable of accounting for the possibility of morality. The key idea is simply that morality, as Kant analyzes it in *Groundwork I* and *II*, requires not merely that our actions conform to duty but that they be "from duty," that is, that the duty-motive of itself provides a sufficient reason to act. Expressed in Kantian terms, this means that the recognition of an obligation brings with it an "incentive" [*Triebfeder*] or "interest" in fulfilling it. Such an interest is termed by Kant a "pure" or "moral" interest. Assuming autonomy, this condition can be met, since *ex hypothesi* an agent with this property is capable of being motivated by a non-sensuous incentive. Lacking this property, however, such motivation is impossible, since an interest stemming from one's needs as a sensuous being would then be required in order to have a sufficient reason (incentive) to act. And on that scenario, which is that of heteronomy, moral requirements would be reduced to hypothetical imperatives, since the only incentive for fulfilling them would be their status as necessary means to the satisfaction of some presupposed interest.

So far we have considered Kant's argument to the effect that autonomy is a necessary condition of the possibility of morality. Kant also claims, however, that it is its sufficient condition and this is where the Reciprocity Thesis comes into play. In order to understand the significance of this thesis, we must recognize that autonomy, as presented above, does not yet involve any necessary connection with morality. The claim that the will has the capacity to legislate to itself, even apart from all sensuous needs and interests, is not equivalent to the claim that the moral law is the law that it legislates. Rather, the introduction of autonomy as a property of the will serves to create the space needed to account for the possibility of moral motivation (the independence condition), but it does not of itself provide anything to fill that space or even to guarantee that it can be filled. For all that we have seen so far, it is conceivable that an autonomous agent might legislate some other law to itself or perhaps determine itself to act on the basis of principles that make no pretence to lawfulness (no claim to universality and necessity). Accordingly, even granting freedom as autonomy, we still need an argument linking it to the moral law. This is the function of the Reciprocity Thesis, which, in the language of the second *Critique*, affirms that "freedom and unconditional practical law reciprocally imply each other" (Kpr V 5: 28; 29).

In the *Groundwork*, Kant introduces this thesis in connection with the distinction between a negative and a positive definition of freedom. After first characterizing the will as "a kind of causality belonging to living beings so far as they are rational," he claims that freedom, negatively construed, is just the capacity of the will "to work independently of *determination* by alien causes." Although incapable of capturing the essence of freedom because of its negative thrust, Kant claims that it leads to a positive definition which does capture this essence: autonomy, here characterized as the "property which will has of being a law to itself" (Gr 4: 446; 114). The argument for this connection turns on the premise that the will, like any "kind of causality," cannot be lawless, that is, it must have a specifiable *modus operandi* or "character." And since, *ex hypothesi*, determination by "alien causes" in conformity with laws of nature is ruled out, nothing remains but to attribute to the will the property of being a law to itself. Moreover, Kant continues, the claim that " 'Will is in all its actions a law to itself' " is equivalent to the "principle of acting on no maxim other than one which can have for its object itself as at the same time a universal law," which is just the formula for the categorical imperative." And from this he concludes that "a free will and a will under moral laws are one and the same thing" (Gr 4: 447; 114).

This argument consists of two moves: one from the negative to the positive conception of freedom or autonomy and the other from autonomy to the categorical imperative. Unfortunately, each of these moves is highly problematic, with the difficulty in both cases stemming from an ambiguity in the central notion of autonomy. To begin with, causal independence (as expressed in the Incorporation Thesis) does not entail autonomy in the full Kantian sense discussed above. As already indicated, the latter involves more than independence from determination by alien causes; it also involves a positive capacity to be motivated by reasons that are totally independent of one's needs as a sensuous being. But this positive capacity simply cannot be teased out of negative freedom, at least insofar as the latter is simply identified with spontaneity.[12] Similarly, with respect to the second move, the claim that the will is a "law to itself" need not mean more than that it is spontaneous, acting on the basis of self-imposed principles (maxims), and from this there is no direct route to the categorical imperative.

As I have argued elsewhere, however, the analytic connection between freedom and the categorical imperative which Kant affirms in the Reciprocity Thesis can be defended if we thicken our initial conception of negative freedom to include motivational as well as causal independence.[13] In addition to the requisite sense of freedom, this argument, which I can only sketch here in a rough manner, is based on the assumption that the agent in question is rational. This entails that its choices must be subject to a justification requirement. In other words, it must be possible for such an agent to offer reasons for its actions; since reasons are by their very nature universal, this means that such an agent must be willing to acknowledge that it would be reasonable (justifiable) for any rational being to act in a similar manner in relevantly similar circumstances.

Now, of itself this claim is relatively non-controversial and yields only a weak sense of universalizability, one that is far removed from the form required by Kantian morality. The move to the categorical imperative and to the strong sense of universalizability it involves turns on the extension of the justification requirement to the agent's most fundamental maxims. This extension is entailed by the nature of the freedom being attributed to the agent. Since such an agent is assumed to have the capacity to determine itself independently of, and even contrary to, its needs as a sensuous being, it cannot simply appeal to a given desire, no matter how strong or "foundational," as if that desire of itself constituted a sufficient reason to adopt a course of action. On the contrary, desire-based action requires a desire-independent warrant. The question thus becomes what could provide such a warrant, and the short Kantian answer is that it can only be provided by an unconditional practical law, that is, one which applies to all rational agents independently of their desires. This is why Kant claims that "freedom and unconditional practical law reciprocally imply each other" (Kpr V 5: 29; 29).[14] Consequently, an agent with autonomy must submit its self-legislation to the condition of its conformity to unconditional practical law. And since it can be shown that this is equivalent to recognizing the authority of the categorical imperative, it follows that an agent with autonomy must recognize the authority of this imperative as the supreme condition of its self-legislation.[15]

Finally, before concluding this section, it is important to determine more precisely the thrust of the Reciprocity Thesis. First, of itself, it does not suffice to show that rational agents such as ourselves really are subject to the categorical imperative, since it presupposes rather than establishes the type of freedom (autonomy) that is both a necessary and a sufficient condition of this imperative. Second, it does not entail that autonomous agents necessarily obey this imperative insofar as they act freely. It shows rather that they must recognize its authority and motivational force (as the source of a sufficient reason for action) even when they violate its precepts. As always, for Kant, what is objectively (in the eyes of reason) necessary remains subjectively contingent. Nevertheless, it does establish the inseparability of Kantian morality from a conception of freedom that is distinct from that of spontaneity, even when this is understood in the absolute sense.

III

Up to this point we have examined the two conceptions of freedom and their respective theses separately; our present task is to consider their relationship in the overall Kantian conception of the self. Now, given what we have seen so far, it would seem that Kant's position should be that the two conceptions have different warrants and operate at different levels of reflection. Since we can act only under the idea of freedom, spontaneity, and with it the Incorporation Thesis, must be presupposed in every exercise of rational agency. Correlatively, autonomy is presupposed as a condition of acting from duty. Finally, since acting from duty is a species of acting, autonomy must presuppose spontaneity (and the Reciprocity Thesis the Incorporation Thesis).

Although something like the above seems to be operative in the *Groundwork*, when we turn to the texts from 1788 on, a rather different picture emerges. Essential to this picture is the thesis, first enunciated in the preface to the *Critique of Practical Reason*, that the moral law is the "*ratio cognoscendi* of freedom*,*" that is to say, apart from our consciousness of standing under the moral law, "we would never have been justified in assuming anything like [*so etwas*] freedom" (Kpr V 5: 4n; 4). Far from being an isolated claim, this doctrine of the total dependence of the conception of freedom on the moral law is a constant refrain of Kant's from then on. For example, in *Religion within the Limits of Reason Alone*, the very work in which the Incorporation Thesis is expressly formulated, Kant states of the moral law that "it is the only law which informs us of the independence of our will [*Willkür*] from determination of all other incentives . . . and at the same time of the accountability of all our actions" (Rel 6: 25n; 21). Similarly, in the *Metaphysic of Morals* he claims that moral laws "first make known to us a property of our choice [*Willkür*], namely, its freedom" (MS 6: 225; 51).

As the citation from *Religion within the Limits of Reason Alone* makes clear, the claim is not that we are free, or even that we are certain of our freedom, only insofar as we act from duty; it is rather that it is the capacity to act from duty (of which we are aware through our consciousness of standing under the moral law) that makes us aware of our general capacity to determine ourselves to act independently of the "causality of nature." In short, it is through the consciousness of our autonomy that we become aware of our absolute spontaneity and, therefore, of the imputability of our acts. Moreover, this account of the connection between the moral law (itself certified through the "fact of reason") and freedom as spontaneity appears to underlie both the "deduction" of freedom and the doctrine of the unity of reason in the second *Critique*. Thus, Kant there maintains that pure practical reason fills the place left "vacant" by speculative reason by providing practical reality (through the moral law) to the "idea of freedom as a faculty of absolute spontaneity," which, with respect to its possibility, is an "analytical principle of pure speculation." And, in the same context, he further contends that "Speculative reason does not herewith grow in insight but only in respect to the certitude of its problematic concept of freedom, to which objective, though only practical, reality is now indubitably given" (Kpr V 5: 49; 50).

Since absolute spontaneity (transcendental freedom) is the conception of freedom indigenous to reason in its speculative use, it seems clear that establishing an intimate connection between morality and such freedom is essential to Kant's systematic project of demonstrating the unity of reason. It seems equally clear, however, that this linkage of absolute spontaneity specifically and solely with the capacity to act from duty raises fresh questions about the overall coherence of Kant's position. First, there is the question of consistency, which arises because of the difficulty reconciling such a view with many of the texts previously considered as well as with the significance attributed to the Incorporation Thesis. Second, the result seems highly counter-intuitive, for assuming that Kant is consistent in maintaining that freedom as spontaneity is a condition of rational agency, it would follow that he is committed to the view that it is only through our consciousness of standing under the moral law that we can become aware of our rational agency, that is, of a capacity to set ends, adopt maxims and the like. But this seems quite implausible; indeed, it is only insofar as we first consider ourselves as agents engaged in a deliberative process that moral claims gain any real hold on us.

One might respond to both the inconsistency and implausibility charges by appealing to texts which suggest that Kant in fact thought that the merely comparative conception of freedom, which can be ascertained through experience, rather than absolute spontaneity, is all that is required to distinguish the *arbitrium liberum* from the *arbitrium brutum* and, therefore, for the attribution of agency in non-moral contexts.[16] On this basis, then, one might simply deny that Kant held that absolute spontaneity is a condition of rational agency *per se*. But even leaving aside the difficulty of reconciling any such reading with the Incorporation Thesis, the real problem with it is that it makes it difficult to see how Kant could then deny the possibility of a naturalized account of action from duty as well.[17] Once the adequacy of a thoroughly naturalistic account of rational agency in general is admitted, then it becomes quite difficult to maintain that action from duty constitutes a unique exception. A capacity to act on the basis of reasons that hold independently of one's needs as a sensuous being is one thing and a capacity to act contra-causally, which is clearly what absolute spontaneity involves, quite another. And if Kant does indeed identify the two, then it would seem that he is guilty of conflating a motivational with a causal independence of nature.

Nor can one defend such a conflation on the grounds that motives or incentives for Kant are the psychological causes of action. On this reading, a capacity to act on the basis of a supersensible incentive is just what is meant by a capacity to exercise a supersensible causality; so it would hardly be surprising that Kant identifies the warrant for affirming the latter with the consciousness of the former capacity. Although it must be admitted that Kant does seem to reason this way at times, it cannot be taken as his considered view, since it makes it completely unintelligible how inclination-based actions (which *ex hypothesi* have sensible incentives) could be imputed. As we have already seen, this is conceivable only insofar as we assume that incentives (whatever their nature) are not of themselves sufficient to determine choice, but must first be taken up or "incorporated" into a maxim. Such a view, however, clearly requires a sharp distinction between the incentive and the causal determinant of action, with the latter (as the Incorporation Thesis affirms) being attributed to the absolute spontaneity of *Willkür*.[18]

Interestingly enough, these difficulties disappear if we identify the freedom for which the consciousness of the moral law serves as the *ratio cognoscendi* with autonomy rather than spontaneity. Since autonomy (in the specifically Kantian sense) is not a condition of rational agency, we no longer have to attribute to Kant the view that our consciousness of duty first makes us aware of our agency. Nor do we need accuse him of conflating motives and causes. On the contrary, it would make perfect sense for Kant to claim that our consciousness of duty first makes us aware of our autonomy; particularly since apart from such consciousness we could have no reason to believe that there might be such a thing as a pure or non-sensuous incentive. In short, what the consciousness of standing under the moral law really provides is a determinate content to the otherwise vacuous idea of a motivational independence from our needs as sensuous beings rather than some kind of guarantee of our causal independence from everything in the phenomenal world. The latter independence is still presupposed as a condition of agency, but this presupposition leaves in place the the epistemic possibility that our putative freedom is illusory, that we are automata rather than agents. Although such a view is practically vacuous, since we cannot act on the basis of it, it remains unrefuted theoretically. Indeed, only when the "primacy of practical reason" is taken in a much stronger sense, as it was by Fichte, for example, could such an argument from morality be thought to undermine the very possibility that our freedom might be illusory.[19] But at that point we are no longer on genuinely Kantian ground.

Admittedly, this seems to conflict with much of what Kant says about freedom in the second *Critique,* particularly with the opening claims in the Preface that "With the pure practical faculty of reason, the reality of transcendental freedom is also confirmed" (Kpr V 5: 3; 3). And one paragraph later, that "The concept of freedom, insofar as its reality is proved by an apodictic law of practical reason, is the keystone of the whole architecture of the system of pure reason and even of speculative reason" (Kpr V 5: 3; 3). In passages such as these, which suggest that the reality of transcendental freedom has somehow been established through the moral law as the fact of reason, Kant certainly seems to be denying *tout court* the possibility that our freedom might be illusory. But to interpret such claims in this way is to ignore the explicitly practical context in which they arise. As Kant makes clear at several points, freedom is known only as a condition of the moral law; this means that, although the law gives practical reality to the notion of an unconditioned, supersensible causality (absolute spontaneity), it does not extend our theoretical insight into such causality – not even to the extent of ruling out the epistemic possibility which theoretical reason leaves open. Once again, then, we find that the most that Kant's argument entails is that the reality of freedom cannot be denied from a practical point of view.

Nevertheless, even this limited result will be rejected by most philosophers, including many who consider themselves Kantians in moral theory. Since the concern of Kantian moral theory is with the question of the nature of moral motivation, why can't we simply abstract from the properly speculative question of transcendental freedom and thus develop a genuinely Kantian moral theory without worrying about this problematic concept? In fact, Kant himself seems to approve of precisely such a procedure when he remarks in the Canon of the first *Critique* that transcendental freedom is a problem, which "does not come within the province of reason in its practical employment" (A803/B831).

The response is to insist once again on the centrality of the Incorporation Thesis and to disarm those who might acknowledge this thesis, or something like it, while denying that this need involve any commitment to even the *idea* of absolute spontaneity or transcendental freedom.[20] In my judgment, this denial is rooted in the mistaken assumption that the appeal to freedom is intended as something like the best explanation for the "phenomenon" of rational agency, understood as our capacity to deliberate, choose, adopt maxims and the like. Indeed, given this assumption, it is all too easy to dismiss the appeal to absolute spontaneity on the dual grounds that any forthcoming "explanation" would involve an illicit appeal to noumenal capacities and that it neglects sophisticated forms of compatibilism, which are allegedly capable of reconciling everything we view as essential to rational agency with a broadly naturalistic account.

As I have argued elsewhere, however, Kant's insistence on the connection between rational agency and spontaneity is to be understood as a conceptual claim rather than a putative metaphysical explanation.[21] In other words, freedom in the sense of spontaneity is not something that we must add to our conception of ourselves as rational agents in order to make some kind of metaphysical sense out of it; it is rather the defining feature of this very conception. This is the force of the claim that we can act only under the idea of freedom. In Hegelian terms, freedom, so construed, is subject and not a mere predicate. And in this sense Kant provided the inspiration for the later idealistic identification of the self, ego or *Geist* with freedom. Leaving aside the complications introduced by the supra-personal nature of *Geist*, the essential difference is that for Kant this remained a mere conceptual claim regarding the manner in which we must conceive ourselves insofar as we take ourselves as rational agents, whereas in his idealistic successors it became inflated into an ontological truth. Whether this conception is necessary and, if so, whether its inflation is warranted are, of course, among the big questions posed for us by German idealism.

10

On a presumed gap in the derivation of the categorical imperative

The recent literature contains a number of relatively successful Kantian responses to the familiar objection, usually associated with Hegel, that the categorical imperative is "empty" in the sense that, of itself, it is incapable of either generating any specific duties or ruling out any maxims as impermissible. Although these responses hardly resolve all of the difficulties regarding the nature and applicability of the categorical imperative, they do show that the emptiness charge rests on a serious misunderstanding of Kant's theory, including a failure to attend to the way in which Kant construes the "contradiction in conception" and "contradiction in will" tests.[1]

These responses fail, however, to address a related but distinct difficulty in the derivation of the categorical imperative that is treated at some length by Bruce Aune in *Kant's Theory of Morals*. This difficulty concerns an apparent gap in Kant's move from the principle that one's actions must conform to universal law, which Aune regards as a non-problematic requirement of rational willing, to the categorical imperative in its canonical universal law formula.[2] Since, according to Aune, the difference between the requirement of conformity to universal law and the categorical imperative consists in the fact that the former does not provide a guide to action, whereas the latter presumably does, this criticism leads to the same conclusion as the emptiness charge: Kant fails to establish a viable, contentful principle of moral discrimination.

In his recent book, *Hegel's Ethical Thought*, Allen Wood raises a similar objection against Kant's derivation and attributes it to Hegel. In fact, according to Wood, the impossibility of deriving a viable moral principle from the mere concept of universal practical law or, as he terms it, an "objective ground," rather than the emptiness of the universal law formula, is the real import of Hegel's critique.[3] Wood's effort to credit Hegel with this line of objection is not totally convincing, since it is based on an appeal to a single ambiguous passage.[4] Nevertheless, setting aside this historical-textual question, the fact remains that both Aune and Wood appear to have called attention to a potentially serious weakness in Kant's metaethical theory that has gone largely unnoticed in the literature.[5] Accordingly, the concern in the present essay is to rectify this situation by attempting to fill in the apparent gap in Kant's derivation of the categorical imperative.

The essay is divided into three parts. The first analyzes the gap as Aune presents it in connection with *Groundwork I;* shows that the same problem arises with respect to the derivation of the categorical imperative in *Groundwork II;* and discusses the implications of such a gap for Kant's moral theory, an issue which Wood emphasizes but Aune largely ignores. The second part considers Aune's contention that the gap cannot be filled and, therefore, that Kant's derivation of the categorical imperative fails. It shows that although there are some difficulties with Aune's account of the categorical imperative and conception of a universal law, the basic problem remains even when these are remedied. It thus concludes that the derivation in the *Groundwork* does, indeed, fail. The third part considers the derivation in the *Critique of Practical Reason*. It argues that the gap is there successfully filled by means of the introduction of transcendental freedom (which in the *Groundwork* is appealed to only in connection with the justification, not the derivation, of the categorical imperative).

I

Groundwork I begins with Kant's famous account of the good will as the sole unconditioned good. Kant contends that both the concept of such a will and the recognition of its supreme worth are "already present in the sound natural understanding" and, therefore, need "not so much to be taught as merely to be clarified" (Gr 4: 397; 64). In the attempt to provide this clarification, Kant introduces the concept of duty, "which includes that of a good will, exposed, however, to certain subjective limitations and obstacles" (Gr 4: 397; 65). From a consideration of the notion of duty Kant then derives three propositions, which collectively constitute the central claims of *Groundwork I:* (1) An action has moral worth when and only when it is done from duty alone *(aus Pflicht);*[6] (2) "An action done from duty has its moral worth, *not in the purpose* to be attained by it, but in the maxim according with which it is decided upon" (Gr 4: 399; 67–68); and (3) "Duty is the necessity to act out of respect for the law" (Gr 4: 400; 68).

Although virtually every step in Kant's analysis involves difficulties and has been subjected to detailed criticism in the literature, our present concern is merely with the consequences Kant draws from his third proposition, which he describes as itself an inference from the first two (Gr 4: 400; 68). This is the crucial part of Kant's analysis, for it is here that he moves from the account of moral motivation to the categorical imperative as the principle on which one acts when one acts from duty.

As is frequently the case, at crucial points Kant's argument proceeds by way of elimination. Assuming a motivational dualism of inclination and duty, Kant rules out inclination as a possible source of moral motivation. This entails that morally worthy acts must be from duty alone, which Kant takes to mean that they must be motivated by respect for a practical law, that is, for a rational principle that governs the choices of rational agents independently of their desires. This naturally raises the question of the nature of this law that is supposed to furnish the principle of a good will, and it is in Kant's attempt to show that the categorical imperative is the only possible candidate for such a law that our problem arises.

Starting with the assumption that the motive to obey any *particular* law must stem from some presupposed end or object of desire and therefore ultimately from inclination, Kant concludes that no particular law could serve as the principle of a good will and, consequently, that there is nothing left to serve as such a principle except "the conformity of actions to universal law as such." But this, Kant suggests, is just to say that "I ought never to act except in such a way *that I can also will that my maxim should become a universal law*" (Gr 4: 402; 70). Since the latter claim contains the first appearance in the *Groundwork* of what is later identified as the categorical imperative, it is clear that Kant is intending to show that this imperative is presupposed in the "natural sound understanding" as the fundamental moral principle. Moreover, since Kant presents this imperative in a parenthetical clause intended to explicate the notion of conformity to universal law as such, it would appear that he regarded these principles as equivalent. At the very least, he must be taken as claiming that the first somehow entails the second.

Here, then, is the "crucial gap" in Kant's argument. As Aune points out, the existence of this gap becomes clear when one notes that the two principles differ significantly with respect to practical import.[7] Put simply, the requirement "Conform your actions to universal law as such," like the requirement "Be authentic," is practically uninformative; it does not provide any useful information about what one ought or ought not to do. By contrast, the categorical imperative does at the very least serve to rule out certain maxims as impermissible. Clearly, Kant's operative assumption is that we conform to universal law just in case we act on maxims that we can will to be universal laws. But, as Aune correctly notes, this claim is far from obvious and Kant needs (but fails to provide) an argument for it.[8]

Moreover, this gap in the argument cannot be attributed to the provisional nature of the discussion in *Groundwork I*, for precisely the same problem arises in connection with Kant's official derivation of the categorical imperative in *Groundwork II*. After presenting the conception of a hypothetical imperative, Kant argues that whereas in the case of such an imperative it is necessary to know the "condition" (the desired end) before it is possible to determine what the imperative "contains" (enjoins), the content of a categorical imperative can be derived immediately from the mere concept of such an imperative. This supposedly follows because:

Besides the law this imperative contains only the necessity that our maxim should conform to this law, while the law ... contains no condition to limit it, there remains nothing over to which the maxim has to conform except the universality of a law as such; and it is this conformity alone that the imperative properly asserts to be necessary (Gr 4: 420–21; 88).

Kant's reasoning here appears to be that since *ex hypothesi* a categorical imperative commands unconditionally (it applies to all rational beings independently of their desires), it must abstract in its legislation from all desired ends, which means that there is nothing left for it to enjoin other than conformity to universal law. Clearly, however, this shows merely that a categorical imperative requires the conformity of one's maxims to universal law as such. But, as before, Kant proceeds from this directly to the conclusion: "There is therefore only a single categorical imperative and it is this: 'Act only on that maxim through which you can at the same time will that it should become a universal law'" (Gr 4: 421; 88). Once again, then, there appears to be a significant gap in Kant's argument that needs to be filled.[9]

According to Allen Wood's analysis, the gap might be more significant than Aune realizes. Whereas Aune locates the weakness in Kant's derivation of the categorical imperative in the unsupported jump from a non-controversial but uninformative principle of practical rationality to one that is action guiding, Wood places it in Kant's failure to distinguish between two senses of universality, which he terms the "universality of applicability" and the "universality of concern" or "collective rationality."[10] By the former is meant simply the principle that if a maxim or course of action is deemed right, reasonable or permissible for any agent in given circumstances, it must also be deemed such for any other rational agent in relevantly similar circumstances. This is essentially equivalent to the rationality requirement depicted by Aune. By contrast, the latter requires not merely that any principle be applicable universally, but also that its universal adoption be somehow collectively beneficial, which includes, but is not limited to, being beneficial to the agent. This clearly goes beyond a minimal rationality requirement, since it requires the agent to be concerned with the desirability of the universal adoption of a maxim, in Kantian terms, its suitability as a universal law. On Wood's reading, then, Kant simply conflates these two senses of universality or at least moves without any apparent justification from the first to the second.[11]

As Wood indicates, the distinction between the two senses of universality and the implications of this distinction for Kant's moral theory are nicely illustrated by the case of the rational egoist. Such an egoist could perfectly well affirm the universality of applicability of his governing principle, since he could endorse the claim that it would be reasonable for every other agent to act on it. Nevertheless, the egoist could hardly claim that the universal adoption of this principle would be universally beneficial and, therefore, rationally desirable. Nor could he will egoism as a universal law, since a universe of egoists would make the furtherance of his own ends extremely difficult, if not impossible. Consequently, it is only by the tacit identification of these two senses of universality that Kant can rule out rational egoism or, for that matter, any other principle that meets a minimal rationality requirement.[12] But, if this is indeed the case, it appears that what Aune describes as a gap is in reality a *non sequitur* of "numbing grossness," perhaps comparable to the one attributed to Kant by Strawson and others in connection with the argument of the Second Analogy.

II

If Wood shows somewhat more sensitivity to the implications of this gap or *non sequitur* for Kant's overall project in moral philosophy, Aune at least attempts to provide an argument in Kant's defense before claiming that the gap cannot be filled. Moreover, this argument has both an initial plausibility and a reasonable claim to reflect the line of thought implicit in Kant's own procedure.

The argument provided by Aune turns crucially on his understanding of the formula of autonomy: " 'Never to choose except in such a way that in the same volition the maxims of your choice are also present as universal law' " (Gr 4: 440; 108). In Aune's gloss, this becomes the principle: "It is morally permissible for s to act on m just when s can consistently view himself as laying down a generalized version of m as a universal law."[13] According to Aune, this requires that the agent be able to view himself as making universal laws, that is, as freely legislating, which he takes to be logically equivalent to the requirement that the agent be able to will his maxims as universal laws.[14] Armed with this equivalence, he then proceeds to formulate the argument needed to support the premise that "we conform to universal law when and only when we act on maxims that we 'can will' to be universal laws."[15] The operative assumption is that this premise or something very much like it is implicit in Kant's derivation of the categorical imperative. Consequently, an argument in support of it is necessary if the gap is to be filled.

As a prelude to the presentation and analysis of this argument, Aune notes that since morally relevant actions for Kant are based on maxims, conformity to universal law must be construed as action on a maxim consistent with universal law. Accordingly, the premise that requires support is reformulated to claim: "The maxim m on which s acts is consistent with universal law just when s can will that m should be a universal law."[16] Clearly, if this could be established, then the gap would be filled and the threat of a *non sequitur* removed.

Initially at least, the formula of autonomy (as construed by Aune) does seem to provide the materials necessary to support this premise. To begin with, it is reasonable to assume that (1) "s can consistently will that m is a universal law just when, as a rational legislator, s can consistently adopt m as a universal law."[17] This is because for an autonomous agent to will m as a universal law is just for that agent to adopt it (freely legislate or "lay it down") as such. It also follows that (2) as a rational legislator or autonomous agent, "s can consistently adopt m as a universal law just when m is consistent with what, as a rational being, s freely legislates."[18] In other words, an autonomous agent can consistently adopt as universal laws those maxims and only those maxims that are consistent with the status of being a universal legislator. But since what a universal legislator freely legislates is just the system of universal law, it follows that (3) "s can consistently will that m is a universal law just when m is consistent with universal law."[19] Moreover, this is logically equivalent to the proposition: "The maxim m on which s acts is consistent with universal law just when s can will that m should be a universal law," which is the premise standing in need of justification.

In spite of its initial plausibility, Aune contends that this argument fails. Eschewing the details of his analysis, the root of the difficulty supposedly lies in the "notion of willing that a maxim shall be a law." As Aune sees it, this is because maxims lack the proper "logical form" to be laws. Consequently, it is not a maxim, but, at best, the *generalization* of a maxim that is a candidate for being willed as a universal law (a point Aune builds into his characterization of the formula of autonomy). But this shift from talk about maxims *simpliciter* to talk about generalized maxims once again opens up a gap in the argument; for what must now be shown is that a maxim is consistent with a universal law "when and only when its *generalization* could be willed to be a universal law."[20] Aune concludes, however, that this cannot be shown, for although it is a logical truth that if the generalization of a maxim is consistent with a universal law the maxim is likewise consistent with that law, the converse does not hold. There is, in short, no absurdity in the supposition that a maxim is consistent with universal law when its generalization is not. In support of this latter claim, he notes that,

> for all we know, the only general law bearing on the maxim m might be to the effect that if a person x acts on m, at least one person y must not do so. In this case m itself (or a particular action on m) may be perfectly consistent with universal law even though $G(m)$ is patently incompatible with it.[21]

Aune is correct in his claim that maxims are the wrong logical type to be laws and, therefore, that it is the generalization of the maxim, not the maxim itself, that is to be tested for its conformity to law.[22] Nevertheless, there is certainly something odd about his account of a universal law, at least in the schematic example of such a law introduced in order to undermine the argument. Put simply, "if a person x acts on m, at least one person y must not do so" is not a universal law of the sort that could "bear on a maxim." If a maxim is to be tested for its conformity to law by means of its generalization, then, presumably, the law in question must be conceivable as the product of the generalized maxim. Otherwise, as in the example offered by Aune, there would be no way to relate the maxim to the law. This is implicit in Kant's entire account of the procedure for applying the categorical imperative, but it is especially clear in the formula of autonomy (admitted by Aune to be equivalent to the first formulation), where we are to consider ourselves as legislating universal laws *through* our maxims.

Aune is also to be faulted for his account of the categorical imperative. As already noted, in the *Groundwork* formulation, the imperative requires us to "*Act only on that maxim through which [durch die] you can at the same time [zugleich] will that it should be a universal law.*" Thus, contrary to what Aune maintains, the test is not whether one is able to will the generalization of one's maxim as a universal law; it is rather whether one's maxims are those *"through which"* one can *"at the same time will"* that they should become universal laws. In other words, what the imperative requires is just that one's maxims be capable of including themselves when regarded as universal laws, which is by no means identical to the requirement that one be able to will one's maxim (or even its generalization) as a law.

The basic point is nicely illustrated by the much discussed example of false promising. Contrary to what is sometimes assumed, the contradiction does not lie in the thought of a world in which everyone makes false promises under certain conditions (according to Kant, it would follow that the institution of promising would die out, but there is no contradiction in that); it lies rather in the incompatibility between such a "law" and the intent expressed in the maxim of false promising, namely, to profit by it. Very roughly, the basic idea is that the policy of promising falsely whenever one believes oneself in need would be self-defeating if universally adopted.[23] Thus, a will that willed both this policy and its generalization would be in contradiction with itself.

Nevertheless, these inadequacies in Aune's account do not vitiate his larger thesis regarding the gap in Kant's derivation of the categorical imperative. In order for the gap to be filled, we would need a premise to the effect that a maxim conforms to universal law just in case that maxim can include itself as universal law. But whereas a maxim that can include itself as universal law, for example, the maxim of honesty, clearly conforms to universal law, the converse does not hold. A maxim might very well conform to universal law (indeed, a law produced through the generalization of a maxim) without being able to include itself as universal law. This can likewise be illustrated by the maxim of false promising. This maxim conforms to universal law or, in Wood's terms, has "universality of applicability," since its proponent might perfectly well be prepared to acknowledge that it is reasonable for any rational agent to act on that principle. For the reasons already given, however, this maxim could not include itself as a universal law. Accordingly, the gap in Kant's argument (or perhaps the *non sequitur*) remains.

III

In view of the failure of the *Groundwork* to provide the materials needed to fill the gap in the derivation of the categorical imperative, it is natural to look to the *Critique of Practical Reason* to see if the argument there meets with any more success. The relevant portion of the text is the opening sections of the Analytic (§§1–7), appropriately termed by Beck the "metaphysical deduction" of the moral law.[24]

Employing the synthetic method rather than the analytic method of the *Groundwork*, Kant begins with a brief typology of the principles of practical reason. For present purposes, the most important type of principle is that of a practical law, which may be characterized as a universally and unconditionally valid practical principle, that is, one applicable to all rational agents independently of their particular interests and desires.[25] Although Kant's overriding concern is to show that there must be such a law if pure reason is to be practical (sufficient of itself to determine the will), he also argues in effect that there is only one conceivable candidate for such a law: the categorical imperative. This corresponds to the move in the *Groundwork* from the bare notion of conformity to universal law to the categorical imperative. Thus, if successful, it would fill the gap in the derivation of the categorical imperative.

At first glance, however, this strategy does not appear to be any more promising than the argument from the concept of a categorical imperative. In fact, the problems are similar to those already noted. For one thing, Kant continues to speak about maxims as if they could themselves be laws, thereby conflating the question of what an unconditional practical law might require of maxims (which is what we wish to learn) with the, strictly speaking, nonsensical question of what form our maxims must possess in order to qualify themselves as practical laws.[26] For another, Kant appears guilty of a slide from one sense of "formality" to another, which parallels the previously noted slide between two senses of universality. Thus, after claiming, reasonably enough, that a universally and unconditionally valid practical law must be formal in the sense that it abstracts from any material (object) of the will (§§2 and 4), he proceeds to argue (§5) that it must be formal in the quite different sense that it concerns merely the legislative form of maxims. Since by "legislative form" Kant means suitability as universal law, this slide turns out to be pivotal in the derivation of the categorical imperative.

The first difficulty can be easily remedied by attention to Kant's actual formulation of the categorical imperative: "So act that the maxim of your will could always hold at the same time as a principle establishing universal law" (KprV 5: 30; 31). Since the imperative requires that one's maxim be suitable to serve as a *principle* establishing universal law, not that it itself serve as a universal law, Kant is not here guilty of treating maxims as if they could themselves qualify as laws. Moreover, since a maxim serves (or holds) as a principle establishing universal law just in case its generalization is suitable as a universal law, in testing a given maxim the appropriate universal law would have to be regarded as produced by the generalization of the maxim in question. And this is sufficient to remove the possibility, insisted on by Aune, that the maxim itself, but not its generalization, might be compatible with universal law.

Nevertheless, this still leaves intact the basic difficulty. For all that we have seen so far, an unconditional practical law might require nothing more than that one's maxim be one on which it would be reasonable for any agent to act in relevantly similar circumstances. As a universal requirement, this principle applies to all agents, independently of the empirical content of their maxims, but it is quite distinct from the substantive requirement expressed in the categorical imperative that one's maxim be able to include itself as a "principle establishing universal law." In fact, since both of these requirements are formal in the sense that they do not address the content of one's maxims, this clarification serves to reinforce the suspicion that Kant's move from a minimal, relatively non-problematic rationality requirement to a viable moral principle turns on the conflation of the two senses of "formality" distinguished above.

Fortunately, however, the situation is not as hopeless as it has so far appeared. What has been neglected is that the argument of the second *Critique* does not move straightforwardly from the concept of a practical law to the categorical imperative as the only conceivable candidate for such a law, but rather from this concept *together with* the assumption of transcendental freedom. In other words, the derivation or metaphysical deduction of the categorical imperative in the *Critique of Practical Reason*, unlike that of the *Groundwork*, has transcendental freedom as an explicit premise.

The key steps occur at §§5 and 6 (Problems I and II), where transcendental freedom is injected into the picture for the first time. Kant first claims in effect that transcendental freedom is a necessary condition of the possibility of a will determinable by the mere legislative form of its maxims (§5) and second that it is a sufficient condition of such a will (§6). Together, they yield the result that "freedom and unconditional practical law reciprocally imply each other" (KprV 5: 30; 29), which I have termed the "Reciprocity Thesis."[27]

In order to evaluate this claim, the first step is obviously to determine the nature of transcendental freedom. Although this is itself a notoriously difficult and controversial topic, a brief discussion of the salient points should suffice for present purposes.[28] To begin with, in the *Critique of Practical Reason*, Kant defines transcendental freedom as "independence from everything empirical and hence from nature generally" (KprV 5: 97; 100). This independence is first of all causal, since, *ex hypothesi*, the choices and actions of a transcendentally free agent are not causally necessitated by features of the phenomenal world.

Independence from causal determination by everything empirical (phenomenal) is not, however, sufficient to characterize the nature of transcendental freedom as Kant understands it, since one can readily imagine a contracausally free agent whose freedom is limited in scope to the choice of means to ends that are ultimately dictated to it by its sensuous nature. In Kantian terms, such an agent would be free, yet ineluctably heteronomous. This suggests that in addition to contracausal freedom, transcendental freedom, in the sense in which it is operative in Kant's moral philosophy, also involves what, for lack of a better term, might be characterized as "motivational independence." By this I mean a capacity to recognize and be motivated by reasons to act that do not stem, even indirectly, from the agent's sensuous nature. Only an agent with this capacity is autonomous in the specifically Kantian sense that its will has the property of "being a law to itself (independently of every property belonging to the objects of volition)" (Gr4: 440; 108).

The relevance of this to our present concerns stems from the fact that this conception of transcendental freedom has important implications for the justification of maxims. This is because, assuming motivational independence, the ground of the selection of a maxim can never be located in an impulse, instinct or anything "natural"; rather, it must always be sought in a higher-order maxim and, therefore, in an act of freedom. Consequently, even if one assumes the existence of a natural drive such as self-preservation, a transcendentally free agent is capable of selecting maxims that run directly counter to its dictates. And from this it follows that the mere presence of a drive or inclination does not of itself constitute a sufficient or justifying reason for acting on the basis of it. On the contrary, as I have argued elsewhere, such a reason could be provided only by a universally and unconditionally valid rational principle of choice, that is to say, a practical law.[29]

If sound, the above line of argument suffices to establish the reciprocity between transcendental freedom and unconditional practical law, which is precisely the thesis that Kant affirms in the second *Critique*, but it still does not establish the reciprocity between such freedom and the categorical imperative, which is presumably what is necessary to fill in the gap and complete the metaphysical deduction of this imperative.[30] Nevertheless, it does finally put us in a position to accomplish this task relatively easily.

As a first step in this direction, we must note that in order to be rationally justified, a maxim must not merely conform to an unconditional practical law, it must be adopted *because* it conforms (keeping in mind that for Kant only a transcendentally free agent has the capacity to adopt maxims by virtue of their conformity to such a law). The point here is simple: unless I adopt a maxim at least in part because I regard it as conforming to the requirements of such a law, I cannot appeal to this conformity in justification of my choice.[31] The conformity would be a purely contingent matter, something incidental to my choice and, therefore, irrelevant to its justification.

Moreover, if I am required to adopt a maxim at least in part because of its conformity to universal law or, equivalently, an unconditional practical law, then, clearly, this maxim must be able to include itself as a "principle establishing universal law," which is just to say that the maxim must have what Kant terms "legislative form." In other words, the intent expressed in the maxim must be compatible with the putative universal law produced by the generalization of that maxim. Otherwise, its conformity to such a law could not possibly be the reason (or even a reason) for adopting the maxim in the first place.

Once again, the point can be illustrated by the maxim of false promising. As we have already seen, this maxim, like the more general maxim of rational egoism, of which it is a specification, conforms to universal law and is, therefore, universalizable in the weak sense that one could consistently maintain that it would be reasonable for any rational agent to act according to it. In Wood's terms, it possesses the universality of applicability. Nevertheless, this property of the maxim or, equivalently, its conformity to universal law, cannot function as the reason for adopting it. If its conformity to universal law were the reason, then the agent, considered as rational legislator, would have to be able to will the law produced by the generalization of the maxim, that is to say, the agent would have to be able to will (rationally endorse) a state of affairs in which people routinely made false promises when it was deemed advantageous to do so. This cannot be done in the present case, however, because, as we have already noted, such a will would be in contradiction with itself; it would will a state of affairs that is incompatible with the attainment of its own freely chosen end, viz., profiting by false promising.

Against this it might be objected that an agent could still adopt a maxim such as false promising, even *because* it conforms to universal law, as long as this is taken to mean merely that it is adopted because it is thought to be reasonable for any rational agent to act accordingly. And since it is precisely this type of possibility that must be ruled out if the derivation of the categorical imperative is to succeed, it might be claimed that we are still faced with the very gap with which we started.

This conclusion would, however, be mistaken. To adopt a maxim such as false promising by virtue of its assumed universality of applicability is not to adopt it because of its conformity to universal law, where the latter is understood as an unconditional practical law. On the contrary, such a policy is deemed reasonable in the first place only because of certain presupposed ends, which derive whatever justification they might possess from the agent's desires. Consequently, these desires and not the intrinsic reasonableness or lawfulness of the policy function as the "determining ground of the will." But this conflicts with Kant's central claim that "the legislative form, insofar as it is contained in the maxim, is the only thing which can constitute a determining ground of the [transcendentally free] will" (KprV 5: 29; 30).

By this line of reasoning, then, which turns crucially on the assumption of transcendental freedom, the apparently empty requirement to conform to universal law and, indeed, even the manifestly empty requirement to act only on maxims possessing the universality of applicability, which presumably even the rational egoist could accept, becomes the non-trivial requirement to select only those maxims which you can also regard as suitable to be universal laws. In short, transcendental freedom is precisely the missing ingredient, which bridges the gap between the idea of conformity to universal law as such, or the mere universality of applicability, and the moral law as Kant defines it.

. . .

Admittedly, it seems strange to find freedom injected into the picture at this stage, where the concern is still merely with the content of a categorical imperative (what it could conceivably enjoin) rather than with the condition of its possibility. Nevertheless, it must be kept in mind that this is precisely how Kant himself proceeds in the *Critique of Practical Reason*. Moreover, there is no need to assume at this point any sharp difference between the doctrine of the *Groundwork* and that of the second *Critique*.[32] First, even in the *Groundwork* the derivation of the categorical imperative from the idea of conformity to universal law is preceded by the account of moral worth as pertaining only to actions from duty, by which is meant actions motivated by respect for the law. Since to act from respect for the law is just to take its dictates as the ultimate norm of action, it could be argued that the necessity of adopting maxims because of their conformity to universal law is already operative in the *Groundwork* as an implicit premise in the derivation of the categorical imperative.[33] Second, and perhaps most important, the analytic method of the *Groundwork* requires Kant to formulate the categorical imperative prior to the introduction of the problematic conception of freedom, whereas the synthetic method of the *Critique of Practical Reason* does not impose any such constraint. At least in this respect, then, the latter provides the more perspicuous presentation of the Kantian moral theory, since it makes it clear that, for better or worse, this theory rests on a thick conception of transcendentally free agency rather than a thin, relatively unproblematic conception of rational agency.

11

Kant's doctrine of obligatory ends

Although Kant insists that the supreme principle of morality must be formal and, as such, abstract from all ends, he also attaches considerable significance to ends in the working out of his moral theory. To be sure, in the *Groundwork* the focus is mainly on ends in the negative sense as limiting conditions or restrictions on choice rather than in the positive sense as goals to be pursued or states of affairs to be produced. Thus, in his summary of the argument of *Groundwork II*, Kant explicitly presents the formula of humanity as an end in itself as providing a "condition limiting all merely relative and arbitrary ends" (Gr 4: 436; 104). Nevertheless, in his initial presentation of this formula Kant clearly takes it to require not merely that we respect humanity as an end in itself in the negative sense that we do nothing that conflicts with this status, but also that we act positively in such a way as to promote this end (Gr 4: 430; 98).

In *The Doctrine of Virtue*, this positive side of Kant's theory occupies center stage and becomes the basis for distinguishing the sphere of ethics or *Tugendlehre* from *Rechtslehre*. The essential claim is that ethics goes beyond the doctrine of law, which consists entirely in imposing limiting conditions on choice, by means of its concept of an obligatory end, that is, an end which it is a duty to adopt. Moreover, in the Introduction to this work Kant argues for the general proposition that there must be some such ends, which he then proceeds to identify as one's own perfection and the happiness of others.[1]

Since it is almost universally maintained by commentators that Kant's arguments for negative duties that impose limits on our permissible choices are more persuasive then the claims for positive duties, it is surprising that more attention has not been paid in the literature to this argument for obligatory (positive) ends. Indeed, it seems even more surprising in light of the zeal with which Kantians endeavor to defend Kant against Hegelian-type objections regarding the "emptiness" of the moral law. After all, if even one obligatory end can be derived from the categorical imperative, then the charge that it is not at all action guiding would have to be abandoned; and if, as Kant contends in *The Doctrine of Virtue*, a whole system of duties of virtue can be derived, then the specter of emptiness would be exorcized permanently. But, in spite of the increased attention paid to *The Doctrine of Virtue* in the recent literature on Kant's moral theory, there is amazingly little that deals directly with Kant's central thesis concerning the necessity of obligatory ends.

Accordingly, my primary concern in the present essay is to analyze this thesis and the role that it plays in Kant's moral theory. After showing the inadequacies of Kant's own arguments in support of it, both in their original form and as reconstructed by Nelson Potter, in the first two parts of the essay, I offer in the third part my own reconstruction, based on the assumption of transcendental freedom. In the fourth and final part I argue that, properly construed, this doctrine of obligatory ends marks an important advance over the treatment of imperfect duties in the *Groundwork*.

I

It is possible to distinguish three separate arguments for the existence of obligatory ends in the Introduction to the *Tugendlehre*. The first, which is the least substantial of the three, occurs within the context of Kant's preliminary analysis of the concept of a duty of virtue. After noting that *Rechtslehre* is concerned only with *formal* conditions of outer freedom, Kant affirms that ethics or *Tugendlehre* goes beyond this in affirming a *matter* or object of free choice. This object is an end *(Zweck)*, in fact, an end of pure reason, which, as such, is objectively necessary and, therefore, as far as human beings are concerned, one that it is a duty to adopt. In support of the claim that there must be such an end (presumably, at least one), Kant remarks:

> For since sensuous inclinations tempt [*verleiten*] us to ends (as the matter of choice) which may be contrary to duty, legislative reason can check their influence only by a moral end set up against the ends of inclination, an end that must therefore be given *a priori* independently of inclinations (MS 6: 380–81; 186).

As it stands, this argument, if it is really intended as such, is totally unconvincing. Presumably, its intent is to show the necessity for acknowledging an end in the positive sense (as the matter or object of choice) as a counterweight to inclination-based ends, which, as such, may lead us to act contrary to duty. But even granting the danger and, therefore, the need for morally legislative reason to check inclination, it by no means follows that it can do this only by prescribing an end in the positive sense. On the contrary, the whole thrust of the negative conception of end developed in the *Groundwork* was precisely to provide such a constraint or limiting condition on choice. Accordingly, whatever force this argument possesses depends on ignoring the distinction between the two conceptions of an end that is central to Kant's project in the *Tugendlehre*.

To some extent at least, this difficulty is addressed in the second argument, which focuses on the positive conception of an end. This argument is prefaced

KANT'S DOCTRINE OF OBLIGATORY ENDS

by the premises that every action aims at some end and that the adoption of any end is an act of freedom. Given these premises, which are fundamental to Kant's theory of action, and the additional non-problematic stipulation that a practical principle that prescribes an end unconditionally must be a categorical imperative, Kant contends:

> Now there must be such an end [one prescribed unconditionally] and a categorical imperative corresponding to it. For since there are free actions there must also be ends to which, as their objects, these actions are directed. But among these ends there must be some that are also at the same time (i.e., by their concept) duties. For were there no such ends, then all ends would be valid for practical reason only as means to other ends; and since there can be no action without an end, a *categorical* imperative would be impossible. This would do away with any doctrine of morals (MS 6: 385; 190).

The argument consists of the following five steps:

(1) Since there are free actions, there must also be ends at which these actions are directed.
(2) But among these ends there must be some that are at the same time duties.
(3) If not, then all ends would be valid for practical reason (rationally justifiable) merely as means to other ends.
(4) And since (*ex hypothesi*) every action aims at some end,
(5) a categorical imperative would be impossible.

Although it does not appear as an explicit premise in the argument, the validity of the categorical imperative (at least for actions) is clearly presupposed. Thus, the argument has a *reductio* form, proclaiming the incompatibility of the conjunction of such an imperative and the principle that every action aims at some end with the assumption that all ends are valid for practical reason merely as means to other ends. In other words, the claim is that the conception of a totally instrumental rationality is incompatible with the existence of a categorical imperative and the end-directedness of action.

Unfortunately, this argument likewise fails. For from the fact that there is a categorical imperative for action, taken together with the non-problematic premise that every action aims at some end, it does not follow that there must also be a categorical imperative for ends (in the positive sense). Why could it not be the case that the only duties we have are strict duties or duties of justice? This would leave us a limited, albeit still categorical, morality, one which would involve the conception of objective ends as limiting conditions on action and a familiar set of negative duties expressing these limiting conditions.

Nor is this problem remedied by the third argument, which is explicitly concerned with the justification of the first principle of the doctrine of virtue:

"Act in accordance with a maxim of *ends* that it can be a universal law for everyone to have" (MS 6: 395; 198). Since by a "maxim of ends" is meant simply a policy to make something one's end, and since an end for which there is a universal law requiring its adoption is just an obligatory end, this principle in effect requires us to adopt obligatory ends (whatever they may turn out to be). As such, it clearly assumes that there are such ends, and this is precisely what Kant's argument in support of the principle endeavors to establish. The situation is complicated, however, by Kant's insistence that, although this principle, in contrast to the analytic first principle of right, is synthetic, it "admits of no proof," but merely a "deduction from pure practical reason." This deduction (in lieu of a proof) proceeds as follows:

> What, in the relation of man to himself and others, *can be* an end, that *is* an end for pure practical reason; for pure practical reason is a capacity for ends generally, and for it to be indifferent to ends, that is, to take no interest in them, would be a contradiction, since then it would not determine the maxims for actions either (because every maxim contains an end) and so would not be practical reason. But pure reason can prescribe no ends *a priori* without setting them forth as also duties, and such duties are then called duties of virtue (MS 6: 395; 198).

In addition to the apparently question-begging characterization of pure practical reason as "a capacity for ends generally," this argument turns on the principle that every maxim contains an end.[2] From this it supposedly follows that pure practical reason cannot provide rules for maxims of actions and, therefore, for actions, unless it also does so for ends. But if pure practical reason provides rules for ends or, equivalently, dictates ends, then there are ends that are at the same time duties for finite rational agents such as ourselves.

Just as the previous argument proceeds from the assumption that there is a categorical imperative, this one starts from the equivalent assumption that pure reason is practical. In both cases the essential claim is that to deny the possibility of obligatory ends (or ends of pure practical reason) is to deny this underlying assumption, thus yielding a *reductio*. This result does not follow, however, from the premise (itself unproblematic) that every maxim contains an end. For all that Kant has shown so far, maxims might contain ends, that is, be policies for attaining freely chosen ends; and pure practical reason, in the form of the categorical imperative, might function as the source of rules for these maxims, without also providing rules for the ends we freely adopt. This would leave us with precisely the limited morality discussed previously, in which the categorical imperative functions as a negative, restricting condition on our choice of ends (and the appropriate means thereto) without itself positively dictating any ends that we are obligated to pursue. As before, then, Kant has done nothing to force us to conclude that such a limited conception of morality is incoherent.

II

To a considerable extent, these difficulties with Kant's "deduction" of the concept of an obligatory end are recognized by Nelson Potter, who offers an interesting reconstruction of Kant's argument that is designed to remedy them.[3] Potter focuses on the second of the three arguments, and his key move is to take "free actions" in premise one to refer to the subset of such actions that are motivated by respect for the law or, equivalently, are from duty. Given this, he attributes to Kant the following argument:

> If there is a categorical imperative, then there are or can be cases of action from duty. Since actions are for the sake of an end, so will actions from duty be for the sake of some end. But this cannot be a merely personal end, for in that case the action mentioned in the maxim would be performed for the sake of realizing a merely personal end, and the action would thus not be an action from duty. Nor can the end of such an action be always merely a means to some further end. Morally motivated actions may involve means–ends relations. . . . But in such cases there is always one end that is not valid merely as a means to a further end, viz., our ultimate end, which has been adopted from purely moral motives. If such an end adopted from moral motives were not possible, there would be no maxim of action which could correspond to the categorical imperative. Thus, unless some end is also itself a duty, there can be no categorical imperative corresponding to any maxim, which means that there can be no categorical imperative at all.[4]

Although Potter presents this as a *reductio* from the assumption of the categorical imperative, it seems to be rather a *reductio* from the assumption of action from duty (an assumption that certainly does not figure explicitly in any of Kant's actual arguments). In any event, the nerve of the argument is clearly the premise that in the case of an action from duty the end of that action cannot be merely a means to a further end, unless either that end or some other end further up the line is an obligatory end. In short, every action from duty must involve an end adopted for purely moral reasons, and from this it supposedly follows that if there is such a thing as an action from duty, there must be ends that are at the same time duties.

Unfortunately, this reconstruction does not really improve matters very much. To begin with, the reading of the initial premise is forced. In support of it, Potter merely cites Kant's characterization of freedom in the Introduction to the *Metaphysic of Morals* as the capacity of *Willkür* to act from the motive of duty (MS 6: 226–27; 52).[5] This hardly clinches the matter, however; particularly since it ignores the fact that Kant develops his account of freedom in the *Tugendlehre* specifically in connection with the analysis of end-setting. Indeed, the close connection between the freedom of *Willkür* and end-setting that Kant emphasizes suggests that his concern is to underscore the agent's responsibility for *all* acts of end-setting so as to bring them under the categorical imperative.

Moreover, even granting Potter's reading, the argument still does not work. In order to see this, we need only keep in mind that for Kant ethics requires that even duties of justice or, more generally, perfect duties, which do not involve obligatory ends (in the positive sense), ought to be performed from the duty-motive. Thus, it does not follow that in order for there to be actions from duty these actions must aim either at ends that are themselves dictated by the categorical imperative or at ends that are (at least indirectly) means to such ends. For example, if an agent tells the truth, independently of any prudential considerations, simply because it is regarded as the morally required course of action, then that agent is acting from duty without (even indirectly) aiming at some further end that is itself a duty to pursue. As before, then, there seems to be ample logical space for a morality that includes the categorical imperative and even actions from duty, yet recognizes ends only in the negative sense as limiting conditions on action.

Nor may it be retorted at this point that in the example given the agent is aiming at a morally required end after all: truthfulness. The problem with this response is that it ignores the essentially negative nature of perfect duties (whether of justice or of virtue).[6] Strictly speaking, there is no duty of truthfulness for Kant; there is rather a prohibition against lying, which in the *Tugendlehre* is treated as a perfect duty to oneself considered merely as a moral being (MS 6: 429–31; 225–27). To be sure, this prohibition often requires telling the truth (although, significantly, it can frequently be met by silence), so in that sense even negative duties are positive. Nevertheless, in refraining from lying from moral considerations, one is not endeavoring to bring about a state of affairs (an end in the positive sense); rather, one is respecting the humanity in oneself and others (ends in the negative sense). Thus, to claim that even such actions aim at an end that is in some sense necessary is to save the inference from the categorical imperative to obligatory ends at the cost of undermining the larger thesis that it is intended to serve: that in addition to the narrow, perfect duties to respect ends in the negative sense there are also broad, imperfect duties to adopt ends in the positive sense.

III

Although Potter's reconstruction fails, he is to be credited for calling attention to the fact that freedom plays a prominent role in at least the second of Kant's arguments, a fact that was largely ignored in our initial analysis. Accordingly, it is worthwhile considering whether the argument can be viewed in a more favorable light, if freedom is included as an explicit premise. The problem, however, is that it is not immediately obvious just what role freedom is supposed to play. Kant prefaces the second argument with the account of the connection between end-setting and freedom, but the only use that he appears to make of it is to claim that since there are free actions there must be ends at which these actions aim. From that point on, the argument proceeds without any further explicit reference to freedom. And, of course, freedom does not appear to play any role at all in the other two arguments.

In spite of these obstacles, it is possible to provide a reconstruction of the argument that is true both to the text of the *Tugendlehre* and the overall structure of Kant's moral theory and that also gives an essential role to freedom. The argument assumes that by freedom is to be understood absolute or transcendental freedom, which Kant defines in the *Critique of Practical Reason* as "independence from everything empirical and hence from nature generally" (KprV 5: 97; 100). As such, it is similar to the one I have elsewhere presented in connection with what I term Kant's "Reciprocity Thesis," that is, the claim that "[transcendental] freedom and unconditional practical law reciprocally imply each other" (KprV 5: 29; 29–30).[7] Underlying the argument are two key premises, which I have argued for in connection with the above and shall simply assume here: (1) since a (transcendentally) free agent is also a rational agent, the choices of such an agent are subject to a justification requirement; that is to say, they must be justified by means of a principle that would apply to all other rational agents in relevantly similar circumstances; and (2) the moral law, as the sole unconditioned practical law, furnishes this principle. Given these premises, it follows that if the ends of a rational agent are freely chosen (which *ex hypothesi* they must be), then the choice of these ends, as well as the choice of the appropriate means to attain them, must be justified or validated by means of the moral law.

The question then becomes how the moral law can justify or validate the choice of ends as opposed to actions. To begin with, since to make something one's end requires acting in ways designed to bring that end about (or at least a willingness to act in such ways), it is clear that if the moral law can prohibit actions it can likewise prohibit ends. For example, it rules out ends such as power over the lives of others, since acting in pursuit of such an end would necessarily require treating others merely as means. Correlatively, some ends, most notably those "subjective" or personal ends in terms of which we define our happiness, can be validated by the moral law as permissible, subject to the condition that we do not violate any duties in pursuit of them.[8] The law thus grants to such ends a conditionally good or permissible status. Otherwise, we would be forced to attribute to Kant the absurdly rigoristic view that the only rationally justifiable ends are those that we have a duty to adopt.

What is noteworthy about ends that are justified (or proscribed) in this manner is that they all stem ultimately from inclination (in the broad sense).[9] This does not mean that such ends are not freely chosen, but rather that in choosing them the will (practical reason) validates, as it were, the claims of inclination.[10] Accordingly, under this scenario the moral law does not of itself provide a sufficient reason to choose or, in Kant's jargon, *pure* reason is not practical. On the contrary, an inclination is presupposed as a condition under which the end is desirable to the agent; apart from the presence of an inclination, the agent would have no reason to choose the end. Thus, with respect to such ends, the law functions merely negatively as a necessary (limiting) condition, ruling out the pursuit of some of them, allowing others as permissible, and stipulating restricting conditions on the means to be used in pursuit of the permissible ends.

It is just at this point that transcendental freedom reenters the picture. The crucial factor is the incompatibility of the operative assumption that all ends are justified in this way or, equivalently, that an inclination must be presupposed if an agent is to have a sufficient reason to adopt an end, with transcendental freedom. Given the Reciprocity Thesis, this would also make it incompatible with the moral law. To recapitulate what I have argued at length elsewhere, the essential feature of transcendental freedom that is relevant to the present issue is that it involves not merely a causal independence, but also what, for want of a better term, I call "motivational independence." In other words, a transcendentally free agent is free not simply in the familiar contra-causal or incompatibilist sense, but also in the sense of having a positive capacity to determine itself to act on the basis of reasons that do not stem, even indirectly, from the agent's sensuous nature.[11] This is at the heart of Kant's positive definition of freedom as autonomy in *Groundwork III*. And since such self-determination is inseparable from the setting of ends, a transcendentally free agent must have the capacity to set ends for itself independently of any appeal to inclination.

But if a transcendentally free agent has the capacity to set ends for itself in this manner, then the moral law, as the supreme norm of transcendentally free agency, cannot be limited merely to the functions of proscribing and permitting ends; it must also prescribe or legislate the choice of ends. This follows from the negation of the assumption that an inclination is required in order to have a sufficient reason to set an end, which, in turn, is entailed by the claim to be rebutted that the moral law is limited to the proscriptive and permissive functions with respect to ends. In short, if end-setting by pure practical reason independently of inclination is possible (as it must be if we are transcendentally free), then pure practical reason must also serve as a law for ends. Moreover, if pure practical reason serves as a law for ends, then any ends prescribed by this law are obligatory. Finally, it follows from this that among the ends of a [transcendentally] free agent "there must also be some that are at the same time (i.e., by their concept) duties" (MS 6: 385; 190).

Expressed schematically, the argument is a *reductio* from transcendental freedom consisting of the following six steps:

(1) Assume that for any potential end x, an inclination or desire for x is necessary in order to have a sufficient reason to choose x (entailed by the

denial of the claim that the moral law or pure practical reason is capable of dictating ends in the positive sense).
(2) There is transcendental freedom (*ex hypothesi*).
(3) But this is incompatible with (1), which means that there are some x's (at least one) that we have sufficient reason to choose independently of inclination.
(4) But inclination (in the broad sense) and pure practical reason are the only sources of reasons to act or adopt ends (Kant's motivational dualism, a fundamental assumption of his moral psychology).
(5) Therefore, pure practical reason must of itself provide sufficient reason for adopting some ends, that is, it prescribes these ends.
(6) Such ends are at the same time duties (by definition).

Notice that this argument does not entail nor does Kant claim either that *all* of the ends of a transcendentally free agent must be regarded as duties or that the choice of an inclination-based end is of itself incompatible with the exercise of transcendental freedom. The claim is only that a transcendentally free agent cannot consistently regard *all* of its ends as necessarily of that nature because that state of affairs would be incompatible with that agent's freedom or autonomy. Consequently, ample room is left for the inclusion of permissible subjective ends based on inclination and, more generally, for inclination-based or heteronomous agency.

Moreover, it cannot be objected at this point that the argument shows merely that pure practical reason has the *capacity* to legislate ends but not that it actually does so. This distinction between a capacity and its exercise would be in place if we were considering *Willkür* or "executive will," which is free to accept or reject the dictates of morality. It is completely out of place, however, with respect to *Wille* or "legislative will," which is here in consideration.[12] To attribute to *Wille* a capacity to legislate is equivalent to attributing an actual legislation, just as the attribution of a "capacity" to explain a given phenomenon to a law of nature is equivalent to claiming that the phenomenon is, in fact, explained on the basis of the given law. Presumably, this was what Kant had in mind, when, in a previously cited passage, he remarks, "What ... *can* be an end *is* an end for pure practical reason" (MS 6: 395; 198). This makes perfect sense if we keep in mind that pure practical reason in this context just is *Wille*.

Finally, this enables us to see just what is wrong with Kant's own formulation of his *reductio* argument. Clearly, the problem is that Kant moves too quickly from the premise that the moral law cannot be concerned merely with actions as means and must, therefore, in *some sense* also relate to freely chosen ends, to the conclusion that it must prescribe these ends as duties.[13] In so doing, he neglects the distinction, crucial to his own theory, between the function of the moral law in ruling out certain ends (as well as actions) on the grounds that they conflict with rational agency as an end in itself (in the negative sense) and its function in prescribing certain ends (in the positive sense) as duties. And this, in turn, leads him to neglect the possibility that the moral law might function to validate or proscribe ends without actually prescribing them. As already indicated, Potter's reconstruction suffers from a similar defect, although it does possess the great virtue of underscoring the essential role that freedom plays in the argument.

Admittedly, the argument provided here proceeds on the basis of strong and highly controversial premises. In particular, it presupposes the validity of the categorical imperative, the practicality of pure reason and the reality of (transcendental) freedom. For present purposes, however, this need not bother us, since in the *Tugendlehre* Kant is explicitly arguing on the basis of the claim made in the *Critique of Practical Reason* that the categorical imperative has been secured as a "fact of reason," which in turn serves as the basis for a deduction of freedom.[14] Presumably, that is why he characterizes it as a "deduction from pure practical reason" rather than as a proof. In any event, our only concern up to this point has been to determine whether, even given all of this, Kant is entitled to claim that there must be obligatory ends, and this question at least has been answered affirmatively.

IV

We now turn to the question of the significance of this result for Kant's moral theory. The consideration of this issue requires: (1) the determination of which ends are to be regarded as duties and for what reason; (2) an analysis of just what is involved in making something one's end; and (3) an examination of the relationship between this new doctrine of obligatory ends and the more familiar treatment of broad or imperfect duties in the *Groundwork*. Until we receive further information on these matters, it is impossible to determine what significance is to be attached to the vague claim that we must acknowledge some obligatory ends.

The first question can be dealt with easily. The two generic obligatory ends which Kant affirms, namely, one's own perfection and the happiness of others, are derived from the conception of the *Summum Bonum*. More specifically, they are precisely those features of the *Summum Bonum* which it is within our capacity to promote. That is why rather than arguing in a straightforward way that we have an obligation to include each of these among our ends, Kant first explains why we cannot regard our own happiness and the perfection of others as obligatory ends and concludes from this that we must regard our own perfection and the happiness of others as such ends (MS 6: 385–86; 190–91). The operative assumption, taken over from the *Critique of Practical Reason* but never made explicit in the *Tugendlehre*, is that the *Summum Bonum*, consisting of the combination of complete virtue and happiness, is the unconditioned object or system of ends of pure practical reason. Accordingly, our obligatory ends would be just those features of the system of ends which we are capable of bringing about or at least promoting.[15]

Since Kant's account of the *Summum Bonum*, including the claim that we have a duty to work for its realization, is widely regarded as the most problematic part of his moral theory, this result is somewhat disappointing.[16] But since Kant later provides independent arguments for the obligations to include these among our ends, the situation is perhaps not as bad as it might appear. Of greater interest is the correspondence of this result with the two imperfect duties affirmed in the *Groundwork*. This correspondence naturally leads one to ask if this new line of argument, by way of the concept of an obligatory end, really marks an advance over the account in the earlier work. It is in order to answer this question that we must consider just what is involved in making something one's end.

In spite of his emphasis on the connection between end-setting and freedom, Kant does not deal explicitly with this crucial question. He does answer it implicitly, however, in his account of the nature of an obligatory end. Only the concept of such an end, he writes, "establishes a law for the maxims of actions by subordinating the subjective end (that everyone has) to the objective end (that everyone ought to make his own)" (MS 6: 389; 193). From this and similar passages, it seems reasonably clear that to make something one's end is just to adopt a maxim to act in ways which will serve to realize this end.[17] In fact, it is precisely because ethical duties are requirements to adopt maxims rather than to perform (or refrain from) particular actions that they (in contrast to juridical duties) are of "wide obligation," allowing "a play-room *(latitudo)* for free choice in following (observing) the law" (MS 6: 390; 194).

We can see more concretely what this involves by considering briefly the duty of beneficence, understood as the requirement to include the permissible ends of others among one's own ends.[18] Since it is merely the adoption of the maxim that is required, this does not involve (except perhaps under certain limiting conditions) an obligation to perform any particular beneficent act.[19] Here is where the "play-room" occurs; the beneficent person, although committed to the policy of helping others, is free to determine under what conditions, to whom and to what extent such help is to be offered. Nevertheless, it does involve a readiness to help others, an openness to their needs and a willingness to act when the occasion requires it. One cannot adopt a maxim without being ready and willing to act on it, indeed, except perhaps in very rare circumstances (such as a sincere moral conversion followed by sudden death), without actually acting on it. In fact, this is just the difference between willing an end and merely wishing for it.[20]

Moreover, as Marcia Baron, following the lead of Warner Wick, has emphasized, the commitment to beneficence is also broad in the sense of being open-ended. She is also careful to note, however, that this is not be taken in the manner of Susan Wolff's example of the "moral saint," who strives to produce as much happiness in the world as possible; it is rather that one cannot regard the requirement as something that can be discharged by a certain amount of beneficent action, that is, "as something to get out of the way" (like mowing the lawn), so that one can then get on with what one really cares about.[21] Someone whose beneficent acts stem from the latter mind-set does not have the maxim of beneficence or, equivalently, has not made beneficence her end.

It is illuminating to contrast this picture of beneficence as an end with the account in the *Groundwork*, where the duty of beneficence is treated first in connection with the "contradiction in will" test of the categorical imperative. The question there is whether an "attitude" (*Denkungsart*) of complete indifference to others could hold as a universal law of nature. Kant maintains that this could perfectly well be *conceived* as a universal law of nature but that a rational agent could not *will* such a law. As he puts it:

For a will which decided in this way would be in conflict with itself, since many a situation might arise in which the man needed love and sympathy from others, and in which, by such a law of nature sprung from his own will, he would rob himself of all hope of the help he wants for himself (Gr 4: 423; 91).

Although this argument has been subject to considerable criticism, our present concern is not with its cogency, but rather with the question of what, assuming its cogency, it would show. Now, on the most charitable reading, all that it can be taken to have shown is that it would be morally unworthy and, therefore, impermissible to adopt a maxim of complete indifference or nonbeneficence.[22] In short, its force, like that of the arguments for perfect duties falling under the "contradiction in conception test," is entirely negative, ruling out the maxim of non-beneficence. Moreover, this limited result is precisely what one should expect if, as seems reasonable, one takes the universalizability test as primarily concerned with the permissibility of maxims.

The problem, however, is there are at least two quite distinct ways of rejecting a maxim of non-beneficence. One way is to adopt the contrary maxim of beneficence, that is, to take a genuine concern with the well-being of others, a concern that may be expressed in a variety of ways and in different degrees, but that virtually always involves some beneficent action.[23] Another is to acknowledge a requirement to act beneficently, but to construe this as something to be gotten out of the way, to be discharged as painlessly as possible, so as to be able to get on to one's real projects. Clearly, the former course is morally preferable and Baron is surely correct in pointing out that someone who opts for the latter does not have a maxim of beneficence.

What she fails to note, perhaps simply because it is not germane to her project, is that the contradiction in conception test of the categorical imperative is incapable of discriminating between these two cases. Both pass the test, since both involve a rejection of a policy of non-beneficence; both, therefore, are permissible maxims. Moreover, the same can be said, *mutatis mutandis*, in the case of the duty to develop one's talents. Here again, the test might be taken as sufficient to rule out a maxim of slothfulness (assuming that the *complete* neglect of one's natural endowments cannot be willed as a universal law), but this is compatible with both a genuine commitment to self-perfection and a grudging recognition that *something* must be done. In short, the categorical imperative, of itself, is incapable of generating such broad, positive duties.

Such a conclusion does not necessarily amount to a criticism of Kant, however, since he claims in the *Groundwork* to be concerned merely with the formulation and establishment of the first principle of morality, the actual derivation of duties being reserved for the system of moral philosophy, that is, the then merely projected metaphysics of morals.[24] This is especially true, if, as suggested, one takes the universalizability test as primarily a test of the permissibility of maxims. Nevertheless, it does show that an auxiliary principle is required for the derivation of positive duties, which is precisely what is provided by the synthetic first principle of the doctrine of virtue: "Act in accordance with a maxim of *ends* that it can be a universal law for everyone to have" (MS6: 395; 198). Assuming that there are such ends (which is just what the "deduction" of this principle endeavors to show) and that the happiness of others is among them, it follows that we are obligated not merely to reject the maxim of non-beneficence, understood as a kind of principled unconcern with the well-being of others, but also to adopt the contrary maxim of beneficence. And, of course, the same reasoning applies to the obligation to develop one's talents or self-perfection. Thus, the first principle of the doctrine of virtue takes us beyond what the categorical imperative alone can accomplish. More specifically, it enables us to apply this imperative to the choice of ends, something that could not be accomplished within the framework of the *Groundwork*.[25]

It must be admitted, however, that it is not so clear that Kant himself saw the situation in just this way. Thus, already in the *Groundwork*, in discussing beneficence under the formula of humanity, Kant insists that the requirement to treat rational agents as ends in themselves positively obliges us to endeavor to further the ends of others: "For the ends of a subject who is an end in himself must, if this conception is to have its *full* effect in me, be also, as far as possible, *my* ends" (MS4: 430; 98). Although this notion of the conception of humanity as an end itself as having its "full effect" (presumably in contrast to its merely partial effect as a limiting condition) is obscure and unanalyzed, Kant is here clearly taking the formula of humanity as requiring us to include beneficence among our ends. As such, it goes beyond what we have just seen may be legitimately derived from the first formulation: the rejection of the maxim of non-beneficence. But, since Kant viewed these formulas as equivalent, this suggests that he might very well have thought that this duty could be derived directly from the non-universalizability of the contrary maxim (as if the opposed maxims were contradictories rather than merely contraries).

Moreover, this cannot be dismissed as a confusion limited to the *Groundwork*, since in the "official" argument for the duty of beneficence in the *Tugendlehre*, Kant once again appeals to the universalizability criterion to rule out non-beneficence and concludes immediately from this that "[T]he maxim of common interest, of beneficence toward those in need, is a universal duty of men, just because they are to be considered fellow men, that is, rational beings with needs, united by nature in one dwelling place so that they can help one another" (MS6: 453; 247).

Fortunately, Kant provides another argument for the duty of beneficence in the *Tugendlehre*, one which is closely connected with the concept of obligatory ends and does not turn on the non-universalizability of non-beneficence. The premise of this alternative line of argument is the inseparability of our self-love from our need to be loved by others, as a result of which "we make ourselves an end for others." From this, Kant concludes, by way of the categorical imperative, that I cannot regard this requirement as binding on others unless I take it as a universal law applicable to me as well (MS6: 393; 196–97).

The questionable feature of this argument is the initial premise about the inseparability of our self-love from our dependence on others, which is a variant of the premise of the corresponding argument in the *Groundwork*. Once again, however, our concern is not with the cogency of this argument, but with its form. In addition to avoiding the problematic move from the rejection of non-beneficence to the affirmation of the contrary, it appeals to the conception of persons as end-setters and applies the universalizability test directly to these ends. But it cannot make the latter move without presupposing the conception of obligatory ends and, therefore, the first principle of the doctrine of virtue. Moreover, the corresponding argument for (natural) perfection as an obligatory end is based explicitly on the conception of persons as end-setters (MS6: 391–92; 195–96). Consequently, it too makes use of (although it does not mention) the first principle of the doctrine of virtue.

In light of these considerations, we may, I think, conclude that, although Kant is far from clear on the point, the conception of an obligatory end and the first principle of the doctrine of virtue with which it is inseparably connected do, in fact, play a significant role in the *Tugendlehre*, providing the basis for a "material" ethic that goes well beyond the "formalism" of the *Groundwork*. At the same time, however, it must also be kept in mind that this result rests ultimately on certain substantive and highly controversial doctrines, most notably that of transcendental freedom.

12

Reflections on the banality of (radical) evil: A Kantian analysis

In her reply to Gershom Scholem's criticism of *Eichmann in Jerusalem: A Report on the Banality of Evil,* Hannah Arendt writes:

It is indeed my opinion now that evil is never "radical," that it is only extreme, and that it possesses neither depth nor any demonic dimension. It can overgrow and lay waste the whole world precisely because it spreads like a fungus on the surface. It is "thought-defying," as I said because thought tries to reach some depth, to go to the roots, and the moment it concerns itself with evil, it is frustrated because there is nothing. That is its "banality." Only the good has depth and can be radical.[1]

Arendt is here contrasting her post-Eichmann view of evil with that of her earlier work, *The Origins of Totalitarianism* (1951). In that work she had explicitly characterized the evil perpetrated by the totalitarian systems of Hitler and Stalin as "radical" in the sense of being "beyond the pale of human sinfulness."[2] In fact, this conception of radical evil underlies the central thesis of this work, namely, that the evil of those regimes is a peculiar phenomenon of the twentieth century, qualitatively distinct from anything that had preceded it in history, including the worst tyrannies of the past. As Young-Bruehl notes, Arendt there seems to have adopted three criteria for such evil: it must be unforgivable, unpunishable and rooted in motives so base as to be beyond human comprehension.[3] Appealing to the etymology of the term 'radical,' Arendt also contends that such evil must be viewed as rooted in some original fault in human nature. Finally, in the same context she asserts that the entire philosophical tradition was unable to conceive of radical evil. Interestingly enough, this includes even Kant, whom she says, "must have suspected the existence of this evil even though he immediately rationalized it in the concept of a 'perverted ill will' that could be explained by comprehensible motives."[4]

As Young-Bruehl makes clear, the change in the Eichmann book concerns mainly the matter of motivation (the third criterion). The Nazi atrocities remain both unforgivable and unpunishable; but instead of viewing them as stemming from inhuman, diabolical motives, Arendt now sees Eichmann's crimes (and by extension, those of the Nazi regime as a whole) as essentially motiveless. Thus, she notes at one point that far from being a Macbeth, Iago or Richard III, "[E]xcept for an extraordinary diligence in looking out for his personal advancement, he [Eichmann] had no motives at all."[5] And with the rejection of anything like diabolical motivation goes the need to assume some deep fault in human nature which could account for its possibility.[6] Accordingly, evil loses its depth dimension and becomes simply banal.

Ironically, by rejecting the notion of diabolical motivation Arendt came closer to the genuinely Kantian conception of radical evil than she was in her earlier work, in which she embraced the concept, if not Kant's understanding of it. She apparently failed to realize this, however, because of a misunderstanding of what radical evil meant for Kant and the systematic role it plays in his moral theory. Radical evil does not refer, as Arendt seems to have assumed throughout, to a particularly great or deeply rooted demonic evil.[7] It refers rather to the root of *all* moral evil, whatever its extent. In Kantian terms, it refers to the universal propensity [*Hang*] to evil, which serves as the precondition of the adoption of maxims contrary to the moral law and, therefore, of evil actions in the familiar sense. Moreover, properly construed, Kant's analysis of evil not only shares certain important structural features with the evil attributed by Arendt to Eichmann, it also provides a philosophical framework in which this latter account of evil can be further analyzed, if not fully understood. Or so I shall argue.

The discussion is divided into four parts. The first sketches the main features of Arendt's conception of the banality of evil as exemplified in the persona of Eichmann. The second considers Kant's denial of the possibility of a diabolical human will in relation both to his own theory and to Arendt's similar denial, which she erroneously takes as equivalent to a denial of radical evil. The third explores the connection between radical evil and self-deception, which is also an important feature in Arendt's account. Finally, the fourth briefly considers and rejects the objection that Eichmann cannot be condemned as evil by Kantian standards, since he scrupulously obeyed the law of the land.

I

According to Arendt, what was most striking about the defendant, Adolf Eichmann, and what created the greatest perplexity for the Israeli judges at his trial, was precisely his chilling ordinariness. Far from the moral monster, the depraved, demonic anti-semite, driven by a passionate desire to exterminate Jews, which the prosecution attempted to depict him as being and which the world had taken him to be, Eichmann appeared as a totally unremarkable human being. As she succinctly puts it, "The trouble with Eichmann was precisely that so many were like him, and that the many were neither perverted nor sadistic, that they were, and still are terribly and terrifyingly normal."[8]

An essential feature of this terrifying normalcy is the claim to have lived according to a moral code, indeed, by no less a code than the Kantian. Thus, we learn that Eichmann repeatedly insisted that, at least up until the time at which he was given the responsibility for carrying out the "Final Solution," he had followed the categorical imperative. And, as Arendt notes, in response to the questioning of an incredulous judge, Eichmann was even able to provide a passable characterization of the categorical imperative and once remarked that he had read the *Critique of Practical Reason*.[9] How, then, could such a person have committed such heinous crimes? And having done so, how could he be so free of a guilty conscience? These are the questions with which Arendt attempts to grapple without any appeal to the conception of radical evil or any comparable philosophical or theological construct.

Now, one might argue that, objectively speaking, all of this is readily understandable precisely in terms of the true nature of the "moral code" to which Eichmann and presumably many other Nazis subscribed. Although Eichmann claimed to be following the categorical imperative, it was clearly a grotesquely distorted form of this imperative. According to Arendt, it amounted to the principle "Act as if the principle of your actions were at the same time that of the legislator or law of the land," which, she suggests, is virtually equivalent to what Hans Frank, the Nazi governor in Poland, had termed "the categorical imperative in the Third Reich": "Act in such a way that the *Führer,* if he knew your action, would approve it."[10]

Moreover, this perverted understanding of duty was reflected in Eichmann's legal defense. Thus, the central claim was not that he was merely following superior orders, which he could not disobey without putting himself in great danger (a matter of *casus necessitatis*), but rather that he was obeying the *legal* order, the law of the land as manifest in the will of the *Führer*.[11] Leaving aside, then, the perverted nature of the principles to which Eichmann subscribed, it would seem that, in his eyes at least, these principles provided an explicitly *moral* justification for his actions. He was doing the morally required thing, not simply what he had to do in order to survive or even to avoid seriously unpleasant consequences. More than that, he was identifying his own will with the principle behind this law, which, in his distorted understanding of the categorical imperative, is precisely what morality requires.[12] No wonder, then, that he did not have a guilty conscience; that while acknowledging his acts, he consistently proclaimed himself to be "Not guilty in the sense of the indictment."[13]

Nevertheless, far from clarifying matters, this serves merely to underscore the central problem, which is just how such a perverted moral standpoint is possible in the first place. At the heart of Arendt's answer, which is scattered throughout the book rather than located in a single section, is her claim that it was the "sheer thoughtlessness" of Eichmann, which she distinguishes from stupidity, which prevented him from ever fully realizing what he was doing and "predisposed him to become one of the greatest criminals of that period."[14] Moreover, for Arendt this thoughtlessness is hardly unique to Eichmann, since

IDEALISM AND FREEDOM

she seems to regard it as a characteristic of virtually all Germans of the Nazi period.[15] What differentiates Eichmann from the many like him, who took no overt part in the "Final Solution," are merely the circumstances in which he happened to find himself.

In order to understand what Arendt terms "the strange interdependence of thoughtlessness and evil,"[16] it is first of all necessary to determine the precise sense in which she construes "thoughtlessness." Clearly, we cannot take it in the usual sense in which thoughtlessness is regarded as a moral failure: as simple inconsiderateness. It would be a misstatement of grotesque proportions to claim that the problem with the Nazis was that they were "inconsiderate"! Equally clearly, it cannot mean a complete neglect of moral considerations. As we have seen, the enigmatic feature of Eichmann's character was not a total lack of moral reflection, but the truncated, grossly distorted form which that reflection took. If Arendt's portrait is accurate (and for purposes of this discussion I am assuming that it is), it would seem that the usual moral considerations regarding appropriate means were in place, but combined with a complete failure to question the nature of the end for which these means were intended. How else can one understand the fact that, while unconcerned about the morality of exterminating millions of Jews, Eichmann was apparently insistent about avoiding causing any unnecessary suffering?[17]

According to Arendt, the unique and pernicious kind of thoughtlessness underlying this attitude consists in a total incapacity to look at things from the other's point of view.[18] It is this incapacity, then, which perhaps one might characterize as an incapacity even to recognize that the other has a point of view, that accounts for Eichmann's peculiar form of moral blindness. And this makes perfect sense *as far as it goes,* for it surely must be a failure to recognize the personhood of the other, in Kantian terms the other's status as an end in itself, that underlies the unprecedented crime of genocide. Moreover, only such thoughtlessness, as contrasted with sheer maliciousness, could account for the above noted combination of a concern to avoid unnecessary suffering with a total unconcern about killing on a mass scale.

As is apparent from her posthumously published *Lectures on Kant's Political Philosophy,* Arendt's analysis of Eichmann's thoughtlessness in terms of an incapacity to recognize the point of view of the other has deep Kantian roots. These roots stem from the *Critique of Judgment,* however, rather than the *Critique of Practical Reason* or *Religion within the Limits of Reason Alone.* Arendt's project in these lectures is to expound and analyze Kant's "unwritten political philosophy," which she finds in the third *Critique.* Central to this philosophy is the account of reflective judgment, particularly the judgment of taste, which presupposes the capacity to abstract from one's own interest and consider the aesthetic object (or its representation) from a universal point of view. Basing her analysis largely on the account of the *sensus communis* in §40, Arendt takes the capacity to judge in this way or, in Kant's terms, to adopt the maxim of an "extended way of thinking," as essential not simply to aesthetics, but to moral and political life.[19] And viewed in this context, Eichmann's thoughtlessness can be seen as the extreme case of the failure of judgment, a failure which Arendt insists was endemic to the whole Nazi era.[20]

More germane to our present concerns, this inability to judge (at one point Arendt equates it with an inability to imagine[21]) is deemed inseparable from an inability to communicate (another familiar third *Critique* theme). In fact, one of the most striking features of Arendt's portrait of Eichmann, one to which she returns again and again, is his use of language. Eichmann could speak only in clichés.[22] This lent a certain comic quality to his performance before and during the trial, making him often seem like a clown, since he frequently expressed himself with ridiculous *non sequiturs*. But Arendt's deeper point is that the "language rules" used by Eichmann and his fellow Nazis were truly invidious rather than comic, playing a large role in blinding them to the moral implications of their acts. As Arendt's account indicates, it is not that they literally did not know what they were doing, it is rather that their use of language enabled them to take their own acts under descriptions which obfuscated their true moral status.[23] Nowhere, of course, is this more evident than in their use of the horrible phrase "Final Solution," which suggests that the extermination of millions of human beings is, at bottom, nothing more than a technical problem.

Given this analysis of thoughtlessness and obfuscation through language, it is not surprising that Arendt locates the real basis of Eichmann's attitude, and that of the Nazis as a whole, in self-deception. To be sure, at one point she asks rhetorically: "Is this a textbook case of bad faith, of lying self-deception combined with outrageous stupidity? Or is it simply the case of the unrepentant criminal . . . ?"[24] Nevertheless, her position is clear; she characterizes Eichmann's own capacity for self-deception as itself "criminal" and notes that, in general, the practice of self-deception by the Nazis had become so commonplace that it was "almost a moral prerequisite for survival."[25] Presumably, her point is that self-deception becomes "criminal" and a "moral prerequisite for survival" by enabling its practitioners to avoid facing both the true moral character of their deeds and their ultimate responsibility for them.

At this point, however, her analysis effectively stops. Although she does link Eichmann's self-deception to that of the German people as a whole, suggesting that the latter somehow made the former possible or at least easier, she does not really pursue the question of the grounds of individual responsibility for such criminal thoughtlessness and self-deception. Admittedly, this procedure is consistent with the historico-sociological, anti-metaphysical thrust of her book as well as with her views about evil. Clearly, if evil is truly banal in Arendt's sense, if it is a surface phenomenon without depth, then there is no need to pursue the topic any further.[26] Nevertheless, this refusal to continue really begs the question regarding radical evil, which is perhaps the point of

IDEALISM AND FREEDOM

Scholem's complaint that Arendt's appeal to the banality of evil in her discussion of Eichmann remained a mere "catchword," standing in need of philosophical analysis.[27] In any event, it seems to be worthwhile considering whether the Kantian conception of radical evil offers any resources for such an analysis. One reason to think that it might is that Kant, like Arendt, explicitly denies the possibility (at least for human beings) of a diabolical will.

II

Since Kant's rejection of a diabolical will is an essential feature of his account of radical evil, whereas Arendt appeals to it in her denial that evil can be radical, it is hardly surprising that they arrived at this shared view by quite different routes. For Arendt, it seems to have been largely a psychological claim, resulting from her experience of and reflection upon Eichmann, as well as her continued study of the literature regarding the Nazi period. For Kant, by contrast, it is clearly an *a priori* matter, following directly from his thesis that we must somehow still respect the categorical imperative even while violating it. Thus, already in the *Groundwork,* after noting that in the transgression of duty we do not actually will that our immoral maxim should become a universal law, but merely "take the liberty of making an exception to it of ourselves" (Gr4: 424; 91), he goes on to reflect:

This procedure, though in our impartial judgment it cannot be justified, proves none the less that we in fact recognize the validity of the categorical imperative and (with all respect for it) merely permit ourselves a few exceptions which are, as we pretend, inconsiderable and apparently forced upon us (Gr4: 425; 92).

In *Religion within the Limits of Reason Alone,* where Kant for the first time explicitly thematizes about evil, this all too human tendency to make exceptions for oneself, to quibble with the stern dictates of the law on behalf of self-interest, is inflated into an innate (yet freely chosen) propensity to evil. The propensity is not to reject the law altogether, to abandon all moral considerations (this is deemed incompatible with our predisposition to the good); it is rather the propensity to subordinate moral considerations to those stemming from self-love. In short, it is to reverse priorities or, in Kant's terms, "the order of incentives." The claim is not that we always in fact do this, but rather that even the best of us have such a tendency; that it is ineliminable or "rooted in human nature" and that we must constantly struggle against it. It is against this background of ideas that Kant writes:

Man (even the most wicked) does not under any maxim whatsoever, repudiate the moral law in the manner of a rebel (renouncing obedience to it). The law, rather, forces itself upon him irresistibly by virtue of his moral predisposition; and were no other incentive working in opposition, he would adopt the law into his supreme maxim as the sufficient determining ground of his will [*Willkür*] (Rel6: 36; 31).

This conception of radical evil is actually the logical consequence of the combination of two essential features of Kant's theory of freedom. One, which I term the "Incorporation Thesis," holds that inclinations themselves do not constitute sufficient reasons or incentives to act for a free agent. They only become such insofar as an agent takes one up or, as Kant puts it, "incorporates it into his maxim" (Rel 6: 23, 19), which means that an agent spontaneously makes it his rule to act on a given inclination in certain circumstances.[28] Otherwise expressed, inclinations do not come with an inherent motivational force, by virtue of which they can move us to act against our will. On the contrary, we are moved to act by means of or, better, on the basis of them only insofar as we allow ourselves to be. This feature of our agency accounts for our responsibility for heteronomous or inclination based action and explains why evil must be rooted in the will rather than in our given sensuous nature.

The other feature is Kant's affirmation of a reciprocal connection between the moral law and a free will (what I have termed the "Reciprocity Thesis").[29] This thesis precludes the possibility of a diabolical will, understood as one which explicitly denies the authority of the law, since it rules out the possibility of such a denial. The reasoning here is simple: if, as the Reciprocity Thesis maintains, the moral law necessarily is the law of a free will in the sense of providing the ultimate norm in terms of which its choices must be justified, then a free rational agent cannot reject the authority of the law without undermining its own agency. Combining both of these, we arrive at the result that evil must be rooted in a free choice against the law (a kind of inner voting in favor of inclination), which recognizes and respects the authority of the law even while contravening it.

At its maximum, evil, so construed, takes the form of wickedness [*Bösartigkeit*], which rather than choosing evil for its own sake intentionally subordinates moral considerations to those of self-love. And since even at this last stage of humanly possible evil the authority of the moral law is recognized, Kant indicates that this is only possible insofar as the agent engages in a kind of systematic self-deception. Basically, the idea is that one tells oneself that one is doing all that morality requires, as long as one's overt behavior (taken under some description) accords with the law. In fact, Kant points out that this stage may even coexist with a certain (ungrounded) moral self-satisfaction, which stems from the fact that one has been fortunate in avoiding circumstances that would have led to actual immoral behavior (Rel 6: 30; 25). In short, moral good luck is self-deceptively identified with virtue. Although Kant himself does not make the point, it would seem to be in accord with his analysis to add that insofar as wickedness leads to actually immoral behavior (which it does not necessarily do), this result is self-deceptively attributed to bad (moral) luck.

In spite of its considerable subtlety and accord with the basic principles of

Kant's moral theory, this conception has seemed to some to stand in blatant contradiction with the facts. Thus, John Silber, in his otherwise highly appreciative account of Kant's views on morality and freedom, maintains that far from being an impossibility, the kind of defiant rejection of the moral law that Kant apparently rules out "is an ineradicable fact of human experience."[30] In support of this claim he appeals to the historical examples of Napoleon and Hitler, the authority of St. Paul, Kierkegaard and Nietzsche, and even the fictional example of Melville's Captain Ahab. These examples and authorities strike quite different notes, but they presumably all bear witness to the fact that evil takes forms that transcend the narrow confines of the Kantian moral framework. More specifically, they suggest that evil cannot be understood simply in terms of the contrast between morality and self-interest, as the subordination of the former to the latter. Great evil, it would seem, can involve as much self-sacrifice (at least as it is usually conceived) and intensification of personality as great virtue. In the end, then, according to Silber, Kant remains very much a child of the *Aufklärung* (or Plato) and, as such, is incapable of recognizing the Dostoevskian depths to which humanity can sink.

Although Arendt could hardly accept Silber's essentially Dostoevskian conception of evil, she would certainly join with him in rejecting Kant's account in terms of the subordination of moral motives to those of self-interest. Indeed, as we have seen, in *The Origins of Totalitarianism* she criticized Kant for rationalizing evil, by which she presumably meant the attempt to account for it in terms of "comprehensible motives" such as self-interest, while in *Eichmann in Jerusalem* she explicitly linked the banality of evil to its motivelessness. Accordingly, it would seem that the Kantian conception is vulnerable to attack from both sides.

In an effort to deal with these difficulties, I shall first consider Silber's affirmation of genuinely diabolical evil and then the objection, shared by both Silber and Arendt, that evil of the quality of Eichmann's cannot be adequately accounted for in terms of motives such as self-interest. To begin with, it is not at all clear that the kinds of examples to which Silber alludes in support of his thesis really amount to choosing evil for the sake of evil. Certainly, we should be careful about identifying evil that seems manifestly counter-prudential (for example Ahab's single-minded, obsessive pursuit of Moby Dick) with evil chosen for its own sake. As we shall see, there are other alternatives.

Moreover, as Allen Wood has pointed out, Silber's whole line of criticism stems from a failure to consider Kant's claim in light of his conception of a predisposition to personality, which is just the capacity to be motivated by respect for the law. So considered, Kant's denial of a diabolical will is not a dubious bit of empirical moral psychology, but rather an *a priori* claim about the conditions of the possibility of moral accountability. Specifically, the claim is that in order to be accountable and, therefore to be *either* good *or* evil, it is necessary to recognize the validity of the moral law. Since a being who lacked this recognition and the concomitant feeling of respect would not be morally accountable, such a being could hardly be thought to have a diabolical will. On the contrary, it would have to be viewed as an unfortunate product of nature (rather than freedom), a non-person, since it lacked the defining characteristic of personality.[31] Thus, the very condition which makes morality possible at all, also rules out the possibility of a genuinely diabolical will.

Of itself, however, this analysis merely reconfirms the incompatibility of a diabolical will with the central principles of Kant's moral theory; thus, it certainly does not address the objection that Kant's moral psychology lacks the resources to account for the motivation (or lack thereof) of villains such as Eichmann. Accordingly, it is worth noting that Kant also has a story to tell (albeit a brief one) about how apparently selfless evil and even the "diabolical vices" [*teuflische Laster*] of envy, ingratitude and spitefulness [*Schadenfreude*] can be grafted on to the original propensity to evil. Moreover, it is at this juncture, which marks the move from *a priori* moral theory to an empirically based moral anthropology, that the Kantian account begins to make contact with Arendt's portrait of Eichmann.

The main thrust of this story, which has been helpfully analyzed by Sharon Anderson-Gold, is that the vices associated with man's inhumanity to man, which seem to differ qualitatively from the mere subordination of moral considerations to self-love, are actually grounded in this very self-love as it is affected by the competitive social context in which human beings find themselves.[32] Given this context, our judgments of personal happiness are essentially comparative, so that we measure our happiness by comparing our state with that of others. This, in turn, leads to a desire "to acquire worth in the opinion of others." Although originally merely a desire for equality, within the competitive context in which everyone else has similar aims, it gradually becomes transformed into the craving for superiority, with which come inevitably jealousy and rivalry. Finally, from these stem what Kant terms "vices of culture," since they only arise in a cultured or civilized state and themselves serve as further spurs to culture. At their most extreme, these vices of culture become the devilish vices (Rel 6: 27; 22n).

As Anderson-Gold indicates, by appealing to our social nature (what he elsewhere terms our "unsocial sociability"), Kant endeavors to show how the bare propensity to evil can account for extreme evil as a cultural phenomenon, without assuming the possibility of a diabolical will. Evil is rooted in self-love insofar as it refuses to limit itself by the moral law, even though in its advanced stages it takes forms that are hardly commensurate with the pursuit of self-interest. As a result of the competitive social context and the effect that it has on our self-conception, an initially innocent self-love can produce the most horrible crimes.

As Anderson-Gold also notes, this suggests "a certain parallel between Kant's concept of radical evil and Hannah Arendt's concept of 'banal' evil."[33]

Although she does not expand on this point, except to remark that Arendt would reject what she terms the "species character" of evil (its universality), it is not difficult to see what she had in mind. In addition to their common rejection of any diabolical motivation, the main point is presumably the way in which Eichmann's character was supposedly molded and corrupted by his social context. Indeed, Arendt does remark that Eichmann was a product of a society in which mendacity had become an ingredient of the national character;[34] that evil in the Third Reich was so deeply ingrained as to lose the capacity to tempt;[35] and that Eichmann committed crimes under circumstances that made it virtually impossible for him to recognize that he was doing wrong.[36]

We must be careful, however, not to push this parallel too far. As already indicated, Kant's account operates at a different level than Arendt's, and this difference is due primarily to the characteristically Kantian emphasis on freedom. Accordingly, Kant's story about the social conditioning of vice must be understood against the backdrop of transcendental freedom. From the Kantian standpoint, if Eichmann truly lacked the capacity to recognize the criminality of his acts, then we must either absolve him of responsibility (as we would someone who has been genuinely "brainwashed") or acknowledge that in some sense his must have been a willful ignorance, a self-imposed thoughtlessness. In an effort to conceptualize such a possibility, we turn now to the notion of self-deception.[37]

III

Perhaps because he refers explicitly to it only in connection with his account of wickedness, the third and highest degree of evil, most interpreters have tended to either downplay or ignore completely the place of self-deception in the overall Kantian account of evil. A careful consideration of Kant's theory, however, suggests that it plays an absolutely crucial role at all levels. Consider the notion of moral weakness or frailty [*Gebrechlichkeit*], which Kant characterizes as the first stage of evil. At this stage, Kant tells us, the good, which objectively considered is an inexpugnable [*unüberwindlich*] incentive, when considered subjectively turns out to be weaker in comparison with inclination (Rel 6: 29; 24). In other words, we recognize and desire to do our duty but find ourselves unable to do so because of powerful countervailing motives.

Now, although this phenomenon is all too familiar, it is by no means an easy matter to reconcile it with the Kantian conception of freedom. After all, how can a philosopher who has as his basic principle that "Man *himself* must make or have made himself into whatever, in a moral sense, whether good or evil, he is or is to become" (Rel 6: 44; 40), allow for a moral *weakness?* Insofar as it is an expression of evil, this weakness must be something for which one is responsible and, as such, an expression of freedom. Consequently, we cannot appeal to any form of constitutive moral luck in order to excuse our frailty (as if a weak will were like a weak heart). But a weakness for which one is responsible is no longer a simple weakness; it is rather a self-imposed or, as Kierkegaard might have put it, a "dialectically qualified" weakness.

The problem thus becomes how one is to understand a self-imposed weakness and here, I have argued, is where self-deception comes into play.[38] To begin with, this "weakness" must be identified with the bare propensity to evil, that is, the ineliminable tendency of even the best of us to subordinate the moral incentive to that of self-love. This expresses itself in moral experience as an openness to temptation, which is really nothing more than a susceptibility to just such a subordination. Self-deception then enters the picture as the means by which an agent transforms this openness into a brute, given fact, a part of one's nature, which one laments because it apparently stands in the way of becoming virtuous, but for which one does not hold oneself responsible. In short, a state of mind for which one is ultimately responsible is self-deceptively taken as a bit of bad moral luck. Similarly, in the case of impurity, the second stage of evil, self-deception explains how we can take ourselves to be acting from duty alone, when, in fact, we require some extra-moral incentive in order to do what duty dictates. Given this, together with the earlier analysis of wickedness, it seems reasonable to conclude that self-deception is already for Kant (as it was to become for Fichte[39] and in our century Sartre) the major mechanism that human beings make use of to evade their responsibility.

Admittedly, Kant does not explicitly argue in this way in the *Religion,* but it is nonetheless, I suggest, precisely how his account of evil must be understood, if it is to be made coherent. Moreover, he gives strong indication in his account of lying in the *Tugendlehre* that this is, indeed, precisely how he understands the situation. Not only does Kant there (in contrast to the various versions of his lectures on ethics) classify lying as a violation of duty to oneself rather than to others, he also puts prime emphasis on the inner lie. Thus, he concludes his account of lying with the reflection:

> But such insincerity in his declarations, which man perpetrates upon himself, still deserves the strongest censure, since it is from such a rotten spot (falsity, which seems to be rooted in human nature itself) that the evil of untruthfulness spreads into man's relations with other men as well, once the highest principle of truthfulness has been violated (MS 6: 430–31; 226–27).

Even granting this, however, it is still not clear that the Kantian conception of self-deception can be used to illuminate the phenomenon of Eichmann. Apparently standing in the way of such a use is Kant's well known view that the difficulty in the moral life consists not in the recognition of what, objectively speaking, is one's duty (since this must be readily apparent to everyone), but in acting as duty dictates. After all, if Arendt's analysis is correct, we have in Eichmann a case of someone whose "thoughtlessness" somehow prevented him from recognizing the most basic obligation, who committed the most heinous crimes without a guilty conscience, and who lived by means of a perverted moral code. And it is by no means immediately obvious that such a possibility can be understood in Kantian terms.

As a first step in dealing with this problem, it must be noted that, in spite of his adherence to the Rousseauian principle that even the humblest intelligence is capable of distinguishing right from wrong, Kant does at times acknowledge the possibility of being mistaken about what is objectively one's duty. For example, in the *Tugendlehre,* while ruling out as an absurdity the notion of an erring conscience, he maintains that incorrigibility applies only to the "subjective judgment" of whether I have consulted my conscience, and that "I can indeed be mistaken at times [*bisweilen*] in my objective judgment as to whether something is a duty or not" (MS 6: 401; 202). Similarly, in his account of moral character as a matter of committing oneself to self-imposed practical principles in the *Anthropology,* he reflects that, "Though it is true that these principles might occasionally [*bisweilen*] be mistaken and imperfect, still the formal element of his volition in general – to act according to firm principles . . . – has something precious and admirable in it; and so it is also a rare thing" (Anthro 7: 292; 157).

Welcome as it is, however, this admission of human fallibility with respect to moral judgment and its principles is only a first step and is obviously not sufficient to deal with the problem at hand. For Kant's circumspect language in both passages (his use of the qualifier '*bisweilen*') makes it clear that he views such mistakes as relatively rare occurrences, which might concern some of the "gray areas" of morality, such as are dealt with in the casuistical questions of the *Tugendlehre,* but not what is fundamental in the moral life. Moreover, insofar as such mistakes are "innocent" errors in moral judgment, it would seem that they do not involve self-deception, at least not in a major way. Accordingly, we find ourselves back at the original problem of trying to understand how Kant's analysis of radical evil can be applied to Arendt's portrait of Eichmann.

In order to make further progress in this direction, it is necessary to consider (albeit briefly) Kant's view of moral deliberation. As is clear to any reader of the *Groundwork,* this consists in subjecting one's maxim to the universalizability test in order to determine whether it can be universalized without contradiction. As is also clear to any student of the literature, however, this is precisely the place where Kant's moral theory is attacked by critics who charge that virtually any maxim, if suitably formulated, can be made to pass the test. Although I can hardly argue for it here, I believe that this much discussed difficulty points more to the failure to recognize the complexity of Kant's moral psychology than to the limitations of his moral theory. Suffice it to say that it is precisely the testing of maxims that provides the major occasion for self-deception, which here takes the form of disguising from ourselves the true nature of the principles upon which we act. In short, immoral maxims appear to pass the universalizability test only because they ignore or obscure morally salient features of a situation.[40] Thus, far from demonstrating the emptiness of the categorical imperative, this shows how the imperative can be misapplied by radically evil agents who continue to recognize its authority.

Let us consider an example which fits nicely into Kant's account of wickedness.[41] Suppose that I have a violent dislike for someone and have come into possession of a piece of information about him, which I know will cause him great pain if he learns of it. With the intent of doing so, I decide to inform him of the matter, but I justify the action on the grounds of his right to know. Accordingly, rather than being a vicious act of causing unnecessary pain, I represent it to myself (and perhaps others) as a laudable act of truth telling. Depending on the degree of my depravity, I might even half-convince myself that it is a sacred duty. In any event, this justificatory procedure is clearly based on self-deception, by means of which I am able to ignore my actual intention, which is here the morally salient factor, defining the very nature of the act.

Admittedly, this still does not quite fit the Eichmann case, since, if Arendt is correct, he was not a rabid anti-semite, who had to hide his true feelings from himself in order to maintain a clear conscience while sending Jews to their death. Even granting this, however, I would still contend that Eichmann can be viewed as a virtual limiting case of Kantian wickedness, on the grounds that his "thoughtlessness" represents an extreme example of the neglect of morally salient features. Once again, what could be more salient than the fact that one is dealing with human beings? And if this neglect is somehow willful, as it must be if it is to be imputable, then it is difficult to see how one can avoid attributing it to something like a propensity to evil.

IV

Up until this point the Kantian analysis has assumed Eichmann's criminality, and in so doing it might seem that we have neglected the obvious objection that in expressly obeying the law of the land, Eichmann was, as he claimed, really following Kantian principles. After all, Kant himself notoriously claimed that revolution and active rebellion are always illegitimate; that we have a duty to obey the most intolerable despot. Given this, Eichmann might seem to provide not so much an illustration of Kant's conception of radical evil as a *reductio* of his political philosophy, and since this supposedly rests on moral grounds, of the categorical imperative itself. Since this again is a large topic to which I can hardly hope to do justice here, I shall limit myself to two brief points.

First, it must be kept in mind that, in spite of his uncompromising views on obedience to the law, Kant did not advocate simple acquiescence to tyranny.

On the contrary, as a zealous advocate of freedom of expression, of the "public use of reason" as a necessary condition of enlightenment, he subscribed to Frederick the Great's famous motto: "Argue as much as you will, and about what you will, but obey!"[42] As Arendt emphasizes, however, Eichmann not only failed to argue with his superiors, he apparently never even really questioned in his own mind the morality of the Final Solution. Accordingly, far from being compatible with Kantian principles, both Eichmann's actions and his pernicious thoughtlessness are clearly opposed to these principles.

Second, it should be noted that on occasion Kant introduced explicit and significant qualifications of the duty to obey.[43] Thus, in *Religion within the Limits of Reason Alone* Kant glosses the Biblical injunction: "We ought to obey God rather than men," to signify that "when men command anything which in itself is evil (directly opposed to the law of morality) we dare not, and ought not, obey them" (Rel 6: 99n; 90). And, in the appendix added to the second edition of the *Rechtslehre,* where, in response to the lengthy criticism of the original version by Friedrich Bouterwork, he affirms as a "categorical imperative" the principle: "*Obey the authority who has power over you* (in whatever does not conflict with inner morality)" (MS 6: 371; 176). Unfortunately, these qualifications of the demand of absolute obedience to the ruling powers remain cryptic remarks, which Kant never integrated into his political theory. Nevertheless, if we assume, as I believe it reasonable to do, that Kant would have regarded the Nazi crimes as "directly opposed to the law of morality" or in "conflict with inner morality," they do suffice to deprive Eichmann of his presumed grounds for a so-called "Kantian defense."

Notes

Introduction

1. Two philosophers within the naturalistic camp who do take the conception of spontaneity seriously in their interpretations of Kant are Wilfred Sellars and Ralf Meerbote. I have discussed Sellars' views on the topic in several places, including "Kant's refutation of materialism," Chapter 7 in this volume. I discuss Meerbote's views at length in chapter 4 of *Kant's Theory of Freedom*.
2. The reader who is familiar with the third *Critique* will no doubt recognize the close parallel between the line of argument I am here attributing to Kant and his account of reflective judgment (particularly with regard to organic beings) in that work. Although I do not discuss this parallelism in any of the essays in this collection, I am keenly aware of it
3. Since this paper was written before the appearance of Paul Guyer's book, *Kant and the Claims of Knowledge* (New York: Cambridge University Press, 1987), it addresses his views as expressed in two earlier papers: "Kant on apperception and a priori synthesis," *American Philosophical Quarterly* 17 (1980), pp. 205–12, and "Kant's tactics in the transcendental deduction," *Essays on Kant's Critique of Pure Reason*, edited by J. N. Mohanty and Robert W. Shaker, Norman, Okla.: University of Oklahoma Press, 1982, pp. 157–99. But since (as far as I can see) nothing essential is changed in the book, I believe that the criticisms expressed in my paper apply to the later and presumably definitive account as well.
4. In addition to the Kant monograph, Gurwitsch's major contribution in this area is his monumental *Leibniz Philosophie des Panlogismus*, Berlin/New York: Walter de Gruyter, 1974.
5. At this point I criticize Nelson Potter, Jr., who in an earlier paper ("Kant on ends that are at the same time duties," *Pacific Philosophical Quarterly* 66 (1985), pp. 78–92) had defended Kant's argument as it stands. He has responded to my critique and defended his original analysis in "Reply to Allison," *Jahrbuch für Recht und Ethik*, Band 1 (1993), pp. 391–400. The major issues between us concern the conception of freedom operative in Kant's argument and our applications of the principle that every action aims at some end to the puzzle case of juridical duties. Although Potter raises some interesting points with regard to the latter issue, I stand by my analysis as contained in the essay.

Chapter 1

1. My first treatment of this problem was in "Transcendental idealism and descriptive metaphysics," *Kant-Studien* 60 (1969), pp. 216–33.

2 Generally speaking, the passages supporting this reading fall into two classes. Sometimes Kant makes it perfectly explicit that he is referring to the things that appear, considered as they are in themselves. For example, he contends that time is nothing, "if we abstract from *our* mode of intuiting ourselves ... and so take objects as they may be in themselves" (A34/B41). Similar passages are to be found at: Bxx, B55, A39/B56, B69, B307, and *Prolegomena* 4: 286; 33. Elsewhere the point is implicit but fairly obvious. Although we there find the expression '*Ding an sich selbst*' or its equivalents, the context indicates that Kant is talking about empirical objects as they are in themselves rather than about entities ontologically distinct from the things that appear. Such places include: A43/B60, A149/B188, A190/B235, A251–52, B312, A276/B332, A205/B341, B430, A496/B524, A566/B594 and *Prolegomena* 4: 284, 287; 31, 35. In addition, there are very many passages in which the reference to things in themselves is ambiguous, which is hardly surprising, given the popularity of the two-object reading. The most thorough textual analysis of this issue has been done by Gerold Prauss, *Kant und das Problem der Dinge an sich*, Bonn: Bouvier, 1974. As Prauss points out (pp. 20ff), when Kant is concerned to articulate the transcendental (as opposed to the empirical) sense of the distinction, he usually uses locutions such as *Ding* or *Sache an sich selbst betrachtet* rather than simply *Ding an sich, Ding an sich selbst* or *Sache an sich*. He also argues convincingly that the shorter forms are to be understood as abbreviations for the longer and canonical versions.
3 See Henry E. Allison, *Kant's Transcendental Idealism: An Interpretation and Defense,* New Haven and London: Yale University Press, esp. pp. 10–13.
4 Ibid., pp. 17–19.
5 See Ameriks, "Reinhold and the short argument to idealism," *Proceedings of the Sixth International Kant Congress,* Vol. II/2, edited by G. Funke and T. M. Seebohm, Washington D.C.: Center for Advanced Research in Phenomenology & University Press of America, pp. 441–53; "Kant, Fichte, and short arguments to idealism," *Archiv für Geschichte der Philosophie* 72 (1990), pp. 174–86; and "Kantian idealism today," *History of Philosophy Quarterly* 9 (1992), pp. 329–40.
6 Malte Hossenfelder, "Allison's defence of Kant's transcendental idealism," *Inquiry* 33 (1990), pp. 467–79, esp. pp. 468–69.
7 Ameriks, "Kantian idealism today," pp. 333–34.
8 For example, I claimed that "transcendental idealism is at bottom nothing more than the logical consequence" of the acceptance of epistemic conditions (*Kant's Transcendental Idealism,* p. 10).
9 I discuss the discursivity thesis and its significance for the analytic–synthetic distinction in chapter 4 of *Kant's Transcendental Idealism* and "The originality of Kant's distinction between analytic and synthetic judgements," *Studies in Philosophy and the History of Philosophy,* Vol. 12, *The Philosophy of Immanuel Kant,* edited by Richard Kennington, Washington D.C.: The Catholic University of America Press, 1985, pp. 15–38. It also plays a significant role in several of the papers in the first part of this collection, particularly in connection with the analysis of the spontaneity of thinking.
10 The contrasting (logically) possible type of cognition according to Kant is "intuitive," which operates by means of a creative "intellectual intuition." Such an intellect is, of course, attributed only to God. Kant's canonical discussion of the

relations between these two forms of "intellect" (discursive and intuitive) is in §76 and §77 of the *Critique of Judgment*.

11 Within the *Critique* the polemic with Leibniz is further developed in the chapter on "The amphiboly of concepts of reflection." For Kant's subsequent analysis of Leibniz, see especially *On a Discovery According to which Any New Critique of Pure Reason Has Been Made Superfluous by an Earlier One*, in *The Kant–Eberhard Controversy*, edited and translated by Henry E. Allison, Baltimore and London: The Johns Hopkins University Press, 1973.

12 This is how I understand passages such as *Prolegomena* 4: 322; 69, where Kant maintains that the nature of things in themselves is independent of the conditions of both sensibility and the understanding.

13 See, for example, A28/B44, A35/B51–52, A206/B251–52, A249–50, B307, A252/B310, A259/B315, A64/B320, A279/B335, A284/B340–41, A500/B528, A525/B553.

14 For my previous discussions, see "The non-spatiality of things in themselves for Kant," *Journal of the History of Philosophy* 14 (1976), pp. 313–21; and *Kant's Transcendental Idealism*, pp. 111–14. The former contains a brief history of the controversy, including an account of the role of Trendelenburg.

15 Paul Guyer, *Kant and the Claims of Knowledge*, Cambridge: Cambridge University Press, 1987, pp. 337–38.

16 See "The non-spatiality of things in themselves for Kant," pp. 320–21.

17 Gerold Prauss, *Kant und das Problem der Dinge an sich*, esp. pp. 139ff. See also note 2.

18 For example, in speculating about a supposed object of a non-sensible intuition, Kant remarks that "its duration is not a time" (B149). This suggests that Kant might not rule out all noumenal analogues to our sensible forms.

19 Lorne Falkenstein, "Kant's argument for the non-spatiotemporality of things in themselves," *Kant-Studien* 80 (1989), pp. 265–83.

20 Allison, "Transcendental idealism: The 'two aspect' view," esp. pp. 160–70.

21 Richard E. Aquila, "Things in themselves and appearances: Intentionality and reality in Kant," *Archiv für Geschichte der Philosophie* 61 (1979), pp. 293–307; and *Representational Mind: A Study of Kant's Theory of Knowledge*, Bloomington, Ind.: Indiana University Press, 1983, esp. pp. 88–118.

22 Aquila, *Representational Mind*, p. 89.

23 In essence, I argued that the term 'appearances' as it enters into the definition of 'world' must be taken in an ontologically neutral sense (which avoids the trivializing charge), and that, given this, the argument shows first that a contradiction emerges if one takes appearances (construed in this neutral sense) as if they were things in themselves in the transcendental sense) and second that the latter manner of conceiving them is the direct consequence of the failure to draw the transcendental distinction. Finally, it concludes from this that the contradiction can be avoided if and only if one regards the spatio-temporal items constituting the world as appearances in the transcendental sense. See "Transcendental idealism: The two aspect view," p. 165. For a full statement of my interpretation of the indirect argument for idealism of the Antinomy, see *Kant's Transcendental Idealism*, pp. 50–61.

24 Ameriks, "Recent work on Kant's theoretical philosophy," *American Philosophical Quarterly* 19 (1982) esp. pp. 6–11.

25 Both the apparent advantages and alleged limitations of the semantic approach are discussed by G. J. Mattey, "Semantical models in Kant's double aspect theory" (unpublished). For similar approaches see also Robert Howell, "A problem for Kant," in *Essays in Honour of Jaakko Hintikka*, Dordrecht: Reidel, 1979, pp. 331–49; Carl Posy, "The language of appearances and things in themselves," *Synthese* 47 (1981), pp. 313–52; and "Dancing to the antinomy: A proposal for transcendental idealism," *American Philosophical Quarterly* 20 (1983).

26 The first passage is in the Fourth Paralogism in the first edition, where Kant remarks: "Though the 'I' as represented through inner sense in time, and objects in space outside me, are specifically quite distinct appearances, they are not for that reason thought as being different things" (A379). The second is from Kant's response to Eberhard, where, among other significant points, he claims that, "[I]t is a complete misunderstanding of the theory of sensible objects as mere appearances, to which something non-sensible must be attached, if one imagines or seeks others to imagine that what is meant thereby is that the super-sensible substrate of matter will be divided according to its monads, just as I divide matter itself" (UE 8: 209n; 125). The latter passage has also been cited by Ameriks, who takes it as evidence that Kant did not hold either to a strict double-aspect theory or to the standard two-world view. Instead, he suggests that, "Really Kant was after a peculiar kind of third position which ultimately identifies reality with a kind of being of which we can say little more (theoretically) than that it definitely is not like either the spatial-physical or the temporal-psychological being with which we are ordinarily familiar" ("Recent work on Kant's theoretical philosophy," p. 10). In my judgment, this indicates his attachment to the very metaphysical picture which I am questioning. I discuss his critique of my own view as non-metaphysical in the next section.

27 Hoke Robinson, "Two perspectives on Kant's appearances and things in themselves," *Journal of the History of Philosophy* 33 (July 1994), pp. 411–41.

28 Ibid., p. 419, note 35.

29 Ibid., p. 420.

30 The other passage (A369) is from the Fourth Paralogism, where transcendental idealism is defined as "the doctrine that appearances are to be regarded as being, one and all, representations only, not things in themselves. . . ."

31 Other illuminating passages in the Aesthetic include A28/B44 and A34/B51, where Kant spells out what he understands by the transcendental ideality of space and time. Moreover, this type of locution is also prominent in the Phenomena and Noumena chapter, where Kant is specifically concerned to contrast our sensible representations and their objects with a problematic non-sensible representation of the same (or other) objects. See, for example, A249 and B306–307. Finally, it should be noted that not all of the passages to which Robinson refers as identifying appearances with representations are as "clear and unequivocal" as he suggests. A case in point is a passage from the B-Deduction, which, as he himself notes, is the only such passage unique to the second edition ("Two perspectives on Kant's appearances and things in themselves," p. 436). To be sure, appearances are there characterized as "mere representations," but this refers back to the preceding sentence, which reads: "But appearances are only representations of things which

are unknown as regards what they may be in themselves" (B164). Thus, seen in its context, even this passage strongly suggests the reading advocated here. Furthermore, the great majority of the passages which Robinson cites are from either the first edition's Transcendental Deduction and Fourth Paralogism, both of which were completely rewritten in the second edition, or the discussion of idealism in connection with the Antinomies, which, I have argued, is not to be taken in the way Robinson suggests.

32 "Two perspectives on Kant's appearances and things in themselves," p. 421.
33 Ibid., pp. 422–23.
34 Ibid., pp. 424–26. In addition, he criticizes my account of affection (pp. 426–27); I shall ignore that here, since a treatment of that issue would lead me well beyond the bounds of the present discussion.
35 I analyze Spinoza's account of the mind–body relation in my *Benedict de Spinoza: An Introduction*, New Haven and London: Yale University Press, 1987, pp. 85–100.
36 See *Kant's Transcendental Idealism*, pp. 240–41. I follow Prauss on this point.
37 See Robinson, "Two perspectives on Kant's appearances and things in themselves," note 58, p. 427. Even in *Kant's Transcendental Idealism*, however, I acknowledged places in which this identification does not hold. Moreover, in an early paper, "Kant's concept of the Transcendental object," *Kant-Studien* 59 (1968), pp. 165–86, I focused on the role of the transcendental object in the A-Deduction, in which it is clearly not identified with the thing as it is in itself.
38 For my previous analysis of these distinctions, see *Kant's Transcendental Idealism*, pp. 242–46.
39 Ameriks, "Kantian idealism today," p. 334.
40 Ibid.
41 This is the central theme of the "ontological school" of Kant interpretation associated mainly with Heinz Heimsoeth. See his *Studien zur Philosophie Immanuel Kants: Metaphysische Ursprünge und ontologische Grundlagen*, Kantstudien Ergänzungshefte 71 (1956); and *Transzendentale Dialektik: Ein Kommentar zu Kants Kritik der reinen Vernunft*, Berlin, New York: Walter de Gruyter, 1971. For a helpful discussion of some of Heimsoeth's views and the issues separating the ontological and the Marburg neo-Kantian schools see Gottfried Martin, *Kant's Metaphysics and Theory of Science*, translated by P. G. Lucas, Manchester: Manchester University Press, 1955.
42 The chapter in the first *Critique* from which this claim comes ("The ground of the distinction of all objects in general into phenomena and noumena") is the major text for interpreting Kant's critical doctrine of the noumenal. For my own account of the nature and function of the concept of the noumenon in Kant's theoretical philosophy see *Kant's Transcendental Idealism*, pp. 242–46.
43 In the Dissertation Kant explicitly held that the use of the intellect with respect to experience is merely logical rather than real; that is, it has merely an organizing rather than a constitutive or determinative function with respect to our sensitive cognitions. See Diss 2: 393–94; 385–86.
44 See Ameriks, *Kant's Theory of Mind, An Analysis of the Paralogisms of Pure Reason*, Oxford: Clarendon Press, 1982, especially the Introduction.
45 For a useful discussion of this issue, see Bernard Rousset, *La Doctrine Kantienne*

de la objectivité, Paris: Librairie Philosophique J. Vrin, 1967, pp. 163–77. Rousset there distinguishes between *"l'en soi immanent"* and *"l'en soi transcendant."*

46 See in particular *Critique of Pure Reason,* A293–309/B349–66 and A338–40/B396–98.

47 See Michelle Grier, "Illusion and fallacy in Kant's first Paralogism," *Kant-Studien* 84 (1993), pp. 257–82; and her unpublished dissertation, *Kant's Doctrine of Transcendental Illusion* (1993). Among the important features of Grier's account is the distinction between the illusion, which is inevitable, and the fallacious inferences based upon it, which are exposed in the Transcendental Dialectic and are avoidable. In particular, she points out how the failure to distinguish between the illusion regarding the soul and the paralogistic inferences vitiates most readings of the Paralogisms, including Ameriks' and, unfortunately, my own in *Kant's Transcendental Idealism.*

48 I offer my overall assessment of Guyer's reconstruction of Kant's argument in the Analytic in my review of *Kant and the Claims of Knowledge, The Journal Philosophy* 86 (1989), pp. 214–21. Also in Chapter 3 in this volume ("Apperception and analyticity in the B-Deduction") I discuss his views on apperception. At present, I am concerned only with his account of transcendental idealism and his critique of my views on this topic.

49 Guyer, *Kant and the Claims of Knowledge,* p. 335.

50 *Kant's Transcendental Idealism,* p. 110. This may be a good place to clear up a confusion stemming from a lack of clarity in my initial formulation of this principle in the book. Initially, I characterized the principle underlying Kant's idealism as follows: "[W]hatever is necessary for the representation or experience of something as an object, that is, whatever is required for the picking out of what is 'objective' in our experience must reflect the cognitive structure of the mind (its manner of representing) rather than the nature of the object as it is in itself" (p. 27). And, in support of this claim, I argued that, "To claim otherwise is to assume that the mind can somehow have access to an object (through sensible or intellectual intuition) independently of the very elements that have been stipulated to be the conditions of the possibility of doing this in the first place. This involves an obvious contradiction." The basic problem here is that there is a distinction between a representation *reflecting* the nature of things as they are in themselves, as I expressed the matter in the first formulation, and being *based upon* or *derived from* an acquaintance with things so considered, as I expressed it in the second (p. 110). Unfortunately, ignoring this difference, I treated the two principles as identical. Understandably, this has caused some confusion for my critics. Thus, Guyer complains with some justification regarding the initial formulation that the description of the contradiction is incoherent (*Kant and the Claims of Knowledge,* p. 339). A similar objection is raised by Terry Greenwood, "Kant and the modalities of space," in *Reading Kant,* edited by Eva Schaper and Wilhelm Vossenkuhl, Oxford: Basil Blackwell, 1989, p. 124. In an effort to eliminate this confusion, I now state that, even in the initial formulation, I intended only the weaker claim that the source of a representation that functions in the manner described (as an epistemic condition) must lie in the mind and not the stronger claim that it cannot (in any sense) apply to things as they are in themselves.

Showing the latter requires a separate argument, since it involves eliminating the so-called "neglected alternative."

51 Guyer, *Kant and the Claims of Knowledge*, p. 342. See also pp. 340–41.
52 For a critique of Guyer's reading of the text along these same lines, see Rolf Peter Horstmann, "Transcendental idealism and the representation of space," in *Reading Kant*, pp. 168–76.
53 Guyer, *Kant and the Claims of Knowledge*, pp. 354–59.
54 Ibid., p. 364.
55 Ibid., p. 363.
56 Ibid., p. 367.
57 See note 50.
58 The point is particularly clear from the contrast Kant draws in both Introductions to the *Critique of Judgment* (Sections III and IV) between the transcendental laws of the understanding to which appearances necessarily conform, and the additional requirement that nature exhibit an empirical lawfulness comprehensible by the human mind, which is contingent precisely because it is not entailed by the transcendental laws.
59 I regard this response as applicable not only to Guyer, but also to the similar critique of Greenwood, who likewise denies that there is any contradiction in the assumption that the representation of space could both function as a condition of experience and be derived from an experience of things as they are in themselves. See his "Transcendental idealism and the representation of space," esp. pp. 118–25. In both cases, the essential point is that Kantian epistemic conditions are to be understood as enabling conditions, for if this is granted, the contradiction follows.
60 I would like to express my thanks to Camilla Serck-Hanssen and Michelle Grier for their helpful comments on earlier drafts of this essay.

Chapter 2

1 Karl Ameriks, "Recent work on Kant's theoretical philosophy." *American Philosophical Quarterly* 19 (1982), pp. 11–13.
2 Ibid., p. 13.
3 Ameriks, "Kant's Transcendental Deduction as a regressive argument," *Kant-Studien* 69 (1978), pp. 273–87.
4 Ibid., p. 282.
5 Ameriks, "Recent work on Kant's theoretical philosophy." p. 12.
6 See H. J. de Vleeschauwer, *La deduction transcendentale dans l'oeuvre de Kant*, Paris: Leroux, 1936, Vol. II, pp. 390–594.
7 Henrich, "The proof-structure of Kant's Transcendental Deduction," *Review of Metaphysics* 22 (1968–69), pp. 640–59. Reprinted in *Kant on Pure Reason*, edited by Ralph G. S. Walker, Oxford, New York: Oxford University Press, 1982, pp. 66–81. All references here will be to the later text.
8 Ibid., p. 70.
9 Hoke Robinson, "Intuition and manifold in the Transcendental Deduction," *The Southern Journal of Philosophy*, 23 (pp. 403–12).
10 See *Critique of Pure Reason*, B145, 159–60.

11 Robinson, "Intuition and manifold in the Transcendental Deduction," p. 405.
12 Ibid.
13 Henrich, "The proof-structure of Kant's Transcendental Deduction," p. 74.
14 Ibid., p. 76.
15 The problem is posed, although not resolved, by Rodolf Zocher, "Kants Transzendentale Deduktion der Kategorien," *Zeitschrift für philosophische Forschung*, 8 (1959); pp. 163–94, esp. p. 165.
16 MAN 4: 475–76; 13. See also R 5923, 18: 385–86.
17 See *Critique of Pure Reason*, B135, 138.
18 This is the crucial Kantian doctrine of the necessity of synthesis or combination, which is the explicit theme of §15. For my account of this doctrine see *Kant's Transcendental Idealism*, New Haven, London: Yale University Press, 1983, pp. 140–49.
19 Ibid., p. 162.
20 It is tempting to attribute Kant's change in the formulation of the general principle of the Analogies to his recognition of this point cf. A177–78 and B218–19.
21 Dieter Henrich, *Identität und Objektivität: Eine Untersuchung über Kants transzendentale Deduktion*, Heidelberg: Carl Winter Universitäts-Verlag, 1976, p. 10.
22 Ibid., esp. pp. 86–88. See also Paul Guyer's review of Henrich's book, *Journal of Philosophy* 76 (1979), p. 162.
23 Guyer, "Kant's tactics in the Transcendental Deduction," *Essays on Kant's Critique of Pure Reason*, edited by J. N. Mohanty and Robert W. Shaker, University of Oklahoma Press: Norman, Okla., 1982, pp. 157–99, p. 190.
24 See Guyer, review of Henrich, pp. 163–64, "Kant on apperception and a priori synthesis," *American Philosophical Quarterly* 17 (1980), pp. 208–209, "Kant's tactics in the Transcendental Deduction," p. 184.
25 *Kant's Transcendental Idealism*, p. 140.
26 Ibid., pp. 137–40.
27 Guyer, "Kant on apperception and a priori synthesis," p. 209.
28 Some possible differences between the two propositions have been pointed out by Michelle Gilmore in an unpublished paper.
29 In his review of Henrich (p. 162) Guyer points to A108 and B134–35, as well as the passage cited above, as affirming this principle. In my opinion, however, none of these passages, particularly the one from the B-Deduction, requires such a reading.

Chapter 3

1 See, for example, H. J. Paton, *Kant's Metaphysic of Experience*, New York: Macmillan, 1936, Vol . 1, p. 518; H. J. de Vleeschauwer, *La Déduction transcendentale dans l'oeuvre de Kant*, 3 vols., Paris etc., 1934–37, reprinted New York & London: Garland Publishing, Inc., 1976, Vol. III, pp. 115–16.
2 Dieter Henrich, "The proof-structure of Kant's Transcendental Deduction," *Review of Metaphysics* 22 (1968–69), pp. 640–59.
3 This aspect of Henrich's view of the Deduction is developed in *Identität und Objektivität: Eine Untersuchung über Kants transzendentale Deduktion*, Heidelberg: Carl Winter Universitäts-Verlag, 1976. I discuss both aspects of Henrich's

interpretation in "Reflections on the B-Deduction," *Southern Journal of Philosophy* 25, Supplement, The Spindel Conference, 1986, pp. 1–15.
4 See Paul Guyer, "Kant's tactics in the Transcendental Deduction," *Essays on Kant's Critique of Pure Reason*, edited by J. N. Mohanty and Robert W. Shahan, Norman, Okla.: University of Oklahoma Press, 1982, pp. 157–99; and *Kant and the Claims of Knowledge*, Cambridge and New York: Cambridge University Press, 1987, pp. 73–90.
5 Guyer, "Kant's tactics," pp. 180–83; *Kant and the Claims of Knowledge*, pp. 132–39.
6 See Guyer, "Kant on apperception and a priori synthesis," *American Philosophical Quarterly* 17 (1980), 205–12; "Kant's tactics," p. 184; and *Kant and the Claims of Knowledge*, pp. 132–33; 140–42.
7 Guyer, "Kant's tactics," p. 184; and *Kant and the Claims of Knowledge*, pp. 134, 136–37, 139–40.
8 Patricia Kitcher, *Kant's Transcendental Psychology*, New York, Oxford: Oxford University Press, 1990, p. 186.
9 For my own account of the relation between the analytic and synthetic unities of apperception and its compatibility with the analyticity of the principle, see *Kant's Transcendental Idealism*, pp. 143–44.
10 Kitcher, *Kant's Transcendental Psychology*, p. 186.
11 Kitcher explicitly discusses and criticizes what she terms my "logical reading of apperception," ibid., pp. 94–95.
12 Ibid., p. 94
13 Ibid., p. 187.
14 Ibid., p. 172.
15 It should be noted here that my quarrel is only with Kitcher's historical thesis that Kant was in fact concerned in the Deduction to reply to Hume's skeptical reflections on mental unity, not with the philosophical thesis that Kant's account is central to the solution of the problem Hume raised in the *Treatise*. Although I interpret Kant's account of apperception in a quite different manner than Kitcher, I readily grant the latter point. The historical thesis is, however, another matter. Under the influence of Kemp Smith, she seems to think that the only obstacle to this thesis is the worry over Kant's access to Hume's *Treatise* (due to his ignorance of English and the lack of a German translation at the time). This obstacle is removed, she thinks, by the fact that a German translation of James Beattie's *Essay on the Nature and Immutability of Truth*, which contains lengthy citations from Hume's discussion of personal identity, appeared in 1772. See *Kant's Transcendental Psychology*, esp. pp. 95–100. At best, however, this shows only that Kant could have had access to Hume's famous discussion, not that his doctrine of apperception was intended, even in part, as a response to it. To prove this thesis it would be necessary to show from Kant's discussions of apperception during the "silent decade" – more specifically, from the time of the *Duisburg'sche Nachlass* to the publication of the *Critique* – that Kant was concerned with the Humean problem. An examination of these texts, which Kitcher completely ignores, suggests a quite different story, however, since Kant's early discussions of apperception assume a knowledge of the unity of the self *qua* mental substance and attempt to connect this knowledge with the categories. For an analysis of this point see

Wolfgang Carl, *Der schweigende Kant: Die Entwürfe zu einer Deduktion der Kategorien vor 1781*, Göttingen: Vandenheck & Ruprecht, 1989, esp. pp. 146–58, which discusses the relevance of Hume to Kant's development during this period.

16 This has also been argued recently by Derk Pereboom, "Kant on justification in transcendental philosophy," *Synthese* 85 (1990), pp. 25–54, esp. pp. 34–36.

17 Paton comes close to this when he suggests that "The proposition can be analytic only if it is made by analysis of the concept of human knowledge," which he further clarifies in a note by stating that for 'human knowledge' it is permissible to substitute 'human thought' or even 'human understanding.' See *Kant's Metaphysic of Experience*, Vol. 1, p. 518 and note 9. What Paton fails to realize here is simply that the concept of discursive thought or understanding is broader than that of human thought or understanding and that this makes all the difference for understanding the claim of analyticity.

18 I discuss this issue in detail in *The Kant–Eberhard Controversy*, Baltimore and London: The Johns Hopkins University Press, 1973, pp. 46–75; *Kant's Transcendental Idealism*, pp. 69–80; and "The originality of Kant's distinction between analytic and synthetic judgements," *Studies in Philosophy and the History of Philosophy*, Vol. 12, *The Philosophy of Immanuel Kant*, edited by Richard Kennington, Washington D. C.: The Catholic University of America Press, 1985, pp. 15–38.

19 In §23 Kant emphasizes that the pure concepts of the understanding have no objective reality with respect to objects of intuition in general, and in §24 he asserts that, so related, they are "*mere forms of thought,* through which alone no determinate object [Gegenstand] is known" (B150). These passages, which are consistent with the doctrine of the Schematism and Phenomena and Noumena chapters, strongly suggest that Kant did not regard the first part of the B-Deduction as establishing anything substantive about the categories with respect to human experience.

20 On the topic of the relation between pure and schematized categories see Paton, *Kant's Metaphysic of Experience*, Vol. II, pp. 41–43, 67–69. As Paton notes (p. 41), Kant does not use the term 'schematized category,' although he does implicitly distinguish between pure and schematized categories.

21 The latter is admittedly a controversial claim, denied by many commentators including Guyer (see particularly his "Kant on apperception and a priori synthesis"); but I think that it is clearly supported by Kant's letter to Herz of May 26, 1789. For my analysis of the relevant portion of this letter see *Kant's Transcendental Idealism*, pp. 153–55.

22 *Kant's Transcendental Idealism*, pp. 137–38.

23 Kant characterizes an intuitive intellect in this manner in *Critique of Judgment* (5: 406; 290).

24 The connection between Kant and James on this point is noted by Norman Kemp Smith, *A Commentary to Kant's "Critique of Pure Reason,"* second edition, revised and enlarged, New York: Humanities Press, 1962, p. 459; and Robert Paul Wolff, *Kant's Theory of Mental Activity*, Cambridge: Harvard University Press, 1963, p. 106.

25 For my discussion of this see *Kant's Transcendental Idealism*, pp. 283–86.

26 Ibid. pp. 144–48.

27 On this point see Wolfgang Carl, *Der Schweigende Kant* and "Kant's first drafts of the Deduction of the Categories," *Kant's Transcendental Deductions: The Three "Critiques" and the "Opus Postumum,"* edited by Eckart Förster, Stanford, Calif.: Stanford University Press, 1989, pp. 3–20.
28 J. Claude Evans, "Two-steps-in-one-proof: The structure of the Transcendental Deduction of the Categories," *Journal of the History of Philosophy* 28 (1990), pp. 553–70, esp. p. 559.
29 See note 2.
30 See, for example, Raymond Brouillet, "Dieter Henrich et 'The proof-structure of Kant's Transcendental Deduction': Réflexions critiques," *Dialogue* 14 (1975), pp. 639–48; and Hans Wagner, "Der Argumentationsgang in Kants Deduktion der Kategorien," *Kant-Studien,* 71 (1980), pp. 352–66.
31 Dieter Henrich, "Diskussion: Beweisstruktur der transzendentalen Deduktion," *Probleme der "Kritik der reinen Vernunft,"* edited by Burkhard Tuschling, Berlin: Walter de Gruyter, 1984, pp. 34–96, esp. pp. 41–42. The whole controversy is discussed by Evans, "Two-steps-in-one-proof," pp. 554–60.
32 For the dating of the composition of the second *Critique* see Lewis White Beck, *A Commentary on Kant's Critique of Practical Reason,* Chicago: The University of Chicago Press, 1960, pp. 13–18.
33 It is interesting to note that by drawing on this analogy with Kant's procedure in the *Critique of Practical Reason,* the interpretation offered here meets one of Dieter Henrich's criteria for an interpretation of the argumentative strategy of the deduction: it must be applicable to the deduction in the second *Critique.* See Henrich's paper, "Kant's notion of a deduction and the methodological background of the first *Critique,*" *Kant's Transcendental Deductions,* p. 30.
34 For my analysis of the reciprocity between the categorical imperative and freedom, see "Morality and freedom: Kant's reciprocity thesis," *Philosophical Review* 95 (1986), pp. 393–425 and *Kant's Theory of Freedom,* Cambridge and New York: Cambridge University Press, chapter 11.
35 For Kant's characterization of objective validity with respect to the categories, see A93/B126 and A97. In *Kant's Transcendental Idealism* I argued that the first part of the Deduction has as its aim the demonstration of the objective validity of the categories and the second, their objective reality (see esp. pp. 134–35). The distinction between objective validity and objective reality and its significance for the Deduction in both editions is also emphasized by Günter Zöller, *Theoretische Gegenstandsbeziehung bei Kant,* Berlin, New York: Walter de Gruyter, 1984.
36 *Kant's Transcendental Idealism,* pp. 158–64.
37 Ibid., pp. 170–72.

Chapter 4

1 P. F. Strawson, *The Bounds of Sense,* London: Methuen & Co. Ltd, pp. 31–32. See also pp. 88 and 97.
2 Patricia Kitcher, *Kant's Transcendental Psychology,* New York, Oxford: Oxford University Press, 1990.
3 Kitcher, *Kant's Transcendental Psychology,* p. 74.
4 Ibid., p. 75.

5 Ibid. Allowing for the shift in terminology from cognitive to mental states, this accords nicely with Sydney Shoemaker's characterization of a functionalist analysis of mental states. According to him, a functionalist analysis holds that "What constitutes a mental state as being the particular mental state it is, and so as having the representational content that it does, are its causal relations to other mental states and to sensory inputs and behavioral modifications." See Shoemaker's "Self-consciousness and synthesis," (commentary to Patricia Kitcher's "Kant's real self"), *Self and Nature in Kant's Philosophy*, edited by Allen W. Wood, Ithaca and London: Cornell University Press, 1984, p. 150.
6 Kitcher, *Kant's Transcendental Psychology*, p. 103.
7 Ibid.
8 See, for example, *Kant's Transcendental Psychology*, pp. 112 and 129.
9 Ibid., p. 107.
10 Ibid., pp. 104 and 187.
11 Ibid., pp. 104–107.
12 Ibid., p. 83.
13 Kitcher, "Kant's dedicated cognitivism," *Historical Foundations of Cognitive Science*, edited by J. C. Smith, Dordrecht/Boston/London: Kluwer Academic Publishers, 1990, p. 200.
14 See, for example, Kant's *Transcendental Psychology*, pp. 111, 126–27. In her more recent work, however, Kitcher has modified her views on apperception somewhat and offered a functionalist analysis of its role in cognition. See "Kant on cognition and self-consciousness" (not yet published).
15 Ibid., pp. 83 and 111.
16 Ibid., p. 121. As places where Kant allegedly denies synthesis watching, she cites A104 and B134, neither of which unambiguously supports her contention.
17 Ibid., p. 127.
18 Ibid., p. 122.
19 Ibid., p. 253, note 5.
20 For a discussion of Kant's contrast between absolute and relative spontaneity (or *spontaneitas secundum quid*) see my *Kant's Theory of Freedom*, Cambridge and New York: Cambridge University Press, 1990, pp. 60–64.
21 Kitcher characterizes Strawson's Kant in this manner in "Kant's dedicated cognitive system," p. 190.
22 Kitcher appears to deny this insofar as she explicitly separates Kant's doctrine of apperception as a reply to Hume's skepticism regarding mental unity from the central concern of the Deduction with the validity of the categories. See *Kant's Transcendental Psychology*, p. 105.
23 See my "Kant's refutation of materialism" (Chapter 7 in this volume), and *Kant's Theory of Freedom*, pp. 37–38.
24 See Kitcher, *Kant's Transcendental Psychology*, pp. 126–27.
25 On this point see Robert Pippin, "Kant on the spontaneity of mind," *Canadian Journal of Philosophy*, 17 (1987), pp. 459–60.
26 See, for example, A50–51/B74–75.
27 Just such a reading was advocated by Wilfred Sellars, who likewise argues for an essentially functionalist interpretation of Kant. See ". . . This I or he or it (the thing) which thinks . . . ," and "Metaphysics and the concept of a person," in

Essays in Philosophy and Its History, Dordrecht/Boston: D. Reidel, 1974, pp. 63–90 and 214–41.

28   For a more fully worked out version of this argument see "Kant's refutation of materialism" (Chapter 7 in this volume).

29   See *Groundwork* 4: 448; 116. For my own more detailed treatment of the issues involved here, see *Kant's Theory of Freedom,* esp. chapters 2 and 13.

30   See Kitcher, "Kant's real self," *Self and Nature in Kant's Philosophy,* pp. 113–47 and *Kant's Transcendental Psychology,* pp. 139–40.

31   Thomas Nagel, *The View from Nowhere,* New York, Oxford: Oxford University Press, 1986, esp. pp. 54–66.

32   I discuss this issue in more detail in *Kant's Transcendental Idealism,* pp. 283–93.

33   Gilbert Ryle, *The Concept of Mind,* New York: Barnes & Noble, 1965, pp. 195–98.

34   I wish to thank Ian Eagleson for his helpful comments on earlier drafts of this paper.

Chapter 5

1   Aron Gurwitsch, *Kants Theorie des Verstandes,* edited by Thomas M. Seebohm, Dordrecht/Boston/London: Kluwer Academic Publishers, 1990.

2   See *Leibniz Philosophie des Panlogismus,* Berlin/New York: Walter de Gruyter, 1974, esp. pp. 127–30, 187–90; and "Der Begriff des Bewusstseins bei Kant und Husserl," *Kant-Studien,* 55 (1964), pp. 410–27, reprinted as Beilage I in *Kants Theorie des Verstandes,* pp. 135–56; and "La conception de la conscience chez Kant et chez Husserl," *Bulletin de la Société française de Philosophie, Séance du 25 Avril 1959,* 54 (1960), pp. 65–96. "The Kantian and Husserlian conceptions of consciousness," an English translation of the French version and subsequent discussion is contained in Aron Gurwitsch, *Studies in Phenomenology and Psychology,* Evanston, Ill.: Northwestern University Press, 1966, pp. 148–74.

3   *Kants Theorie des Verstandes,* pp. 165–66.

4   Leibniz, *New Essays on Human Understanding,* Book II, chapters 1 and 2, p. 111. The now standard English translation by Peter Remnant and Jonathan Bennett, Cambridge: Cambridge University Press (1981), uses the pagination of volume 5, the edition of C. I. Gerhardt, which Gurwitsch likewise cites.

5   Ibid., p. 52.

6   Ibid.

7   *Kants Theorie des Verstandes,* p. 5.

8   For helpful recent discussions of Leibniz's views on apperception see R. M. McRae, *Leibniz: Perception, Apperception and Thought,* Toronto: University of Toronto Press, 1976; and Nicholas Jolley, *Leibniz and Locke: A Study of the New Essays on Human Understanding,* Oxford: Clarendon Press, 1984.

9   *Kants Theorie des Verstandes,* pp. 77–78, and 165.

10 Ibid., p. 58.

11 *Kants Theorie des Verstandes,* chapter 5, pp. 49–63, is devoted to Kant's appropriation of Leibniz's theory of "petites perceptions."

12 See *Leibniz Philosophie des Panlogismus,* p. 190; *Kants Theorie des Verstandes,* pp. 103–106.

13 *Kants Theorie des Verstandes,* p. 107.

14 *Leibniz Philosophie des Panlogismus*, pp. 128–29.
15 *Kants Theorie des Verstandes*, pp. 83–86.
16 Ibid., p. 2, note 1.
17 Ibid., pp. 11–12.
18 Ibid., p. 14.
19 Allison, *Kant's Transcendental Idealism*, p. 218.
20 *Kants Theorie des Verstandes*, p. 38.
21 Ibid., 39. The reference to Cassirer is from *Kants Leben und Lehre*, Berlin: Bruno Cassirer, 1911, p. 170.
22 *Kants Theorie des Verstandes*, p. 19. See also, pp. 35ff, 51ff, 79–81.
23 For Gurwitsch's discussions of this letter see *Leibniz Philosophie des Panlogismus*, p. 129; *Kants Theorie des Verstandes*, pp. 79 and 167–70.
24 Br 11: 52; 153–54.
25 Allison, *Kant's Transcendental Idealism*, esp. pp. 14–58.
26 *Kants Theorie des Verstandes*, pp. 21–22. See also p. 31, where he criticizes Cassirer's purely logical reading of the conception of "consciousness in general," which is the *Prolegomena*'s surrogate for apperception, on the grounds that it fails to deal with the question of the root and origin of the (transcendentally) logical conditions expressed in the idea of consciousness in general.
27 Ibid., pp. 21–22.
28 Ibid., pp. 24–25.
29 Ibid., p. 29.
30 In the recent literature such a view is advocated by Malte Hossenfelder, *Kants Konstitutions-theorie und die Transzendentale Deduktion*, Berlin: de Gruyter, 1978. See also Hossenfelder's critique of my own position in "Allison's defence of Kant's transcendental idealism," *Inquiry* 33 (1990), pp. 467–79.
31 *Kants Theorie des Verstandes*, p. 39.
32 Ibid., pp. 40–42, 101–102.
33 Ibid., p. 50.
34 Ibid.
35 Ibid., p. 52. It may be noted that I use virtually the same expression in *Kant's Transcendental Idealism*, p. 139, referring to the "necessity of the possibility." Although I do not recall Gurwitsch having used such a locution in his Kant seminar, he may very well have done so, in which case my own use of it might be taken as evidence of the importance of those *petites perceptions*.
36 Ibid., p. 53.
37 Ibid., pp. 55–63.
38 See *Kant's Transcendental Idealism*, pp. 142–44.
39 *Reflexion* 5661, 18: 318–19. For my analysis of this text see *Kant's Transcendental Idealism*, pp. 275–78.
40 For a fuller discussion of this topic see my *Kant's Theory of Freedom*, pp. 36–38 and "On naturalizing Kant's transcendental psychology"; and "Kant's refutation of materialsim" (Chapters 4 and 7 in this volume).
41 *Kants Theorie des Verstandes*, pp. 28 and 95.
42 For my analysis of this see *Kant's Transcendental Idealism*, pp. 137–48; and "Apperception and analyticity in the B-Deduction" (Chapter 3 in this volume).

43 *Kants Theorie des Verstandes*, pp. 123–32. See also, "The Kantian and Husserlian conceptions of consciousness," esp. pp. 155–59.
44 I attempted to deal with the latter issue some years ago in "The *Critique of Pure Reason* as transcendental phenomenology," volume 5 of *Selected Studies in Phenomenology and Existential Philosophy*, edited by R. Zaner and D. Ihde, The Hague: Martinus Nijhoff, 1974, pp. 136–55. Among recent commentators, the role of intentionality in Kant's thought has been emphasized by Richard Aquila. See his *Representational Mind: A Study of Kant's Theory of Knowledge*, Bloomington: Indiana University Press, 1983; and *Matter in Mind: A Study of Kant's Transcendental Deduction*, Bloomington: Indiana University Press, 1989.
45 *Kants Theorie des Verstandes*, p. 127.
46 Interestingly enough, Gurwitsch deals only in passing with the problem of intersubjectivity or, more precisely, of an intersubjectively identifiable world in Kant and does not integrate it into his criticism, although he easily could have done so. In contrast to Paton, who attempts to account for this identity in terms of the universality of the conditions of experience, Gurwitsch sees the Kantian response to this problem to lie in the thing-in-itself. But rather than regarding this as a solution, he sees it as an explanation of why the problem never really arose for Kant. See *Kants Theorie des Verstandes*, pp. 44–47.
47 For the full version of this analysis see *Kant's Transcendental Idealism*, pp. 217–28.

Chapter 6

1 See also, A127–28, B165, A159/B198, A216/B263, *Prolegomena*, §36.
2 Buchdahl, like most English language commentators, including Michael Friedman, does not recognize any significant distinction between reason in its hypothetical function and reflective judgment. Serious questions regarding their identification have been raised, however, in the German literature. For a survey of this literature and the issues involved, see Helga Mertens, *Kommentar zur Ersten Einleitung in Kants Kritik der Urteilskraft*, München: Johannes Berchmans Verlag, 1973, pp. 33–46.
3 Gerd Buchdahl, *Metaphysics and the Philosophy of Science*, Cambridge, Mass.: M.I.T. Press, 1969, esp. pp. 651–65; "The Kantian 'dynamic of reason' with special reference to the place of causality in Kant's system," in *Kant Studies Today*, edited by L. W. Beck, La Salle, Ill.: Open Court, 1969, pp. 187–208; "The conception of lawlikeness in Kant's philosophy of science," in *Kant's Theory of Knowledge*, edited by L. W. Beck, Dordrecht: Reidel, 1974, pp. 128–50.
4 See Lewis White Beck, "A Prussian Hume and a Scottish Kant," *Essays on Hume and Kant*, New Haven and London: Yale University Press, 1978, pp. 111–29, esp. p. 126.
5 See Arthur Lovejoy, "On Kant's reply to Hume," *Kant: Disputed Questions*, edited by Moltke S. Gram, Chicago: Quadrangle Books, 1967, pp. 284–308; and P. F. Strawson, *The Bounds of Sense, an Essay on Kant's Critique of Pure Reason*, London: Methuen, 1966, pp. 137–38.
6 For this line of response to the *non sequitur* objection see Buchdahl, *Metaphysics*

and the Philosophy of Science, pp. 670–71; and Lewis White Beck, "Is there a non sequitur in Kant's proof of the causal principle?" *Kant-Studien* 67 (1976), reprinted as "A non sequitur of numbing grossness," in *Essays on Kant and Hume*, pp. 147–53; and Henry E. Allison, *Kant's Transcendental Idealism*, New Haven and London: Yale University Press, 1983, pp. 232–34.

7   The main paper in which this challenge is presented is "Causal laws and the foundations of natural science," *The Cambridge Companion to Kant*, edited by Paul Guyer, Cambridge: Cambridge University Press, 1992, pp. 161–97. Also relevant is "Regulative and constitutive," *Southern Journal of Philosophy*, Vol. XXX, Supplement, The Spindel Conference, 1991, pp. 73–102; and earlier papers such as "Kant on space, the understanding, and the law of gravitation: *Prolegomena* §38," *Monist* 79 (1989), pp. 236–84.

8   Friedman, "Causal laws and the foundations of natural science," pp. 165–70.

9   This claim was contained in a draft version read at Princeton in the fall of 1990 but deleted from the published version.

10 Friedman, "Kant on causal laws and the foundations of natural science," p. 171.

11 Ibid., p. 171.

12 Ibid., pp. 172–75.

13 Other passages cited in support of the same point include: A127–28; B165; A216/B263; etc.

14 Friedman, "Kant on causal laws and the foundations of natural science," p. 176; "Regulative and constitutive," p. 81.

15 Friedman, "Kant on causal laws and the foundations of natural science," p. 182.

16 Friedman, "Regulative and constitutive," p. 80.

17 In "Regulative and constitutive," note 17, p. 98, Friedman refers to both texts in support of this reading.

18 Friedman, "Kant on causal laws and the foundations of natural science," pp. 176–78.

19 Ibid., pp. 185–86.

20 Ibid., p. 189.

21 Ibid., pp. 190–91.

22 This point is put clearly by J. D. McFarland, *Kant's Concept of Teleology*, Edinburgh: University of Edinburgh Press, 1970, esp. pp. 8–11.

23 See H. J. Paton, *Kant's Metaphysic of Experience*, London: George Allen & Unwin Ltd., 1951, Vol. 2, pp. 275–78.

24 Paul Guyer, *Kant and the Claims of Knowledge*, Cambridge and New York: Cambridge University Press, 1987, p. 252. For my critique of Guyer on this point, see my review of his book, *Journal of Philosophy* 86 (1989), pp. 214–21.

25 An interesting variant of this view is held by Philip Kitcher, who claims that the Second Analogy is intended to show that one cannot justify judgments about "Hume facts," that is, tokens of objective succession, apart from the justification of causal claims, but that these claims are only justified by an appeal to reason's or reflective judgment's principle of systematicity. Kitcher thus combines the view that appeal to causal laws is necessary for the experience of objective succession with an essentially Buchdahlean view of the function of the principle of systematicity. See "Projecting the order of nature," in *Kant's Philosophy of Physical Science*, edited by Robert Butts, Dordrecht and Boston: Reidel, 1986, pp. 210–35.

26 See McFarland, *Kant's Concept of Teleology*, pp. 5–6.
27 See, for example, Friedman, "Kant on causal laws and the foundations of natural science," pp. 164, 168, 169, 170, 186.
28 Compare, for example, A91/B123–24 and A192/B237.
29 Allison, *Kant's Transcendental Idealism*, esp. p. 223.
30 Friedman, "Kant on causal laws and the foundations of natural science," pp. 178 and 186.
31 Buchdahl, *Metaphysics and the Philosophy of Science*, pp. 651–55.
32 Paul Guyer, *Kant and the Claims of Knowledge*, pp. 258–59, 315, 326.
33 For my analysis of this argument see *Kant's Transcendental Idealism*, pp. 224–28.
34 Buchdahl, "Dynamic of reason," p. 342, note 11, "Conception of law-likeness," p. 136.
35 Friedman, "Kant on causal laws and the foundations of natural science," p. 190. The passage is from KU 5: 183; 23.
36 Friedman, "Kant on causal laws and the foundations of natural science," manuscript version, note 47, pp. 34–35.
37 See Guyer, "Reason and reflective judgment: Kant on the significance of systematicity," *Nous* 24 (1990), pp. 17–43, esp. pp. 39–43, and "Kant's conception of empirical law," *Proceedings of the Aristotelian Society*, Supplementary Volume (1990), pp. 221–42, esp. pp. 236–42.
38 Friedman discusses the role of regulative principles in more detail in "Regulative and constitutive," especially section II, pp. 83–90.

Chapter 7

1 See *Reflexionen* 4218, 4294, 4336, 4723, 4904, 5109, 5441, 7440, 7041 and ML, 28: 267–69. The issue is discussed in detail by Karl Ameriks, *Kant's Theory of Mind*, Oxford: Clarendon Press, 1982, pp. 194–96. I also discuss these texts briefly in "The concept of freedom in Kant's 'semi-critical' ethics," *Archiv für Geschichte der Philosophie* 68 (1986), Heft 1, 109–11.
2 *Reflexion* 5442. The importance of this *Reflexion* is noted by Dieter Henrich, "Die Deduktion des Sittengesetzes," in *Denken im Schatten des Nihilismus*, edited by Alexander Schwan, Darmstadt: Wissenschftliche Buchgesellschaft, 1975, pp. 55–112.
3 See Wilfred Sellars, "... this I or he or it (the thing which thinks)...." and "Metaphysics and the concept of a person" in *Essays in Philosophy and its History*, Dordrecht: D. Reidel, 1974, pp. 63–90 and 214–41; and Patricia Kitcher, "Kant on self-identity," *Philosophical Review* 91 (1982), 41–72, "Kant's Paralogisms," *Philosophical Review* 91 (1982), 515–47 and "Kant's real self," in *Self and Nature in Kant's Philosophy*, edited by Allen Wood, Ithaca, N.Y., and London: Cornell University Press, 1984, pp. 113–47.
4 Sellars, "Metaphysics and the concept of a person," p. 240.
5 Kant draws this distinction explicitly in sections 24 and 25 (B152–59). The non-experiential nature of the latter mode of self-consciousness is the topic of the important *Reflexion* 5661: "Is it an experience that we think?" 18: 318–19. I discuss this *Reflexion* and the whole question of the relationship between apperception and spontaneity in *Kant's Transcendental Idealism*, pp. 274–78.

6. See, for example, Patricia Kitcher, "Kant on self-identity," pp. 60–61, 66; and "Kant's real self," p. 119.
7. The necessary reflexiveness of experience and its connection with spontaneity has been very helpfully explicated by Robert Pippin, "Kant on the spontaneity of mind," *Canadian Journal of Philosophy* 17 (1987), 449–75, 459–63.
8. See *Kant's Transcendental Idealism*, pp. 138–47, for such an account of apperception in the B-Deduction.
9. See Pippin, "Kant on the spontaneity of mind," pp. 459–60.
10. Gilbert Ryle, *The Concept of Mind*, New York: Barnes & Noble, 1965, pp. 195–98.
11. See *Critique of Pure Reason*, A346/B404, A402, B422; and *Kant's Transcendental Idealism*, pp. 290–93.
12. See *Kant's Transcendental Idealism*, pp. 283–86.
13. The "critical" version of the anti-materialist claim is first made, albeit without argument, in Prol 4: 332, 82. Similar arguments were used in the "pre-critical" metaphysics lectures to establish the full-blooded doctrine of the soul's simplicity. For an account of the history of Kant's views on the topic see Karl Ameriks, *Kant's Theory of Mind*, esp. pp. 27–37.
14. For an account of the Leibnizian position on this issue, which in many ways is quite close to Kant's, see Margaret Wilson, "Leibniz and materialism," *Canadian Journal of Philosophy* III (June 1974), 495–513.
15. Ameriks, *Kant's Theory of Mind*, pp. 32–47. The other four are appearance, phenomenal, noumenal and transcendental materialism. The latter is also called "materialism in the extended sense."
16. Fort 20: 308.
17. Wilson, "Leibniz and materialism," p. 511.
18. Ibid. p. 512; and Ameriks, *Kant's Theory of Mind*, p. 40.
19. Gr 4: 448; 116.
20. The most explicitly Kantian formulation of this argument in the contemporary literature is by Warner Wick, "Truth's debt to freedom," *Mind* 73 (1964), 527–37.
21. Critics who take this line include A. J. Ayer, "Fatalism," *The Concept of a Person and Other Essays*, London: Macmillan, 1963; D. M. Armstrong, *A Materialist Theory of the Mind*, London: Routledge and Kegan Paul, 1968, p. 200; G. E. M. Anscombe, "A reply to Mr. C. S. Lewis's argument that naturalism is self-refuting," *Metaphysics and the Philosophy of Mind, Collected Philosophical Papers, Volume II*, Minneapolis: University of Minnesota Press, 1981, pp. 224–32; Patricia Smith Churchland, "Is determinism self-refuting?" *Mind*, XC (1981), 99–101.
22. The compatibility of Kant's views with functionalism is a central theme in the work of Patricia Kitcher (see note 3 above). Recently, an interpretation of Kant's views of agency in terms of Davidson's "anomalous monism" has been advocated by Ralf Meerbote. See his "*Wille* and *Willkür* in Kant's theory of action," *Interpreting Kant*, edited by Moltke S. Gram, Iowa City: University of Iowa Press, 1982, pp. 69–89; "Kant and the nondeterminate character of human actions," *Kant on Causality, Freedom and Objectivity*, edited by William A. Harper and Ralf Meerbote, Minneapolis: University of Minnesota Press, 1984, pp. 138–63; and "Kant on freedom and the rational and morally good will," *Self and Nature in Kant's*

Philosophy, pp. 57–72. Since Meerbote's interpretation is concerned mainly with Kant's theories of agency and freedom I shall not deal with it explicitly in the present essay. It should be noted, however, that he certainly holds that Kant's account of the spontaneity of the understanding can best be understood in the "spirit of anomalous monism."

23 This is noted by James N. Jordan, "Determinism's dilemma," *Review of Metaphysics*, 23 (1969–70), 48–66, esp. 51–52.
24 See Adolph Grünbaum, "Science and man," in M. Mandelbaum, et al., eds., *Philosophic Problems*, 2nd edition, New York: Macmillan, 1967, p. 457.
25 RSV8: 14.
26 This version of the argument is advocated by James N. Jordan, "Determinism's dilemma," 61–64.
27 The clearest formulation of this version is by William Hasker, "The transcendental refutation of determinism," *Southern Journal of Philosophy* 11 (1973), 175–83.
28 In formulating this line of objection to his argument, Hasker refers explicitly to Alvin Goldman's notion of a "simultaneous nomic equivalent," as presented in "The compatibility of mechanism and purpose," *Philosophical Review* 78 (1969), 468–82. I believe, however, that the basic point can be more simply expressed in terms of supervenience.
29 See Hasker, "The transcendental refutation of determinism," 179–81.
30 Thomas Nagel, *The View from Nowhere*, New York, Oxford: Oxford University Press, 1986, esp. pp. 54–66. Although Nagel certainly emphasizes the ineliminability of the I or subjectivity from a complete account of the world, he does not take this thought in the Kantian direction attempted here.
31 Paul Churchland, *Matter and Consciousness*, Cambridge, Mass.: MIT Press, 1984, p. 48.
32 Ibid.
33 Ibid.
34 Ibid., p. 31.
35 I wish to thank Karl Ameriks, Patricia Kitcher and Robert Pippin for their extremely helpful criticism of earlier versions of this essay. The mistakes that remain are, of course, entirely my own.

Chapter 8

1 Stephen Engstrom, "Allison on rational agency," *Inquiry* 36 (1993), pp. 405–18.
2 See *Religion within the Limits of Reason Alone*, 6: 24; 19, and *Kant's Theory of Freedom*, Cambridge, New York: Cambridge University Press, 1990, pp. 40–41.
3 For a discussion of this issue with textual references, see *Kant's Theory of Freedom*, pp. 54–59.
4 In *Kant's Theory of Freedom* I frequently used the term 'incompatibilism' in connection with Kant's conception of freedom because it is radically opposed to the Leibnizian and Humean positions against which Kant defined his own view. It has been pointed out, however, by Hud Hudson in his review of my book (*Kant-Studien* 82 (1991), pp. 219–22, by Lewis White Beck in personal correspondence and by several others that this is quite misleading, since Kant is indeed a compatibilist in the sense that he holds that freedom of the will is compatible with causal

determination. This is, of course, correct and, strictly speaking, Kant's conception of freedom should be characterized as 'indeterministic' rather than 'incompatibilistic.' Nevertheless, I have maintained this terminology because its use with respect to Kant is already fairly common in the literature (Karl Ameriks and Allen Wood are two examples) and because I wish to emphasize the sharp difference between Kant's conception of freedom and the contemporary naturalistic forms of compatibilism with which it is frequently compared. Accordingly, in the essays in this volume I shall regard 'incompatibilist' and 'indeterminist' (and their cognates) as equivalent and use them interchangeably.

5 Ibid., pp 59–61.
6 For a different account of the spontaneity–autonomy contrast see Lewis White Beck, *A Commentary on Kant's "Critique of Practical Reason,"* Chicago: University of Chicago Press, 1960, pp. 176–78; and "Five concepts of freedom in Kant," in *Philosophical Analysis and Reconstruction*, a Festschrift to Stephan Körner, edited by J. T. J. Srzendnick, Dordrecht: Martinus Nijhoff, 1987, pp. 35–51.
7 Since Kant sometimes defines transcendental freedom as absolute spontaneity, which must be distinguished from autonomy, it might seem mistaken or, at the very least, misleading to link practical freedom with spontaneity and transcendental freedom with autonomy. Part of the problem here is due to the fluidity of Kant's terminology, part to the ambiguity of the concept of practical freedom (which I explored in *Kant's Theory of Freedom*) and part to the significant shift in Kant's moral theory brought about by the introduction of the principle of autonomy. Setting the terminological problems aside, however, the main point on which I insist is that the spontaneity presupposed by the Incorporation Thesis does not entail autonomy as Kant came to understand it. Thus, he cannot move directly from a general reflection on the conditions of rational agency to the authority of the categorical imperative. I analyze this issue in more detail and in connection with Kant's later writings in "Autonomy and spontaneity in Kant's conception of the self" (Chapter 9 in this volume).
8 For my analysis of Kant's moral theory at the time of the publication of the first edition of the *Critique of Pure Reason*, see *Kant's Theory of Freedom*, pp. 66–70.
9 See *Groundwork* 4: 417; 85. As Kant himself there notes, this proposition is analytic.
10 Engstrom, "Allison on rational agency," p. 410.
11 Ibid., pp. 411–13.
12 See *Groundwork*, 4: 418–19; 85–86. *Critique of Practical Reason*, 5: 25–26; 24–25.
13 *Groundwork*, 4: 418; 85; and *Critique of Practical Reason*, 5: 26; 25.
14 See, for example, *Groundwork*, 4: 415; 82; *Metaphysic of Morals*, 6: 386; 190.
15 For my interpretation of Kant's conception of interest, see *Kant's Theory of Freedom*, pp. 89–90.
16 Engstrom, "Allison on rational agency," p. 113.
17 Andrews Reath, "Intelligible character and the Reciprocity Thesis," *Inquiry* 36 (1993), pp. 419–30.
18 Ibid., p. 427.
19 For my discussion of the *Wille–Willkür* distinction, see *Kant's Theory of Freedom*, pp. 129–36.

20 See *Metaphysic of Morals*, 6: 226; 52.
21 For my discussion of these topics, see *Kant's Theory of Freedom*, chapters 7 and 8.
22 It should be noted that this view of maxims as ordered hierarchically is itself controversial and conflicts with the views of commentators such as O'Neill and Höffe. For my defense of this interpretation see *Kant's Theory of Freedom*, pp. 91–94; for direct textual support see *Metaphysic of Morals*, 6: 411; 211.
23 For this last step in the argument, which I cannot deal with here, see *Kant's Theory of Freedom*, pp. 210–13; and "On a presumed gap in the derivation of the categorical imperative" (Chapter 10 in this volume).
24 See *Groundwork*, 4: 412; 80.
25 See *Groundwork*, 4: 424; 91 and *Religion within the Limits of Reason Alone*, 6: 35–36; 31.
26 Reath, "Intelligible character and the Reciprocity Thesis," pp. 427–29.
27 Ibid., p. 429.
28 The need for rational justification underlies Kant's conception of conscience. See *Metaphysic of Morals*, 6: 438–40; 233–35.
29 Marcia Baron, "Freedom, frailty, and impurity," *Inquiry* 36 (1993), pp. 431–41.
30 Ibid., p. 432.
31 See *Kant's Theory of Freedom*, pp. 90–91.
32 In a note to the published version of her account, Baron offers a clarification of her view. As she now puts it, "It may seem, as Allison suggests in his reply, that I have in mind a two-step process: first, get yourself a maxim; second, incorporate an incentive into it. That is not my view. I am imagining, rather, that I might have a maxim that would be permissible were it not for the nasty incentive ... and I am asking: Is it part of my freedom that I can 'revise' the maxim by jettisoning the incentive, replacing it by another? Or can I say 'No' to the incentive only by saying 'No' to the entire plan of action?" ("Freedom, frailty, and impurity," note 3, p. 440). Although this certainly clarifies her position, I do not think that it affects the main point, for she still seems to assume that the maxim or "plan of action" and the incentive are merely externally related to each other. Thus, as I see it, the question she raises concerns the structure of rational agency rather than the limits of freedom.
33 Baron, "Freedom, frailty, and impurity," pp. 433–35.
34 Ibid., p. 435.
35 Ibid., 437–38.
36 Allison, *Kant's Theory of Freedom*, p. 167.
37 See *Groundwork*, 4: 399; 67; *Critique of Practical Reason*, 5: 93; 97; *Metaphysic of Morals*, 6: 388; 193.
38 See note 4.
39 Karl Ameriks, "Kant and Hegel on freedom: Two new interpretations," *Inquiry* 35 (1992), pp. 219–32; Paul Guyer, Book Review, *The Journal of Philosophy* (1992), pp. 99–110.
40 Guyer, Review, 99, 101.
41 Ibid., 101.
42 Ibid., 102.
43 Ibid., 100–101.

44 Ibid., 102.
45 Ameriks, "Kant and Hegel on freedom," p. 224.
46 The major exception to this compatibilist trend in the recent literature is Peter van Inwagen, *An Essay on Free Will,* Oxford: Clarendon Press, 1983; but he does not consider Kant or the distinctively Kantian view that one and the same occurrence might be both causally determined and a free act in a contracausal sense.
47 Ameriks, "Kant and Hegel on freedom," pp. 223–24, acknowledges this point but claims that it is perfectly compatible with also attributing to Kant a traditional noumenal metaphysic. This may be true, but my point is that there is no need to appeal to any such metaphysic, involving timeless choice and the like, because Kant is not appealing to freedom as an *explanans.*
48 Cf. Guyer, Review, p. 103.
49 Cf. *Critique of Practical Reason* 5: 94–95; 98–99; *Religion within the Limits of Reason Alone,* 6: 49n; 45.
50 Allen W. Wood, "Kant's compatibilism," in *Self and Nature in Kant's Philosophy,* edited by Allen W. Wood, Ithaca, N.Y., and London: Cornell University Press, 1984, p. 74.
51 I develop a similar anti-mechanist argument with respect to the theoretical capacity of reason in "Kant's refutation of materialism" (Chapter 7 in this volume).

Chapter 9

1 Lewis White Beck, *A Commentary on Kant's "Critique of Practical Reason,"* Chicago: University of Chicago Press, 1960, pp. 176–81; and "Five concepts of freedom in Kant," in *Philosophical Analysis and Reconstruction,* a Festschrift to Stephan Körner, edited by J. T. J. Srzednick, Dordrecht: Martinus Nijhoff, 1987, pp. 35–51.
2 See, for example, Beck, who correlates freedom as autonomy specifically with *Wille* and freedom as spontaneity with *Willkür, Commentary,* pp. 199–200.
3 For my discussion of this issue see *Kant's Theory of Freedom,* Cambridge, New York: Cambridge University Press, 1990, pp. 129–36.
4 These are *Reflexionen,* 5611–20, 18: 252–59. For an analysis of these *Reflexionen,* see Heinz Heimsoeth, "Freiheit und Charakter nach den Kant-Reflexionen Nr. 5611 bis 5620," *Tradition und Kritik,* edited by W. Arnold and H. Zeltner, Stuttgart: Friedrich Frommann, 1967, pp. 123–44.
5 Karl Ameriks, "Kant on spontaneity: Some new data," *Akten des Siebenten Internationalen Kant-Kongresses,* edited by G. Funke, Bonn: Bouvier, 1991, p. 478.
6 See also *Reflexion,* 6077, 18: 443.
7 Another important, frequently discussed text in which Kant argues in a similar manner is RSV 8: 14.
8 See my *Kant's Theory of Freedom,* pp. 214–21.
9 On the latter point see *Reflexion,* 5661, 18: 318–19, where Kant explicitly denies that we can experience ourselves as thinking.
10 This is argued by Rüdiger Bittner, "Maximen," *Akten des Kongresses,* edited by G. Funke and J. Kopper, Berlin: de Gruyter, 1974, pp. 485–98; and by Gerold Prauss, *Kant über Freiheit als Autonomie,* Frankfurt am Main: Vittorio Klostermann, 1983.

11 This claim is, of course, controversial. I argue for it in "The concept of freedom in Kant's 'semi-critical' ethics," *Archiv für Geschichte der Philosophie* 68 (1986), pp. 96–115; and *Kant's Theory of Freedom*, pp. 66–70. For a similar analysis, see E. G. Schulz, *Rehbergs Opposition gegen Kants Ethik*, Köln: Böhlau Verlag, 1975, pp. 105 note 35, 162–67.

12 Although he does not draw the contrast between spontaneity and autonomy as two species of freedom, the basic point is also noted by Thomas Hill, who likewise distinguishes between the two kinds of independence and argues that the move from negative to positive freedom requires attributing both kinds to the former. See *Dignity and Practical Reason in Kant's Moral Theory*, Ithaca, N.Y., and London: Cornell University Press, pp. 93–94; 106–10.

13 See "Morality and freedom: Kant's Reciprocity Thesis," *Philosophical Review*, 95 (1986), pp. 393–425; and *Kant's Theory of Freedom*, chapter 11.

14 In *Kant's Theory of Freedom*, "On a presumed gap in the derivation of the categorical imperative" (Chapter 10 in this volume) and "Kant's doctrine of obligatory ends" (Chapter 11 in this volume) I have correlated the categorical imperative with transcendental (as opposed to mere practical) freedom rather than autonomy. But in each case the point was that what is required is motivational and not simply causal independence. In some of my later discussions, I have linked it specifically with autonomy in order to bring out this very point. Accordingly, this marks merely a terminological change. For a discussion of the terminological point, see Chapter 8 in this volume, note 7.

15 For the argument linking the notion of an unconditional practical law with the categorical imperative, see *Kant's Theory of Freedom*, pp. 210–13; and "On a presumed gap in the derivation of the categorical imperative," Chapter 10 in this volume.

16 See *Critique of Pure Reason*, A801–803/B829–31; *Metaphysik der Sitten Vigilantius*, 27: 503–507; and Karl Ameriks, "Kant on spontaneity: Some new data," who refers to somewhat similar passages from *Metaphysik K*$_3$, *Metaphysik Mrongovius* and *Moral Mrongovius II*.

17 This is the main thrust of the very influential critique of Kant by August Wilhelm Rehberg, who held that even our consciousness of the moral law ought to be regarded by Kant as an appearance in inner sense and, therefore, as subject to the causality of nature. For a discussion of Rehberg's views, see E. G. Schulz, *Rehbergs Opposition gegen Kants Ethik*.

18 Something like the view criticized in this paragraph seems to be proposed by Allen Wood. See his "Kant's incompatiblism," in *Self and Nature in Kant's Philosophy*, edited by Allen W. Wood, Ithaca, N.Y., and London: Cornell University Press, 1984, pp. 73–101; and "The emptiness of the moral will," *Monist* 73 (1989), p. 454–83. For my critique of Wood's reading, see *Kant's Theory of Freedom*, pp. 48–52.

19 I take this to have been Fichte's project in the chapter added to the second edition of his first published work, *Attempt at a Critique of all Revelation*, in which he takes up specifically the question of whether the consciousness of spontaneity might be illusory. See *Johann Gottlieb Fichtes sämmtliche Werke*, edited by I. H. Fichte, reprinted Berlin: Walter de Gruyter & Co., 1971, Vol. 5, pp. 16–33.

20 For a recent expression of that viewpoint, see Nancy Sherman, "Person-relativity in ethics," *Monist*, 76 (1993), note 46, p. 263.
21 See "Kant on freedom: A reply to my critics," Chapter 8 in this volume.

Chapter 10

1 See, for example, Marcus Singer, *Generalization in Ethics*, New York: Alfred Knopf, 1961, pp. 292–95; Andreas Wildt, *Autonomie und Anerkennung*, Stuttgart: Klett-Cotta Verlag, 1982, pp. 84–96; Onora Nell (now O'Neill), *Acting on Principle*, Columbia University Press: New York and London, 1975, chapter 5; and Christine Korsgaard, "Kant's formula of universal law," *Pacific Philosophical Quarterly*, 66 (1985), pp. 24–47.
2 Bruce Aune, *Kant's Theory of Morals*, Princeton: Princeton University Press, 1979, pp. 29–30.
3 Allen W. Wood, *Hegel's Ethical Thought*, Cambridge, New York: Cambridge University Press, 1990, pp. 161–64. It should be noted, however, that Wood also emphasizes that Hegel's emptiness charge is directed against Kant's identification of morally worthy actions with those motivated by the thought of duty alone (*aus Pflicht*). The basic claim is that since the pure thought of duty is itself empty it cannot motivate. This aspect of Wood's analysis is touched on in the present work (167–73) and is more fully developed in "The emptiness of the moral will," *Monist* 73 (1989), pp. 454–83. I discuss this topic in my book, *Kant's Theory of Freedom*, Cambridge, New York: Cambridge University Press, 1990, 184–91.
4 See Wood, *Hegel's Ethical Thought*, p. 163.
5 An exception is Thomas Hill, who offers a similar objection in "Kant on the argument for the rationality of moral conduct," *Pacific Philosophical Quarterly*, 66 (1985), p. 19. Hill, however, apparently endorses the objection without considering the implications for Kant's moral theory.
6 As is frequently noted, Kant fails to formulate this principle explicitly, although it is clearly the first of the three consequences he intends to draw from the concept of a good will. I analyze and defend this principle in chapter 6 of *Kant's Theory of Freedom*.
7 Aune, *Kant's Theory of Morals*, pp. 29–30.
8 Ibid., p. 30.
9 Ibid., p. 43.
10 Wood contrasts the "universality of applicability" with both the "universality of concern" and "collective rationality" or "collective benefit." Although he never makes the connection explicit, it does appear that he regards the latter two expressions as at least roughly equivalent to "universality of concern." See *Hegel's Ethical Thought*, pp. 135–36, 165–66.
11 Ibid., pp. 163–67.
12 This argument is obviously a restatement of a familiar line of objection to Kantian appeals to universalizability as the criterion of moral correctness. Wood had already advanced this criticism of Kant, albeit without any reference to Hegel, in "Kant on the rationality of morals," *Proceedings of the Ottawa Congress on Kant in the Anglo-American and Continental Traditions Held October 10–14, 1974*, edited by P. Laberge, F. Duchesneau, B. C. Morrisey, pp. 94–109. The same

objection is also affirmed by Gilbert Harman, *The Nature of Morality*, New York: Oxford University Press, 1977, pp. 76–77. In Harman's case, however, there is absolutely no attempt to connect the criticism to the Kantian texts.
13 Aune, *Kant's Theory of Morals*, p. 86.
14 Ibid.
15 Ibid., p. 87.
16 Ibid.
17 Ibid.
18 Ibid.
19 Ibid.
20 Ibid., p. 88.
21 Ibid., p. 89.
22 I discuss this issue in *Kant's Theory of Freedom*, chapter 5.
23 On this point see Onora O'Neill, *Acting on Principle*, p. 78; Christine Korsgaard, "Kant's formula of universal law," pp. 24–47; and Thomas W. Pogge, "The categorical imperative," in *Grundlegung zur Metaphysik der Sitten: Ein kooperativer Kommentar*, edited by Otfried Höffe, Frankfurt am Main: Vittorio Klostermann, 1989, pp. 174–76.
24 Lewis White Beck, *A Commentary on Kant's "Critique of Practical Reason,"* Chicago: University of Chicago Press, 1960, pp. 109–25.
25 I am here distinguishing, as Kant himself frequently fails to do, between objective practical principles in general and the subset of such principles that count as laws in the strict sense. The contrast corresponds to the one that Kant sometimes draws between moral and pragmatic laws (*Critique of Pure Reason*, A802/B830), where only the former are universally and unconditionally valid, that is, valid independently of the inclinations or desires of an agent. The main point is that a principle could be objectively valid under a condition, that is, given a certain end or object of desire that is not itself an end of pure reason. For a further discussion of some of the complexities involved in this issue and in the distinction between objective and subjective practical principles (maxims), see Allison, *Kant's Theory of Freedom*, pp. 86–90.
26 This conflation seems to run through Kant's analysis, but it becomes explicit in §4 (Theorem III), KprV 5: 27; 26.
27 See Allison, "Morality and freedom: Kant's Reciprocity Thesis," *The Philosophical Review*, 95 (1986), pp. 393–425, and *Kant's Theory of Freedom*, chapter 11.
28 What follows is essentially a summary of the analysis provided in various places of my book, *Kant's Theory of Freedom*. See in particular pp. 54–70, 207–208.
29 See Allison, "Morality and freedom: Kant's Reciprocity Thesis," and *Kant's Theory of Freedom*, chapter 11.
30 My analysis in "Morality and freedom: Kant's Reciprocity Thesis" has been criticized for, among other reasons, failing to explain the move from practical law to the categorical imperative by Rüdiger Bittner, *What Reason Demands*, English translation by Theodore Talbot, Cambridge and New York: Cambridge University Press, 1989, note 187, pp. 170–171. This criticism is well taken, and I had recognized and tried to deal with the problem in *Kant's Theory of Freedom* prior to seeing the English version of Bittner's book. What I offer here is a further development of the line of argument sketched in my book.

31 The qualification "at least in part" is needed here in order to capture the dual function of the categorical imperative as both the source of a sufficient reason to act in the case of obligatory actions and as a merely necessary or limiting condition in the case of permissible but morally indifferent actions. The fact that a maxim or action is morally permissible obviously is not of itself a sufficient reason to choose it, but its non-permissibility would be a sufficient reason not to do so. The best discussion of this feature of the categorical imperative is by Barbara Herman, "On the value of acting from the motive of duty," *The Philosophical Review*, 90 (1981), pp. 359–82.

32 I say "at this point," because I do believe that there is a significant difference between the two works with respect to the justification of the categorical imperative. For this topic, see Allison, *Kant's Theory of Freedom*, chapters 12 and 13.

33 This point was suggested to me by Carl Posy.

Chapter 11

1 John E. Atwell, *Ends and Principles in Kant's Moral Thought*, Dordecht/Boston/Lancaster: Martinus Nijhoff, 1986, p. 96, notes that Kant never uses an expression that could be translated literally as "obligatory end," and criticizes Mary Gregor for using it in the original version of her translation of the *Tugendlehre* to render Kant's "*Zweck, der zugleich Pflicht ist.*" Atwell thinks that this is misleading, since it suggests (wrongly) that Kant is committed to a form of consequentialism. In the revised version of her translation, Gregor has dropped this expression, perhaps under the influence of Atwell. But since, for reasons that should become clear in the course of this paper, I do not believe that this worry is well founded, I shall continue to uses Gregor's original rendering, which is equivalent to, and much less cumbersome than, the more literal alternative.

2 According to Mary J. Gregor, *Laws of Freedom*, Oxford: Basil Blackwell, 1963, p. 89, human action is the third term linking the subject and predicate concepts in the deduction. Although no doubt correct, this does not appear to help very much.

3 Nelson Potter, "Kant on ends that are at the same time duties," *Pacific Philosophical Quarterly* 66 (1985), pp. 78–82.

4 Ibid., p. 81.

5 Ibid.

6 The topic of Kant's division of duties into juridical, ethical, perfect, imperfect, broad, narrow (as well as duties to oneself and to others) is an extremely complicated one. At the heart of the problem is the fact that Kant affirms a set of perfect duties to oneself, which, as such, are both narrow and non-juridical. Fortunately, however, we need not deal with all of the nuances of this division here, since our concern is solely with the set of duties to pursue certain ends, which are all broad and imperfect and which, for present purposes, can be contrasted with all the rest. For helpful discussions of this issue, see Gregor, *Laws of Freedom*, pp. 95–112; and Onora Nell (now O'Neill), *Acting on Principle: An Essay in Kantian Ethics*, New York and London: Columbia University Press, 1975, pp. 46–51.

7 For my analysis of this thesis and the argument in support of it, see my "Morality and freedom: Kant's Reciprocity Thesis," *The Philosophical Review*, 95 (1986),

pp. 393–425; *Kant's Theory of Freedom,* Cambridge and New York: Cambridge University Press, 1990, chapter 11; and Chapters 8, 9 and 10 in this volume.

8 In the *Groundwork* (4: 427; 95) Kant distinguishes between subjective ends and objective ends. The latter are based on reason, that is, grounds valid for all rational agents, and this presumably includes both the negative and positive sense of ends.

9 By "inclination in the broad sense" I mean the sense it has when it is contrasted with duty as one of the two possible sources of motivation. For my discussion of this topic and of its connection with Kant's own definitions of inclination see *Kant's Theory of Freedom,* pp. 108–109.

10 This amounts to what I have termed Kant's "Incorporation Thesis." For my discussion of this see *Kant's Theory of Freedom,* esp. pp. 40, 103, 126, 147–48, 189–90.

11 See *Kant's Theory of Freedom,* pp. 54–70, 207–208, and Chapters 8, 9 and 10 in this volume.

12 For my analysis of the *Wille–Willkür* distinction see *Kant's Theory of Freedom,* pp. 129–36.

13 The failure to recognize this possibility is one of the basic weaknesses of Mary Gregor's overall very helpful account of Kant's argument. See particularly *Laws of Freedom,* p. 86.

14 For my analysis of the argument of the second *Critique* see *Kant's Theory of Freedom,* chapter 13.

15 The connection between obligatory ends and the *Summum Bonum* is a central feature of Mary Gregor's analysis of the doctrine of obligatory ends. See *Laws of Freedom,* pp. 85–94. The point is also noted by Paul Eisenberg, "From the forbidden to the superogatory: The basic ethical categories in Kant's Tugendlehre," *American Philosophical Quarterly* 3 (1966), p. 9; and Potter, "Kant on ends that are at the same time duties," p. 84.

16 See, for example, Lewis White Beck, *A Commentary on Kant's "Critique of Practical Reason,"* Chicago: University of Chicago Press, 1960, esp. pp 244–55.

17 See Mary Gregor, *Laws of Freedom,* p. 86.

18 Eisenberg notes, "From the forbidden to the superogatory," p. 9, that Kant is inconsistent in his characterizations of beneficence, sometimes construing it as the duty to make the permissible ends one's own and sometimes as the duty of helping others in distress. This distinction is an important one and Eisenberg makes use of it in his critique of Kant's classification of duties, but I shall limit discussion to the first sense here because this is the one explicitly connected with the doctrine of obligatory ends.

19 For a discussion of when such conditions might obtain, see Eisenberg, "From the forbidden to the supererogatory," pp. 9–10.

20 Kant distinguishes between willing and wishing in the Introduction to the *Metaphysic of Morals,* 6: 213; 9–10.

21 Marcia Baron, "Kantian ethics and supererogation," *The Journal of Philosophy* 84 (1987), p. 250.

22 On this point, see, for example, Onora O'Neill, *Constructions of Reason: Explorations of Kant's Practical Philosophy,* Cambridge and New York: Cambridge University Press, 1989, pp. 98–100.

23 Baron, "Kantian ethics and supererogation," pp. 258–59, offers a nice account of such differences within the framework of a beneficent maxim.
24 See, for example, Gr 4: 392; 60. Accordingly, the much discussed examples are to be taken as illustrations of how this principle functions in the context of deliberation rather than as attempts to derive particular duties. For a thorough treatment of the issues regarding the relation between the *Groundwork* and the *Metaphysic of Morals* see Gregor, *Laws of Freedom*, pp. 1–33.
25 This conclusion is to be contrasted with the view of John Atwell, *Ends and Principles in Kant's Moral Thought*, esp. pp. 98–100. On his reading, the only reason why we should adopt certain ends such as the happiness of others is that a maxim excluding such an endeavor cannot be willed as a universal law of nature. Any other conclusion, on his view, would commit Kant to a form of consequentialism that would be incompatible with the main thrust of his theory. Atwell, like many interpreters, fails, however, either to distinguish between the two ways of rejecting non-beneficence or to consider the systematic role of the first principle of virtue.

Chapter 12

1 Hannah Arendt, *The Jew as Pariah*, edited by Ron H. Feldman, New York: Grove, 1978, p. 251, cited by George Kateb, *Hannah Arendt Politics, Conscience, Evil*, Totowa, N.J.: Rowman & Allanheld, 1984, p. 79.
2 Hannah Arendt, *The Origin of Totalitarianism*, New York: Harcourt, Brace & World, Inc., 1951, p. 459.
3 Elisabeth Young-Bruehl, *Hannah Arendt: For Love of the World*, New Haven and London: Yale University Press, 1982, p. 369.
4 Arendt, *The Origins of Totalitarianism*, p. 469.
5 Hannah Arendt, *Eichmann in Jerusalem: A Report on the Banality of Evil*, New York: The Viking Press, revised and enlarged edition, 1964, p. 287.
6 Young-Bruehl, *Hannah Arendt*, p. 368.
7 Arendt says this explicitly in *The Human Condition*, Chicago: The University of Chicago Press, 1958, p. 241.
8 Ibid., p. 276.
9 Ibid., p. 136.
10 Ibid.
11 See, for example, *Eichmann in Jerusalem*, pp. 93, 136–37, 148–49, 292–93.
12 Ibid., pp. 136–37.
13 Ibid., p. 21.
14 Ibid., pp. 287–88.
15 See, for example, her account of how the judges ought to have addressed the defendant in rendering their verdict. *Eichmann in Jerusalem*, pp. 277–79. On the other hand, she also suggests, op. cit., p. 288, that thoughtlessness of the scope of Eichmann's was hardly commonplace.
16 Ibid., p. 288.
17 Ibid., p. 109.
18 Ibid. pp. 47–49.

19 *Lectures on Kant's Political Philosophy*, edited by Ronald Beiner, Chicago: University of Chicago Press, 1982, esp. pp. 70–74.
20 *Eichmann in Jerusalem*, pp. 294–95.
21 Ibid., p. 287.
22 Ibid., p. 49.
23 Ibid. p. 86.
24 Ibid., pp. 51–52.
25 Ibid., p. 52.
26 Presumably, it is in light of this view of evil, as well as the focus of the book on the concrete matter of the judgment of Eichmann and the other Nazis rather than on general metaphysical considerations, that we must understand Arendt's emphatic statement that, of all the things that the book is not, it is "least of all, a theoretical treatise on the nature of evil." *Eichmann in Jerusalem*, p. 285. If evil is truly as she depicts it, such a treatise would be pointless.
27 Scholem raises this criticism in a letter to Arendt of June 23, 1963. See *The Jew as Pariah*, p. 245.
28 For my discussion of the "Incorporation Thesis" see *Kant's Theory of Freedom*, especially chapter 2, and Chapters 8 and 9 in this volume.
29 See my "Morality and freedom: Kant's Reciprocity Thesis," *Philosophical Review* 95 (1986), pp. 393–425; and *Kant's Theory of Freedom*, chapter 11, and Chapters 8, 9, 10 and 11 in this volume.
30 John Silber, "The ethical significance of Kant's religion," in *Religion within the Limits of Reason Alone*, translated by T. M. Greene and H. H. Hudson, p. cxxix.
31 Allen W. Wood, *Kant's Moral Religion*, Ithaca, N.Y., and London: Cornell University Press, 1970, pp. 210–15.
32 Sharon Anderson-Gold, "Kant's rejection of devilishness: The limits of human volition," *Idealistic Studies* 14 (1984), pp. 35–48. I am here basically following Anderson-Gold's analysis.
33 Ibid., p. 48, note 30.
34 Arendt, *Eichmann in Jerusalem*, p. 52.
35 Ibid., p. 150.
36 Ibid., p. 276.
37 Interestingly enough, Fichte, who in his account of evil follows Kant in the denial of the possibility of devilishness, appeals explicitly to a kind of freely chosen thoughtlessness in the effort to explain how a being who recognizes the authority of the moral law might yet fail to act on it. See *Das System der Sittenlehre nach den Principien der Wissenschaftslehre*, 16, IV, *Fichtes Werke*, edited by I. H. Fichte, Berlin: Walter de Gruyter & Co., 1971, Vol. 4, pp. 191–98. In the same context he also emphasizes the role of self-deception.
38 See Kant's *Theory of Freedom*, pp. 158–61.
39 See note 37.
40 This notion of moral salience is suggested by the work of Barbara Herman, who develops an account of rules of moral salience and their role in moral judgment. See her "The practice of moral judgment," *The Journal of Philosophy* 82 (1985), pp. 414–36; reprinted in *The Practice of Moral Judgment*, Cambridge, Mass.: Harvard University Press, 1993, chapter 4.

41 This example was suggested to me by Marcia Baron, who used a similar one for a quite different purpose in a symposium on my *Kant's Theory of Freedom*. For my response to Baron's use of this example see Chapter 8 in this volume.
42 See, for example, "What is enlightenment," 8: 37 and 41.
43 Frederick Beiser, in *Enlightenment, Revolution, & Romanticism, The Genesis of Modern German Political Thought 1790–1800*, Cambridge, Mass., and London: Harvard University Press, 1992, suggests (on p. 36) that Kant temporarily modified his uncompromising views on obedience in *Reflexion* 8055, dating from the late 1780s, only to return to them from 1793 on. But, as Beiser himself acknowledges, since this text is an unpublished fragment, in which Kant may very well be tentatively considering a view rather than firmly committing himself to it, it is difficult to know how much weight to place upon it. Moreover, Beiser ignores both the response to Bouterwork, which dates from after 1793, and the passage from the *Religion*.

Index

Ameriks, Karl, xv, 4, 5, 6, 11–12, 17–18, 19–21, 27–28, 31, 97, 109, 124–126, 131–32, 186n, 200n, 204n
Analogies of Experience, 80–81, 83, 85, 89; Second Analogy, xvii, 55, 72, 78, 80–91 passim
Antimony of Pure Reason, 5, 11
appearances: relation to representations, 12–14; relation to things in themselves, 3, 6–17, 17–21; transcendental conception of, 7; unifiability of, 36–37
apperception, xvi, xvii, 53–66 passim, 69, 71–74, 74–77; analytic principle of, 31–32, 35–52 passim, 77; empirical, 73–74; and inner sense, 62, 94; Leibniz' conception of, 68–70; and materialism, Kant's critique of, 93–95, 101–4; numerical identity of, 37–40, 42, 48; ontological status of, 65–66; and spontaneity, 62–66; and synthesis, 53–66 passim, 76; synthetic unity of, 41, 43–49, 75; in transcendental deduction, 27, 29, 32, 35–40, 41–52 passim. *See also* Gurwitsch, Aron; Guyer, Paul; Henrich, Dieter; Kitcher, Patricia
Anderson-Gold, Sharon, 177–78
anomolous monism, 98, 102
Aquila, Richard, 11–12
Arendt, Hannah, xx–xxi, 169–82, 210n, 211n
Atwell, John E., 208n, 210n
Aune, Bruce, xix–xx, 143–49, 151
autonomy, xiii, xix, 111–14, 117–18, 129–38; and categorical imperative, 134, 136–38; and consciousness of moral law, 139–42; vs. heteronomy, 134–35; and Incorporation Thesis, 134–35; and moral agency, 129, 135–38; as motivational independence, 111, 117, 135–36, 141; and Reciprocity Thesis, 130, 136–38; and transcendental freedom, 129–42

Baron, Marcia, 109, 118–22, 123, 165–66, 203n, 210n, 212n
Beck, Lewis White, xvii, 80, 129, 150, 201–2n
Beiser, Frederick, 212n
beneficence, duty of, 122–23, 165–68
Berkeley, George, 5
Bird, Graham, 6
Bittner, Rüdiger, 207n
Buchdahl, Gerd, xvii, 80, 85, 88, 90–91, 197n

Canon of Pure Reason, the, 109–10, 113, 142
Carl, Wolfgang, 192
Cassirer, Ernst, 70, 72, 74, 196n
categorical imperative: derivation of, xx, 143–54; transcendental freedom as premise in, 151–54; formula of autonomy, 147–49; and obligatory ends, 157–58, 160, 162–64; universal law, formulation of, 145–46, 150. *See also* Aune, Bruce; Wood, Allen
categories: as conditions of possibility of experience, 29–31, 51–52; logical vs. real use of, 7; objective validity of, 58–60; transcendental deduction of, 27–52 passim, 58–60. *See also* concepts, pure; transcendental deduction
causality, xvii, 80–91; concept of, 82, 86–88; of freedom, 127, 132, 136–41; and reflective judgment, 80, 85, 90–91; schema of, 89–90; in Second Analogy, 80–91 passim; transcendental principle of, 80, 82–85, 91; and uniformity of nature, 80–81. *See also* causal laws; Friedman, Michael; Guyer, Paul
causal laws, xvii, 80–91 passim; grounding of, 82–85, 90–91; "grounding" vs. "guaranteeing," 90–91; hybrid status of, 82–85; and "instantaneous laws," 86; and judgment of objective succession, 86–90; and metaphysical principles of mechanics, 83–85;

213

INDEX

causal laws (*cont.*)
  necessity of particular, 82–85, 86; and objectivity of experience, 86–90; and principle of systematicity, 85, 90–91; and reflective judgment, 80, 85, 90–91; and transcendental principle of causality, 80, 82–85, 91. *See also* causality; Friedman, Michael; Guyer, Paul
cause. *See* causality; causal laws
Churchland, Patricia S., xviii
Churchland, Paul, xviii, 105–6
concept, pure, 6, 29–31, 51, 58–59
consciousness: empirical, 73–74, 94–96; intentionality of, 77–79; and "taking as," 101–4; unity of, 96–98, 102. *See also* apperception

Davidson, Donald, 102
Dennett, Daniel, 57, 102
diabolical will: impossibility of, 174–78; and respect for moral law, 176–77
discursivity thesis, 6–8, 18, 31, 46, 47–48, 93–94. *See also* intellect, discursive
duty: imperfect, 160, 164–68; of beneficience, 122–23, 165–68; and summum bonum, 164–65; perfect, 160

Eberhard, J. A., 23, 186n
Eisenberg, Paul, 209n
Engstrom, Stephen, 109–14, 118, 123, 125
epistemic condition, 4–7, 8, 14, 22, 25–26
evil: Arendt's analysis of, 169–82. *See also* radical evil
experience: and causal laws, 86–90; conditions of possibility of, 29–32, 42, 51–52

Falkenstein, Lorne, 10–11
Fichte, J. G., xiv, 141, 179, 205n, 211n
frailty. *See* radical evil
freedom, xii, xviii, xx, 129–42; and autonomy, 134–42; causality of, 136–41; and consciousness of moral law, 138–42; and derivation of categorical imperative, 151–54; idea of, 124, 126, 133–34, 139, 142; and obligatory ends, 160–164; positive vs. negative, 136; and spontaneity, 57, 54–65, 110–11, 130–34, 138–42; transcendental vs. practical, 109–11. *See also* autonomy; spontaneity
Friedman, Michael, xvii–xviii, 80–91 passim
functionalism, 53, 54–55, 63, 92, 98

Garve–Feder review, 32
Gottfried, Martin, 187n
Greenwood, Terry, 188–89n
Gregor, Mary, 208n, 209n
Grier, Michelle, 21, 188n, 190n
Gurwitsch, Aron, xvii, 67–79 passim, 196n, 197n
Guyer, Paul, xv, xvi, 4, 5, 9, 15, 18, 21–26, 28, 37–40, 42–45, 50, 82, 86, 89, 91, 109, 124–26, 183n, 188–89n, 190n

happiness: as end, 113–14; indirect duty to cultivate, 123; principle of personal, 116–18
Harman, Gilbert, 206–7n
Hasker, William, 201n
Hegel, G. W. F., xx, 142, 143, 206n
Heimsoeth, Heinz, 187n
Henrich, Dieter, xvi, 28, 32–39, 42, 50, 193n
Herman, Barbara, 208n, 211n
heteronomy, 111–14
Hill, Thomas, 205n, 206n
Hossenfelder, Malte, 5, 6
Hudson, Hud, 201–2n
Hume, David, 4, 5, 43, 44, 53, 54, 55, 66, 70, 73, 77, 80–81, 191n
Husserl, 67, 71, 77–79
hypothetical imperatives, 112–14

idea. *See* freedom, idea of; transcendental idea
idealism. *See* transcendental idealism
imagination, 54–56, 59, 62; transcendental synthesis of, in Deduction, 35–36, 52
inclination, and end-setting, 161–63
Incorporation Thesis, xviii, 109, 113, 118–23, 126, 130–35, 139–42; and spontaneity, 132–34
intellect, discursive, 31, 46–48. *See also* discursivity thesis; judgment
intelligible world: idea of, 19–20; as standpoint, 128
intentionality. *See* consciousness, intentionality of
intuition, unity of, in Deduction, 33–34, 37. *See also* sensibility, forms of; space; time

James, William, 48
judgment: and apperception, 59–61; and discursivity thesis, 6–8, 18, 94; of perception, vs. of experience, 73–74; as "taking as," 61, 63–64, 95–98, 103–4

214

INDEX

Kant's works:
  Anthropology from a Practical Point of View, 180
  Critique of Judgment, 80, 81, 90, 172, 173
  Critique of Practical Reason, 51, 172; on categorical imperative, xx, 150–54, 164, 171; on freedom, xviii, xix, 19, 111, 132, 136, 138, 139, 141, 161
  Critique of Pure Reason, 92, 112; on causality, 80–91 passim; on freedom, 109, 123–24, 128, 131, 142; on spontaneity, xiv, 53–66; on Transcendental Deduction, 27–40, 41–52; on transcendental idealism, 3–26 passim
  Duisburg Nachlaß, 23
  Groundwork of the Metaphysics of Morals, xviii, 19, 155, 174, 180; on categorical imperative, xx, 144–46, 149, 150, 151, 154; on imperfect duties, 156, 164–68; on Incorporation Thesis, 131–32; on freedom, 133–38; on materialism, 93, 98–99
  Inaugural Dissertation, 8, 17–18, 30
  letter to Herz, 72–73
  Metaphysical Foundations of Natural Science, xvii, 35, 84, 85, 91
  Metaphysics of Morals, xx, 121, 129, 139, 182; obligatory ends, xx, 155–168 passim; on radical evil, 179, 180
  Metaphysik K3, 131
  "On a Discovery According to Which Any New Critique of Pure Reason Has Been Made Superfluous by an Earlier One," 23
  "On the Progress of Metaphysics," 97
  Opus Postumum, 68
  Prolegomena to Any Future Metaphysics, 12, 42, 59, 73, 88
  Reflexion 5611, 131
  Religion within the Limits of Reason Alone: on Incorporation Thesis, 130–32, 139, 175; on radical evil, 120, 172, 174, 178–79, 182
Kemp Smith, Norman, 33
Kitcher, Patricia, xvi–xvii, 43–44, 53–66 passim, 92, 191–92n, 194n, 200n
Kitcher, Philip, 198n

law(s): moral 115–18, 150–54; practical 115–18; universal, or unconditioned practical, 147–49, 150–53. *See also* causal laws; moral law

Leibniz, Gottfried W., 7, 10, 23, 29–30, 67–77 passim, 96
Locke, John, 22, 24, 68, 69, 72, 77

Marburg neo-Kantianism, 67, 71, 79
materialism: eliminative, 103, 104–6; Kant's critique of, xviii, 92–106; non-reductive, 98–104
maxims, 115–16, 134–35; and conformity to universal law, 147–49, 150–53; and Incorporation Thesis, 119–20, 131; and obligatory ends, 158, 165–68; as self-legislated, 134
Meerbote, Ralf, 183n, 200–1n
metaphysical principles of mechanics: and empirical laws, 83–85. *See also* causality; causal laws
moral law: authority of, 115–18; and freedom, 134–38, 139–42; "metaphysical deduction" of, 150–54; validity of, 116–17. *See also* categorical imperative
moral weakness. *See* radical evil
motivation, moral: and autonomy, 135–36, 140–42; and Incorporation Thesis, 130–31, 140; and radical evil, 175–76

Nagel, Thomas, 6, 65, 103, 201n
Newton, Isaac, 68, 81, 84, 87, 89
noumena, 18–21; concept of, 18; and relation to freedom, 19. *See also* phenomenal–noumenal distinction; things in themselves

object(s): concept of, in Deduction, 49; and "filtration model," 14–16; intelligible, 20; noumenal, 21; numerical identity of, 77–79; representation of, 3–8, 12–14, 31, 47, 54–55, 58–61, 77–79, 94–97; transcendental, 16–17. *See also* appearances; things in themselves; transcendental idealism
obligatory ends, xx, 155–68; and categorical imperative, 157–58, 160, 162–64; "deduction" of, 155–64; vs. ends as limiting conditions, 155, 156, 160, 162; and maxims, 158, 165–68; and transcendental freedom, 160–64
O'Neill (Nell), Onora, 203n, 208n

Paralogisms, 20, 43, 45, 48, 92–93, 96, 97
Paton, 74, 192n

215

INDEX

phenomenal–noumenal distinction, 11–12, 14–17, 18–20; and distinction between things in themselves and appearances, 20; ontological status of, 4, 18–20; relation to freedom, 19. *See also* transcendental idealism

Pippin, Robert, 57, 200n

Potter, Nelson, 156, 159–60, 164, 183n

Prauss, Gerald, 9, 14, 184n

principles, practical, 114–18; distinction between objective and subjective, 115; fundamental, 114–16; and *Wille–Willkür* distinction, 115–16

psychology: rational, 97–98; transcendental, xvi–xvii, 53–66 passim, 71–77

purposiveness, 90–91

Putnam, Hilary, 6

radical evil, xx–xxi, 120–23, 169–182; and authority of moral law, 174–76; and impurity, 179; and Incorporation Thesis, 175; and moral weakness or frailty, 120–23, 178–79; and motivation, 175–76; as propensity to evil, 170, 174; and Reciprocity Thesis, 175; and self-deception, 173–74, 175, 178–81; wickedness, 175, 178, 18. *See also* Arendt, Hannah; evil, Arendt's analysis of

rational agency, 109, 113, 117–18, 129, 130–34, 139–40; and freedom, 124–28, 130–34, 139–42; and obligatory ends, 160–64. *See also* autonomy; spontaneity

reasons–causes distinction, 100–4

Reath, Andrews, 109, 114–18, 123

Reciprocity Thesis, 114, 117, 130, 136–38, 140, 142

reflective judgment, 80, 85, 90–91

Refutation of Idealism, 76, 94

Rehberg, August Wilhelm, 205n

representations, 54–55, 58–61; vs. appearances, 12–14; of objects, 4–8, 31, 47, 54–55, 58–61, 94, 97; unifiability of, 41–42, 44

representing, act of, 61; as "taking as," 61, 63

Robinson, Hoke, xv, 4, 12–17, 33–34, 186–87n

Ryle, Gilbert, 66, 96

Scholem, Gershom, 169, 174

self-consciousness. *See* apperception

self-deception, 173–74, 175, 178–81

self-determination. *See* autonomy; freedom; spontaneity

self-love, 175–77

Sellars, Wilfred, 92, 183n, 194n

sensibility, forms of, 6–7, 8–11, 22, 25–26. *See also* space; time

Shoemaker, Sydney, 194n

Silber, John, 176

space: as epistemic condition, 8, 22–26; as form of sensibility, 8–11, 14; unity of, in Deduction, 37

Spinoza, Benedict de, 15

spontaneity, xiii, xiv–xv, xix, 53, 56–57, 62–66, 71, 75, 110–11, 126–28, 129–34, 138–42; absolute vs. relative, 57, 62–64, 127, 132; and apperception, 94–96, 106; and autonomy, 110, 125; and Incorporation Thesis, 130–34, 142; Leibniz' conception of, 68; and materialism, 92–98, 101–4; practical, 119; and rational agency, 19–34, 139–42; of understanding, 31, 36, 47, 57, 62–66, 93, 101–4. *See also* freedom

Strawson, P. F., xvi, 3, 22, 27, 43, 53, 57, 58, 81, 147

succession, objective: of representations, 78–79, 86–90

sympathy, feeling of, 121–23; duty to cultivate, 121–23

synthesis, 54–64, 71–74, 78–79; of apprehension, 71–74, 78–79; of imagination, transcendental, 35–36, 52; three-fold, 71–74, 78–79; in Transcendental Deduction, 35–36, 52; of understanding, 55–57, 59, 62–64

systematicity, principle of, 80, 85, 90–91; and causal laws, 80, 85, 90–91; and reflective judgment, 85, 90–91

temporal order, objective, 86–90

things in themselves: vs. intelligible objects, 20; non-spatiality of, 8–11, 15, 22–23; relation to appearances, 3, 6–24; and transcendental object, 16

time, 8, 10, 14; as epistemic condition, 22–26; unity of, in Deduction, 37

Transcendental Aesthetic, 5, 7, 10, 13, 14, 22–23, 36

Transcendental Analytic, xiv, 7, 56

Transcendental Deduction, xv–xvi, 27–66 passim, 69, 72–77; A edition, 34, 43, 45, 57, 60, 73, 74, 76; and analytic principle of apperception, 31–32, 35–40, 41–52 passim; and apperception, 27, 29, 32, 35–40, 41–

216

52; B edition, 27–52 passim, 61, 69, 72–77, 94; proof structure of, 27–28, 32–37, 41–52; and transcendental synthesis of imagination in, 35–36, 52. *See also* Ameriks, Karl; Guyer, Paul; Henrich, Dieter

Transcendental Dialectic, 20, 109–10

transcendental distinction, things in themselves vs. appearances, 3, 6–26; and appearance–reality distinction, 17–18; and distinction between things in themselves and intelligible objects, 20; "double-aspect" conception of, 3–26; metaphysical conception of, 12, 16

Transcendental Exposition, 10, 23

transcendental freedom, *see* freedom; spontaneity

transcendental idea: and things in themselves, 20; and intelligible objects, 20; and unconditioned, 20–21; of freedom, 133–34, 139, 142

transcendental idealism, xiii, xv, 3–26; and discursivity thesis, 6–8, 18; dogmatic reading of, 21–24; "double-aspect" reading of, 3–26, 124, 128; and the "neglected alternative" problem, 3, 8–11, 25; ontological reading of, 3, 11–13, 17–22. *See also* Ameriks, Karl; Guyer, Paul; Robinson, Hoke; transcendental distinction, between things in themselves and appearances

transcendental illusion, 20–21, 96

transcendental object. *See* object, transcendental

transcendental pscyhology. *See* psychology, transcendental

transcendental reflection, 3, 7–9, 104

Trendelenburg, Adolf, 8

unconditioned, 20–21

understanding: activity of, 75; and Leibniz' conception of, 70; spontaneity of, 31, 36, 47, 93, 101–3; and synthesis, 75. *See also* spontaneity

van Inwagen, Peter, 204n

vice, 177–78

Walker, Ralph, 6

Wick, Warner, 165

will, 134–38; animal vs. free, 130–31; as law to itself, 136–37

Wille–Willkür, distinction between, 115–18, 129

Williams, Bernard, 114–15

Wilson, Margaret, 97–98

Wolff, Susan, 165–66

Wood, Allen, xx, 128, 143, 144, 146, 147, 149, 153, 176, 206n

Young-Bruehl, 169

Zöller, Günter, 193n